MYSTERIES AND SECRETS OF VOODOO, SANTERIA, AND OBEAH

LIONEL AND PATRICIA FANTHORPE

MYSTERIES AND SECRETS OF VOODOO, SANTERIA, AND OBEAH

DUNDURN PRESS
TORONTO

Copy-editor: Jennifer Gallant
Typesetting: Jennifer Scott
Printer: Webcom

Library and Archives Canada Cataloguing in Publication

Fanthorpe, R. Lionel
    Mysteries and secrets of Voodoo, Santeria and Obeah / Lionel and Patricia
Fanthorpe.

ISBN 978-1-55002-784-6

    1. Voodooism. 2. Santeria. 3. Obeah (Cult). I. Fanthorpe, Patricia II. Title.

BL2565.F36 2008   299.6   C2008-900677-1

1   2   3   4   5   12   11   10   09   08

 Conseil des Arts du Canada   Canada Council for the Arts   Canadä ONTARIO ARTS COUNCIL CONSEIL DES ARTS DE L'ONTARIO

We acknowledge the support of the **Canada Council for the Arts** and the **Ontario Arts Council** for our publishing program. We also acknowledge the financial support of the **Government of Canada** through the **Book Publishing Industry Development Program** and **The Association for the Export of Canadian Books**, and the **Government of Ontario** through the **Ontario Book Publishers Tax Credit** program, and the **Ontario Media Development Corporation.**

Care has been taken to trace the ownership of copyright material used in this book. The author and the publisher welcome any information enabling them to rectify any references or credits in subsequent editions.

J. Kirk Howard, President

Printed and bound in Canada.
Printed on recycled paper.

www.dundurn.com

All images are courtesy of the authors from their private collection.

Dundurn Press
3 Church Street, Suite 500
Toronto, Ontario, Canada
M5E 1M2

Gazelle Book Services Limited
White Cross Mills
High Town, Lancaster, England
LA1 4XS

Dundurn Press
2250 Military Road
Tonawanda, NY U.S.A.
14150

This book is dedicated to all those whose religion inspires them to do their best to help and heal others, to alleviate poverty, loneliness, and sadness — and to make this mysterious old world a happier and better place for us all to share and enjoy.

TABLE OF CONTENTS

FOREWORD

ONE OF THE authors of this book is a priest of the Church in Wales and, as it happens, so am I, the writer of the foreword. We were both brought up in Christian homes and we have been part of all things Christian all our lives. By that faith we have lived and in that faith we shall die. We make no apology for it. Indeed, we are proud of it. Some of the authors' earlier books were written to help others in or towards the faith of their birth.

Christianity claims to be a faith for the whole world. How could it be anything other with the words of Christ so clear and definite? "Go ye into all the world and make disciples of all nations."

However, it's not the only religion to claim the allegiance of large numbers of the now teeming millions of the world. Muslims are equally proud of what they believe, as are Buddhists, Hindus, Jews, and the followers of other long-established faiths. The presence of so many churches, mosques, synagogues, pagodas, and shrines is witness to some universal longing to believe in a power greater than man himself. History records the names of many who preferred to die rather than surrender one iota of what they believed.

Sadly, it must be admitted, in the western world at least, that a growing number have now come to deplore the very existence of all such worldwide faiths, or, indeed, faith of any kind. They see them as harmful, divisive, and sources of conflict. Shakespeare's pungent phrase "A plague on all your houses" would sum it up for them. Such loss of a faith, naturally, hurts those of us who continue to believe. We affirm, and always will, that the world we share would have been immeasurably retarded, and our lives impoverished, had not the great faiths been there to guide, to inspire, and, when needed, to correct us. All great religions have had something special to give and, in doing so, have shaped our destinies, transforming the laws we live by and the people we become. Christianity, for one, can claim to have inspired characters the world will never forget: Francis of Assisi, Kagawa of Japan, Schweitzer of Africa, Mother Teresa of Calcutta, and a host of others. All faiths have their own honoured lists of martyrs and those who led dedicated lives.

In its long history, Christianity has shown itself at its noblest and at its most frail. It has produced the best in individuals and in society and also the worst. It has both glorified its Creator and shamed Him. The slave trade alone will forever stand as a betrayal of everything Christ taught us. But Christianity has repented and survived and it always will. St. Paul once wrote, "All things work together for good for those who love God."

So it does and will ever do so. The main thrust of this book, the latest in a long series the Fanthorpes have researched for us, is to show what happened when, true to the words of its founders, the Christian religion moved into Africa and from Africa through the ships of the slavers to other far distant parts of the world. It met head-on already long established tribal religions, with their gods and goddesses of primitive beliefs and practices. The result was the birth of what the authors call a "hybridized" faith, the angels of the Christians blending with the Orishas of the Africans, the altar bearing the weight of pagan sacrifices, incense becoming incantations, Christian rituals in worship surrendering to drumming, spells, even mass hysteria. On the surface, the faiths collided and much that was basic to Christianity seems to have been overwhelmed. The powers of Voodoo, Santeria, and Obeah were too strongly entrenched. The Fanthorpes themselves never sit in judgement. They make no comments, no criticisms, no protestations. They are researchers, brilliant at what they do. They leave all judgements and conclusions to us.

Perhaps, if pressed, the authors might have considered a final chapter to this book. I would have loved to do it for them. Clearly, the story did not end there. Neither Santeria nor Obeah prevailed. The Orishas were not greater than the angels. The Christian religion is not so easily over-whelmed. The Church in Africa is now strong, the Christian religion well grounded. It feels itself strong enough to make its voice heard throughout the world. Where countries once turned to Africa for slaves, they now turn to Africa for missionaries. African Christians are well rooted in the faith and an influence in the world. Truly, all things work out well for those who love God.

Reverend Canon Stanley Mogford, MA
Cardiff, Wales, UK, 2007

(As always, the authors are deeply grateful to Canon Mogford, who is rightly regarded as one of the most profound scholars in Wales.)

INTRODUCTION

SHAKESPEARE (1564–1616) wrote in *Hamlet* (act 1, scene 5), "There are more things in Heaven and Earth, Horatio, than are dreamt of in your philosophy." Forty and more years of researching, writing, lecturing, and broadcasting about every aspect of the paranormal have led us to much the same conclusion. As Sir Arthur Eddington (1882–1944) once warned humanity, "We live in a universe that is not only stranger than we imagine: it is stranger than we are *able* to imagine."

So where do the syncretized mystery religions like Santeria, Obeah, and Voodoo fit into this mysterious universe? Our research began with the ancient origins of African magic and the gods of prehistoric Africa. In order to understand Santeria and the others it was necessary to go into the history of the slave trade, to try to discover what the African peoples had brought with them in the way of culture and ideas.

Theology and philosophy are like cocktails: the more they are mixed, the more potent they become. When traditional Christianity collided with the old African religions, something very powerful grew out of their meeting: the new, syncretized mystery religions of which Santeria was one example. Because the slave owners in the New World were mortally afraid that their prisoners would find strength and unity in their old African religions, everything possible was done to inhibit and suppress the old Yoruba faiths. But the slave owners failed, and the old African deities, the Loas and Orishas, became identified with the Christian saints!

Our research led us to examine the quasi-hypnotic processes that formed an essential part of these new, syncretized mystery religions. Drumming, music, and dancing were also among their vital components. Priests and priestesses with great knowledge of ancient African magic became charismatic leaders, healers, seers, and magicians. We researched the sources of their power. We investigated their spells, talismans, amulets, and Voodoo dolls. We also examined cases of zombiism and looked to see whether or not there were rational explanations for some of the darker and more sinister reports concerning it.

These syncretized mystery religions also include powerful sexual magic, and some of the Voodoo spells are based on it. Finally, we brought all our research together — including our own meeting with an Obeah man in Barbados — and looked at the main question: when Voodoo works, *how* does it work?

Chapter 1

THE ANCIENT ORIGINS
OF AFRICAN MAGIC

THE SCOTTISH anthropologist Sir James George Frazer (1854–1941) first published *The Golden Bough: A Study in Magic and Religion* in 1890. He was primarily concerned with ancient religions that he thought of as fertility cults, such as those of the Canaanite Baal and Ashtoreth in the Old Testament. Frazer concentrated on the concept of a sacred, sacrificial king, whom he interpreted as the incarnation of a dying and reviving god. This linked with a solar deity, who died, revived, and mated with an earth goddess. Frazer took his title from an episode in the *Aeniad* in which Aeneas, advised by the Sybil of Cumae (to whom he had presented the sacred golden bough), is admitted by the gatekeeper of Hades in order to talk to the ghost of his father, Anchises.

Sex goddess Ashtoreth from Assyrian cylinder.

The famous golden bough grew in the sacred grove by the shores of Lake Nemi, which was ruled over by the Rex Nemorensis, the Priest of Diana at Aricia in Italy. The hazardous situation of the Rex Nemorensis can best be summed up in the words of the English poet Thomas Babington Macaulay:

> Those trees in whose dim shadow
> The ghastly priest doth reign —
> The priest who slew the slayer,
> And shall himself be slain.

You got the job by challenging the current holder and killing him in single combat — after presenting him with the golden bough.

Frazer walked into a storm of controversy when *The Golden Bough* was published because he included the idea of the dying and resurrected Christ among his examples, but modern scholarship accepts that he was largely on the right track when he investigated sympathetic magic along with magical symbolism.

Crucifix.

One of Frazer's most memorable quotations can be found in Chapter 4, which he entitled "Magic and Religion": "If the test of truth lay in a show of hands or a counting of heads, the system of magic might appeal, with far more reason than the Catholic Church, to the proud motto, '*Quod semper, quod ubique, quod ab omnibus,*' as the sure and certain credential of its own infallibility." (The Latin motto translates as "At all times, in all places, to all people.")

A second comes from Chapter 21, in which Frazer examines the subject of "Tabooed Things": "The danger, however, is not less real because it is imaginary; imagination acts upon a man as really as does gravitation, and may kill him as certainly as a dose of prussic acid."

Before magic and religion can be studied in the comprehensive way that Frazer did (his third edition of *The Golden Bough* ran to eleven volumes — plus a twelfth that was the index!), a working definition of both concepts is needed.

Magic may be regarded as the result of a magician's attempt to control his or her environment and everything in it — including other human beings — by means of spells, enchantments, philtres, potions, charms, liturgies, and other rituals. These enactments may be thought to exert the magician's power directly over nature: rain, clouds, storms, earthquakes, illnesses in animals or people, injuries, death, and the arousal of feelings of love. In other cases, the magician's work is indirect: calls are made on powerful psychic entities, often demons, to do the job that the enchanter wants done — in return for some favour that the magician is doing the entity.

The nexus between magic and religion can be traced to this recognition by the worker of magic that he or she cannot control some aspects of nature directly — but that other more powerful beings can.

Religion may then be defined as an attempt to form a relationship with a god — or gods — to whom petitions and requests can be presented in prayer. Some religious enthusiasts believe that they can reinforce their prayers by offering sacrifices, fasting, maintaining all-night vigils, enduring various types of self-deprivation, abstaining from physical pleasure, or even self-inflicting pain and discomfort as in the wearing of a hair shirt.

Other religious theorists emphasize a self-emptying of the personality, so that the worshipper is absorbed by his or her gods and becomes a mere drop of water in some sort of divine ocean.

It may, however, be argued that the highest religious concept is of an infinitely loving god who cares for all creation and wills only their welfare and happiness. This god of love asks nothing of them other than to reflect that divine compassion onto one another and to work for the welfare and happiness of others. It is the nature of love to seek the happiness of the beloved — and to do so is the highest and most acceptable form of worship that can be achieved. It is also the nature of love to enhance, enrich, and reinforce the personality of the beloved — never to diminish it or seek to absorb it. A further aspect of this highest religious concept is that the worshipper's own pleasure is very much a part of the divine will. As the brilliant C.S. Lewis expressed it, "When we have learnt to love our neighbours as ourselves, we are then permitted to love ourselves as much as we love our neighbours."

Having considered the basic nature and substance of magic and religion, it is possible to proceed to a consideration of their African origins.

Historically, the Olduvai Gorge is a truly awesome place. Situated in the Serengeti Plains in northern Tanzania, and forming part of the Great Rift Valley, it is frequently referred to as the Cradle of Civilization. The Olduvai Gorge contains human artifacts and other prehistoric remains dating back at least 2 million years — and perhaps considerably more. Fossilized traces of the earliest humanoid occupants of the area go back at least another half-million years.

The popular name Olduvai dates back to 1911, when Wilhelm Kattwinkel, a distinguished German entomologist searching for rare East African butterflies, came across the gorge. He asked one of his local Maasai friends what it was called, but because of translation difficulties his companion thought Wilhelm was asking about the name of the plants lining the gorge, rather than the name of the gorge itself. Accordingly, his guide told him that it was *Oldupaai* — actually the Maasai name for East African wild sisal plants, or Blue Sansevieria (*Sansevieria ehrenbergii*), which grew there in profusion.

Kattwinkel later pronounced it with a *v* instead of a *p* — hence its present form *Olduvai*.

The plant was well understood locally and was known to have significant healing properties. It was beneficial in controlling bleeding and helping wounds to heal. When Bill Montagne, the paleoanthropologist, was injured while working in the gorge in the 1970s, his Maasai friends treated his wounds with a Sansevieria bandage. Bill was so impressed with its antiseptic qualities that he initiated research into its potential pharmaceutical properties.

Traditional African medical knowledge of this kind forms an important part of the long history of the links connecting ancient magic, religion, herbalism, and healing with developments in our own twenty-first century.

It is no exaggeration to say that the Olduvai Gorge is one of the most important prehistoric sites on Earth, and the brilliant pioneering excavations carried out by Louis and Mary Leakey in the 1950s were of the greatest possible importance. Fortunately, their family members are still continuing with this extremely important work.

A large lake seems to have occupied the site millions of years ago, a lake that was subjected to periodic depositions of volcanic ash. More recently — probably about half a million years ago — a small river cut its way through these successive volcanic deposits. From a contemporary scientific point of view this is an ideal situation, as it allows the artifacts found in the ash strata to be dated using modern radiometric techniques. Stone tools made from the local basalt and quartz date back well over 2.5 million years. These ancient toolmakers, *Paranthropus boisei* and *Homo habilis*, would almost certainly have practised an early form of magical religion — the earliest African roots, perhaps, of modern Santeria and similar religions.

A limestone cliff situated on the southern cape coast in South Africa contains the ancient and mysterious Blombos Cave. Nearly 100,000 years ago — still relatively modern by the standards of Olduvai — the inhabitants of the Blombos Cave were using jewellery made from nassarius shells. Biologically, the nassarius mollusc measures just over a centimetre across and can be found thriving in warm seas and coral reefs in most parts of the world. It has an oval shell and breathes via a siphon.

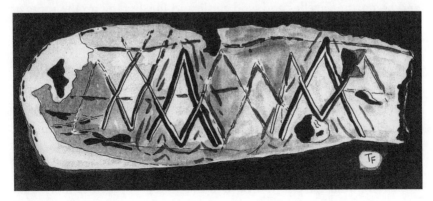

Blombos cave in Africa.

Feeding mainly on dead and decaying organisms or other detritus matter, the nassarius can also be carnivorous.

It is highly probable that nassarius shells were used as a simple form of currency or jewellery — perhaps both — by some of the earliest paleolithic people. They would almost certainly have had religious significance as well. The samples found in the Blombos Cave in South Africa are at least 75,000 years old, and other examples have been found in the Skhul Cave (known as the Cave of the Goats) on the side of Mount Carmel in Israel. Another sample turned up in Oued Djebbana in Algeria that dated to a similar period.

Because examples of the shells of *nassarius gibbosulus* — to give the little marine gastropod its full scientific title — have been found at three different sites, it is reasonable to suggest that very early human beings were using them purposefully: as currency, as ornaments, as jewellery, and as magical and religious symbols. Careful archeological-chemical analysis of the sediment surrounding nassarius shells from the Skhul Cave placed them in the same strata as ten or twelve ancient sets of human remains going back perhaps as many as 140,000 years.

University archeologists have suggested that the finds in and around the Skhul Cave provide evidence of cult and ritual burials, and of belief in an afterlife. Another Mount Carmel cave is known as the Tabun Cave — the Cave of the Oven. It could have been first occupied as many as half a million years ago. Remains show that the earliest inhabitants used hand axes made from flint and limestone for killing and preparing gazelles and wild cattle and for digging up the roots of plants. It is theorized that these hunter-gatherers may have indulged in sympathetic magic in the hope of a successful hunt. Other remains in the Tabun Cave date from the Mousterian culture, which flourished between 200,000 and 40,000 years ago. The Tabun Cave also contained the skeletal remains of a female buried in Neanderthal style, and there are archeologists who accept the possibility that *Homo sapiens* and the Neanderthals coexisted for a considerable time before the latter became extinct.

The El-Wad Cave — the Cave of the Valley — provides more than a hundred burial sites from less than 20,000 years ago. The bodies were buried in the fetal position, often with their ornaments of bone or shell: further evidence of cult ritual and ideas about a future life.

Remains from Olduvai, Blombos, Mount Carmel, and Oued Djebbana all point to the similarities between contemporary human beings and our earliest ancestors. The nassarius beads served much the same social, cultural, and psychological purposes that clothes, body adornments, and accessories do in our own sophisticated twenty-first century: they say things about the wearer. They proclaim leadership, group membership, status, sexuality, strength, ambition, ferocity, and power. They may be an invitation or a warning, a welcome or a challenge. They may say that the wearer is a man or woman with magical powers — a priest or priestess, a wizard or witch.

Because of the great barrier of the Sahara, it is easy to forget that the green and fertile territories of Africa away to the south of that vast desert are an inseparable part of Egypt and the North African Mediterranean coast. For thousands of years, and perhaps up until as recently as five thousand years ago, the hot, dry, barren Sahara contained grass and trees as well as lakes and rivers. It was teeming with aquatic life as well as life on land.

People of that period enjoyed these natural resources and amenities. Fish were taken from lakes and rivers. Sorghum and millet were grown, as was a type of wheat native to Africa. Cattle herding and pottery developed. Then — just as with threats of global warming today — the climate of the Saharan region began to change for the worse around 4000 BC: grass and woodland dried out into formidable and inhospitable desert.

Some of the ancient Saharans fled to Egypt. Others retreated southwards. These refugees took their seeds, their animals, and their agricultural knowledge with them. They also took their ancient religious ideas and their beliefs about magic.

Down from Mesopotamia came the secrets of using bronze, the art of writing like the Sumerians, and deep secrets of ancient Sumerian religion and magic.

Early Egyptian government was administered by the families and trusted friends of the pharaoh. The biblical account of Joseph being put in charge of the Egyptian anti-famine measures, as second-in-command to the pharaoh, is in harmony with what archeologists and Egyptologists know of early administrative techniques there. As distance grew between the pharaohs and their people, the priests devised special religious rituals that were applicable to the divine autocratic pharaoh but not to anyone outside the highest ranks of his court and government. The Egyptian concept of an afterlife also seems to have been an exclusive preserve of pharaohs, nobles, and priests — not something for the ordinary citizens to look forward to.

Egyptian science and technology made remarkable progress considering that they seem to have been severely handicapped by the idea that nature was controlled by capricious and unpredictable gods. Yet despite their inconsistency, these divinities gave a certain stability and order to the universe. Not surprisingly, these gods clung tenaciously to their secrets.

It is worth giving a few moments of serious consideration here to the hypothesis that highly developed, technologically advanced aliens from *elsewhere* would endeavour to control a less advanced terrestrial human population by keeping the secrets of the controlling technology well away from any intrepid and independent-minded terrestrials. Egyptian religion also encompassed the belief that spirits could invade material objects and people, and these spirits were the generators both of illness and dream phenomena. This again corresponds to the biblical account of Joseph's reputation and rise to power in ancient Egypt.

Solar worship was another essential ingredient of this early Egyptian religion, which was preoccupied with myths purporting to explain how and why certain things had come into existence. For example, the sun god had climbed a mountain to rise above the primeval, chaotic waters and had then created everything from his mountaintop. Having made the other gods and then the flora and fauna that filled the earth, the sun god, known as Re or Ra, died in the west every evening and resurrected himself in the east every morning.

As various pharaohs saw themselves as descendants or incarnations of Re they felt it necessary to keep their divinely royal bloodline separate from all others, so pharaohs frequently married their sisters.

Mummification of the pharaoh became another ingredient of this early Afro-Egyptian religion. It was believed that as long as the dead pharaoh's body remained more or less intact his spirit would retain the power to protect and guard his people.

The story of Isis and Osiris became an extremely important part of ancient Egyptian religion and magic. Murdered by his jealous and evil brother Set, or Seth, Osiris's mutilated body was thrown piece by piece into the Nile. His devoted wife, Isis, recovered the pieces, incurred the help of the gods, and enabled Osiris to rule in the underworld as he had once ruled on earth. As an especially benign deity, and one with greater magical powers than most, Osiris benefited crops and taught humanity how to make agricultural tools and instruments. He became a much revered god of agriculture and fertility, while the evil Set became a god of sterility and barrenness. Osiris, who made the Nile flood, was the god of the prosperous, agricultural Nile valley, while Set was more or less exiled to the Saharan wilderness. The lovely and loving Isis was associated with happy and lasting marriage, and she was revered as a perfect goddess throughout Egypt. She also inspired weaving and the skill of grinding corn into flour.

She and Osiris had a son, Horus the Falcon. He became the god of vengeance and tracked down evildoers.

Of even greater significance to serious students of Egyptology is the wise and benign god Thoth, who was associated with the moon, just as Re was associated with the sun. Thoth was said to have been the scribe of the gods, the keeper and protector of all their magical secrets. He knew and recorded everything in the universe that was worth knowing.

Horus the Egyptian god.

The authors tend to agree with those historians and theologians who suggest that Thoth and Hermes Trismegistus (Hermes the thrice-blessed), upon whose awesome Emerald Tablets were written all the greatest and most powerful ancient secrets, were one and the same. Thoth and Hermes were also identified with Melchizedek, the Priest-King of Salem at the time of Abraham. Melchizedek was a being of immense power and was thought to be immortal, "having neither father nor mother, neither beginning of life, nor end of days." Regardless of by which of his three names Thoth is most accurately known, his wife, Ma'at, was the goddess of ethics, morality, justice, and truth. Good Egyptians aspired to be like her. "To live as Ma'at" was an Egyptian ideal — to harm none and to benefit all.

Any deep and worthwhile understanding of early African religion and magic is inseparable from the beliefs and practices of ancient Egypt — because so much of the sophisticated Egyptian belief system came, in its earliest form, from the surrounding areas of what is now referred to as sub-Saharan Africa.

Egyptians revered and worshipped cats, largely because their war goddess was a lioness. Dead cats were respected and mummified. Bulls were venerated because of their great strength and fertility, and in one Egyptian magical ceremony, women who were hoping for children would strip and display themselves to the great "Bull of Bulls" in order to ensure their own fertility. There is almost certainly a connection between this Egyptian bull magic and the legend of the Minotaur that lived within the labyrinth on Crete. Pasiphae, the wife of King Minos, concealed herself inside a hollow model cow and was made pregnant by a sacred white bull. Their offspring became the Minotaur — part bull and part human — which was eventually slain by Theseus of Athens with help from Ariadne. The nexus between the Cretan Minotaur legend and the Egyptian fertility magic reveals the way that early religious-magical ideas and practices spread throughout the ancient world. It is also significant to note that when the Egyptian "Bull of Bulls" died, it was embalmed and mummified as though it had been a pharaoh — and a new bull was solemnly chosen as its replacement.

But there was a great deal more to Egyptian-African magic and religion than rituals, incantations, and spells that sought power, wealth, or fertility. The importance of the just and fair Ma'at, Thoth's consort, is an essential part of understanding the equation. At least some of this mysterious ancient magic and religion was concerned with ethics and morality. As time passed, and powerful new pharaohs established and then re-established peace, order, and justice in their Afro-Egyptian domains, there were writers of conscience who argued that what the gods really required of human beings was hard, honest work, contentment, and tolerance of others.

One of the most controversial of the African religious mysteries concerns the Dogon people, who live in Mali, south of the River Niger, close to Bandiagara in the region known as Mopti. Although fewer than a million strong, the Dogon people have a very long and distinguished cultural history. It is one of their tragedies that they were frequent victims of slave traders, but that tragedy has meant that their knowledge of many ancient and mysterious things has been disseminated across the world.

Dogon religion acknowledges a great ancestral spirit whom they refer to as Nommo. Under his care and guidance, they are basically a very happy and harmonious people. They are sometimes referred to by outsiders as the *sewa* people, because it is part of Dogon culture to greet friends and relatives with a question as to their health and welfare and always to be answered by the word *sewa*, which translates broadly as "Everything is fine, thanks for asking."

The magical-religious issue at the heart of the controversy over the Dogon is their apparently inexplicable knowledge of astronomy and cosmology. They put Sirius at the centre of the cosmos and refer to it as Po Tolo. According to Dogon theories, Sirius was the focal point from which the Milky Way galaxy came into being. Their thinkers describe the known universe as measurable, yet infinite, and they populate it with numerous *yalu ulo*, star systems with spiral patterns. In a similar way to western astrologers and the Persian magi, the Dogon believe that Sirius, Orion, and the Pleiades can exert a great influence not only over human lives but also over the whole of human history.

From the development of the earliest humanoids in places like the Olduvai Gorge, through the Afro-Egyptian mysteries, and on to the strange, seemingly pre-emptive stellar knowledge preserved by the Dogon people, the origins and developments of magic and religion in Africa are very old and enigmatic. Are there really grounds for believing that someone — or some*thing* — from *out there* visited earth long ago, bringing awesome new knowledge from beyond the stars? Was it genetic engineering that created the Minotaur? Was Thoth (alias Hermes Trismegistus, alias Melchizedek) a highly advanced extraterrestrial alien whose knowledge was engraved on gleaming green tablets? Was there warfare between these godlike superbeings? Between Osiris and her hawklike son Horus on one side, and Set, her husband's murderer, on the other?

Almost every pantheon of the ancient religions had its heroes and villains: were they rivals for possession of this earth when our ancestors had nothing but flints with which to fight back? Were the "good" invaders the moral equivalent of Isis and Osiris, of Thoth, Ma'at, and Horus? Were Set and the other "evil" invaders mere land-grabbers who wanted to enslave our remote ancestors? To a man with Stone Age technology, anything much beyond that would have seemed like magic — and those who could control that technology would have seemed like gods to a paleolithic people.

It may reasonably be assumed that the ancient origins of African magic and religion formed part of the culture of the pioneering peoples who once inhabited the Olduvai Gorge,

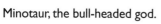

Minotaur, the bull-headed god.

who used *nassarius gibbosulus* in their rituals, and who might have made amazing discoveries via the intervention of extraterrestrial aliens.

Neither can the rich possibilities of the existence of Atlantis and its hypothetical inhabitants be ignored. From submerged Atlantis to North Africa via the Pillars of Hercules is no long journey. What if that journey was made by Atlantean survivors of the deluge and inundation that destroyed their continent? Did they bring a technology that seemed like magic to the pre-desert inhabitants of the Sahara? Was Egyptian technology the child of Atlantean technology? Was it Atlantean astronomers who brought knowledge of cosmology in general, and of Sirius in particular, to the wise Dogon people?

It is not beyond the bounds of possibility that African religion and magic originated many millennia ago — and far beyond this earth. How many of those vital, ancient secrets are still preserved and encoded today within what appear to be religious liturgy and ceremonials, and in magical spells, incantations, and enchantments?

By a careful examination and analysis of Santeria and similar religions, and by tracing their convoluted historical pathways — which have sometimes converged and sometimes separated widely — it should prove possible to find at least some of the deep and ancient secrets that form their common denominator.

Chapter 2

THE GODS OF
PREHISTORIC AFRICA

ALTHOUGH A number of traditional African gods and goddesses may be traceable for only a few centuries, the primary *ideas* from which they developed are much older, going back into the earliest dawn of human history. The mystery of their origins can be approached from seven different perspectives giving rise to a number of diverse theories.

The first perspective accepts the possibility of visits to earth by highly intelligent extraterrestrial aliens who seemed magical and godlike to our distant ancestors. Like the well-known deities in the pantheons of Greece, Rome, and Scandinavia, these supposed extraterrestrials had their own particular characteristics and responsibilities. They also exhibited behavioural failings that were suspiciously similar to our familiar human weaknesses. A variant of this hypothesis is that the so-called gods were humanoids with superior powers — like those of the supposed extraterrestrials — but that these abnormal entities came from Atlantis or Lemuria, or even from vast labyrinthine caverns deep below the surface of the earth.

This has led to a second theory put forward by some social psychologists who suggest that our earliest ancestors creatively *imagined* their gods as beings like themselves but with vast powers. The discreditable behaviour of certain pantheon members can then be understood in terms of what terrestrial human beings would like to do *if only they had the power with which they credited their imaginary deities.* This harmonizes with what James Frazer wrote in *The Golden Bough:* "Primitive man creates his gods in his own image."

A third theory embraces the concept of *tulpa,* or thought-forms. These are also referred to in psychical research literature as *egrigors* (spelling varies and includes *egrigori* and *egrigore*). The theory suggests that the human mind — especially when collaborating with a group of other minds — can actually bring something physical into existence. A classic example of tulpa creation occurred when Alexandra David-Neel was travelling through Tibet, early in the twentieth century. She worked hard, exerting great concentration and mental energy, to produce an amiable little monk, plump, smiling, and totally benign. There are various accounts of what went wrong, but the tulpa she had created surreptitiously escaped from Alexandra's control and became what can only be described as some kind of independent entity. It was no longer plump and amiable. The smile became a triumphant sneer. Other members of the expedition could now see it clearly. The tulpa had become decidedly sinister. It took Alexandra a great deal of time and energy to destroy her creation, and in some accounts she also needed considerable help from experienced local lamas.

In 1972, the Toronto Society for Psychical Research conducted an exceptionally interesting and intriguing piece of research. Their work involved a totally fictitious character named "Philip" whom they had deliberately created. Something purporting to be Philip then answered questions that the group posed with knocks, raps, and table turning. The life story that the Toronto experimenters compiled for the non-existent Philip Aylesford settled him in Diddington Manor in Cambridgeshire, England, a few miles north of the market town of St. Neots. Married to a cold and generally unpleasant wife named Dorothea, the unhappy Philip met a beautiful, young, raven-haired gypsy girl named Margo. Unsurprisingly, he fell in love with her and moved her secretly into the gatehouse of his estate. When the cruel and cunning Dorothea found out about her beautiful and passionate young rival, she accused Margo of witchcraft and had her burned at the stake. The pusillanimous Philip made no attempt to save her. In the story, he had a Catholic royalist background — at a time when Cromwell's merciless puritans were in power in England. Terrified that any adverse publicity associating him with witchcraft would lead to the confiscation of his wealth, his manor house, and his estates, Philip let Margo die in the flames. Soon afterwards, overcome with remorse, he committed suicide.

The 1972 Toronto experiment was by no means an isolated case. Other serious psychical research groups in Canada produced beings similar to

Philip. These entities included Lilith, who was given the character of a French-Canadian espionage agent of the Second World War; an alchemist named Sebastian, who had practised his profession during the Middle Ages; and a time traveller called Axel, who came from an imaginary future.

Another experiment along these lines took place in Sydney, Australia, where the imaginary entity was a teenaged girl named Skippy Cartman, who had been seduced and made pregnant by one of her religious teachers, the fictitious Brother Monk. He had strangled her and buried her body under the floorboards of an abandoned shearing shed — in much the same way that the real Foxy Corder had murdered his equally historical nineteenth-century victim, Maria Marten, and buried her body under the Red Barn on his farm in Polstead, Suffolk, England. Skippy's fictional murderer had moved away long before his victim's body was discovered.

The fourth theory regards the pantheon of ancient African gods as *personifications* of abstractions such as beauty, power, love, and fertility, and as personifications of processes such as hunting, agriculture, and harvest. This theory extends to views

Above: Maria Marten, murder victim.

Right: William "Foxy" Corder, murderer of Maria Marten.

of the pantheon as the *personalized powers* within natural phenomena such as volcanoes, earthquakes, storms, thunder, lightning, winds, rain, seas, and rivers. Within yet another subdivision of this theory, every waterfall, every mountaintop, and every tall tree can be thought of as either the manifestation of a divine being or the dwelling place of a divine being.

A fifth theory speculates on the existence of a range of what might be termed *intermediate* beings — a lot less powerful than the One Supreme God, but a great deal more powerful than *Homo sapiens*. The ancient sacred literature of many religions refers to hierarchies of superior spiritual beings: cherubim, seraphim, angels, and archangels. There are also records of various levels and sub-levels of demons and fallen angels. Logically, if there are infinite gradations of complexity and intelligence between viruses and human beings, there could well be infinite gradations of complexity, power, and intelligence between *Homo sapiens* and the One Supreme God. This fifth theory, therefore, looks at the idea that the gods of the ancient pantheons are more or less as the sacred texts describe them: the African, European, American, Asian, and Australasian gods actually exist.

The sixth hypothesis retreats into a haze of unknowing — and a passive acceptance that some things are by their very nature unknowable and inexplicable: *they are because they are.* According to this theory, belief in the existence of gods — ranging from supreme creators to the lowly spirits of trees and waterfalls — is simply something inevitable. It just goes with the territory, given that the human mind and the pathways of human thought *are as they are.* This theory argues that because *Homo sapiens* can observe the universe only within certain limits, and because human reason can function only within certain limits, it is more or less inevitable that our observations — and our *interpretations* of what we observe — will lead to various theological conclusions incorporating the existence of gods. Seeing what we see of the universe, and processing our data with the limited neurological equipment available to us, gods, religion, and magic are likely to be put forward as explanations.

The seventh theory is ecumenical and inclusive. It argues for toleration, for interpretation and translation of different theological

terms, and for a global assortment of divine entities. It suggests that
the Supreme Creator, who is called by many different names by many
different peoples, is nevertheless the One Supreme Creator God. It also
argues that any subordinate divine power with delegated responsibility
for thunder, volcanoes, rain, or earthquakes remains one and the same
assistant god irrespective of the name that human beings use to label that
sub-deity.

A common factor uniting almost every ancient African religion is
the idea of one great, supreme god at the back of everything. In many
of the earliest African faiths, this great creator is reckoned to have lived
originally on earth. Various reasons are given in the different religions,
but there seems to be a general agreement that because of human sins and
failings, the all-powerful creator god left to dwell in a Sky Kingdom or
Heaven, literally and metaphorically *above* the problems made by human
beings. This supreme god is understood as transcendent, a being of pure
spirit, formless and abstract. Despite its immeasurable distance from
humanity, the supreme god has left a trace of its divine breath, *anima*, or
spirit within each human being.

A belief in Cagn, for example, is part of the ancient religious traditions
of the San and Basarwa peoples of the Kalahari Desert, which includes
areas of Angola, Botswana, Namibia, and South Africa. Archaeological
and genetic evidence suggests that the San and Basarwa tribes, who
describe themselves as Bushmen, are among the oldest surviving human
races on the planet. For them, Cagn, who is also known as Kho and
Thora, is a supreme creator god who once lived with humanity on earth
but left for a transcendent place beyond the skies after people became
sinful. His people also credit Cagn with being a god of shape-shifting
and other types of magic. In any examination of Santeria and similar
religions, a thorough investigation of the very ancient belief in Cagn and
his association with sorcery is particularly important. His counterpart
in the realm of magic and shape-shifting was a sorcerer-god of the
Hottentots known as Heitsi-Eibib.

Lesser gods were created to act as the Sky God's deputies in various
areas. Regions of authority were given to each of them. They were
responsible for rain, for seedtime and harvest, for fire, wind, hunting

animals, sex, and reproduction. Every aspect of life on earth had a god or goddess in charge of it.

In most ancient African faiths, these minor deities listened to human prayers and those that were benign did their best to listen and answer by granting the individual worshipper's request. When something was beyond their remit, however, the benign minor gods would act as intermediaries and take the worshippers' requests to the all-powerful Creator.

In East Africa this great transcendent deity is known as Mulungu. In the west of Africa the name is Nyambe, a slight variation from the name in Ghana, where it is Nyame (just one letter, the *b*, is different). Central Africans refer to the Supreme Creator as Leza. Other ancient African names for the Supreme Being include Wamtatakuya, Tumbuka, and Chiuta, who combined his self-created status and omniscience with the role of rain god. Chiuta in particular was also seen as a god who was prepared to help his people.

The Ibo peoples of East Nigeria refer to their supreme creator deity as Chuku or Chineke: the first great cause. He is also thought of as the father of the earth goddess, and, like Chiuta, he is thought of as a benign and helpful deity.

The Macouas of Zambezi called their supreme creator god Mukuru, but they also gave him special interests in agriculture, the harvest, and architecture. This singles him out from many of the other ancient African deities. If a powerful being from elsewhere is esteemed for his mastery of *architecture*, does it link him with the theory that the Freemasons can trace their origins back for many millennia? They address God in their Masonic prayers as "Great Architect of this stupendous universe." This theory about the earliest origins of Freemasonry is covered in depth in another of our books, *Mysteries and Secrets of the Masons* (Dundurn, 2006).

Ancient African versions of the story of creation differ from the six biblical days, followed by the Jewish Sabbath, or Shabbat, regarded as a sacred rest day. The African creation narratives allow four days for the actual work of creation, and have a sacred fifth day that is devoted to the worship of Orisha Nla. The role of Orisha Nla needs careful explanation. In some accounts he is understood as the First Deputy of Mulungu, or Leza. He is regarded as the chief, or leader, of the minor deities to whom the different subordinate tasks were delegated by Mulungu. It was to Orisha Nla that Mulungu gave the special task of creating human beings from earthly soil — just as Adam was created from the dust of the earth in the Genesis account. Although Orisha Nla had oversight of this *physical* part of the work of creation, it was the Almighty Mulungu who lit the flame of life within them. Just as Adam was placed in the Garden of Eden, so Mulungu placed this new human creation on earth.

The idea of a transcendent, ultimate, and totally benign *spiritual* god like Mulungu, who works with a *physical* god like Orisha Nla, comes very close to the volatile ideas that split the early Christian Church during the first few centuries of the Christian era. Gnostics such as the Paulicians, the Bogomils, and later the Cathars of southwestern France believed that the one great and supreme creator god was a being of pure spirit. According to them, the physical universe had been created by another powerful, but inferior, deity referred to as the demiurge. The Greek δημιουργός, Latinized as demiurgus, simply meant a workman. The Mandaeans referred to the demiurge as Ptahil, and it was also referred to as Yaldabaoth. Gnostics regarded it — and all physical matter — as evil.

There may well be some connection here with Juok, also known as Shilluk, a god whose worshippers were situated in the area of the White Nile. Juok — like the demiurge — is credited with creating human beings.

Adroa is another very mysterious and theologically puzzling ancient African deity. He belongs to the Lugbara people who occupy parts of Zaire and Uganda. Like Orisha Nla and the mighty Mulungu, he enjoys a creative function, but he has evil aspects too. Sometimes he is conceived of as being very tall and only partially complete: often an eye, an arm, and a leg are missing from his tall frame. Adroa is thought of as a god of law, order, and justice — as well as a god of death.

The descendants of Adroa, referred to as the Adroanzi, became nature gods with individual responsibilities for certain territories, for rivers, waterfalls, whirlpools, and trees. Their mixed nature — like that of their divine parent Adroa — gave them a curious relationship with their human worshippers. They would follow and protect their people in dangerous places, defending them from thieves or dangerous animal predators. However, if the protected worshipper looked around to make sure that his guardian Adroanzi was actually there, the former guardian would immediately slay the worshipper instead of protecting him or her.

The Turkana of Kenya had a deity whom they called Akuj. He was their god of divination, of soothsaying and of peering into the clouded mysteries of the future.

The ancient goddess Ala, also referred to as Ane, was sacred to the Ibo peoples. Like Orisha Nla, Ala was a creator, who also reigned over the dead. She was the goddess to whom oaths were sworn by her devotees, and, like Adroa, Ala was concerned with law, order, and justice. Harvests were also her responsibility.

Among the 2 million Temne people of Sierra Leone, there are those who refer to Anayaroli as a river god — or demon — and he is also a god of wealth and financial success. For serious students of Santeria, the significance of Oba, sometimes called Obba, another river goddess, must not be overlooked. According to the historical legends, she was the first

and only legitimate wife of Shango, second king of the Oyo Empire. He is also the god of thunder and lightning in the complex Yoruba mythology. Shango is in some ways very similar to the Nordic Thor, and is armed with an axe, similar to Thor's great hammer. Freudian psychoanalysts would be particularly interested in the symbolism of Oba's offering Shango her ear to eat. When he declined, she was overcome with sadness at his rejection of her, and was transformed into the River Obba. There was a rival wife, named Osun, who also became a river goddess. Where her River Osun joins the River

Orisha Shango Yoruba's double-headed axe.

Obba there are dangerous and spectacular rapids that symbolize the furious animosity between the two wives. So important is this Santeria river goddess in the minds of the Iwo people that they are called the Sons of the River Obba in her honour. Ymoja, yet another river goddess, is venerated by the Yoruba peoples and exercises her protective care and blessings over women and children.

Since the arrival of Islam and Christianity, however, devotion to these local river gods and goddesses like Obba, Anayaroli, and Ymoja has declined noticeably despite the great antiquity of the cults of such river divinities.

Some of the Akamba of Kenya acknowledge Asa as a "strong lord" or even as a "father god." He is regarded as a god of intervention and miracles who frequently gives help to his worshippers. They also view him as the deity who helps his followers to survive the impossible.

The Ashanti people from Ghana in West Africa have a pantheon leader referred to as Nyame, or Nyankopon, who is thought of as omniscient and omnipotent. His wife, the goddess Asase Ya, is an earth goddess, thought of as the creator of human beings and strongly associated with fertility, agriculture, and the harvest. She is also the goddess who receives the spirits of the dead.

Neptune, also well known as Poseidon, was the sea god of classical Greek and Roman mythology. He was the husband of the sea goddess Amphitrite, who bore their son Triton — part man and part fish. The ancient African religions also include sea gods and goddesses, among whom Behanzin, the fish god of Fon in Dahomey, was prominent. Fishermen in particular would beg him for a good catch when they ventured out. Aquatic gods in these ancient African belief systems suggest possible connections with accounts of Dagon, the fish-god of the Phoenician peoples, mentioned in the Bible. There is some discussion among theologians as to whether Dagon was originally a corn and harvest god who was transformed into a fish-god in the pantheon of the seagoing Phoenicians.

Oannes was also thought of as a fish–god by the Babylonians. Berossus, a Babylonian writer dating from the third century BC, credits Oannes with having the body of a fish, or the *appearance* of a fish, but with a human body underneath. Again, according to Berossus, it was the benign and powerful Oannes who taught humanity wisdom in general and science, literacy, and art in particular.

There are two main schools of thought regarding the origin of Oannes. One theory suggests that he was based on Ea, a god of ancient Babylon. The weight of current scholarly opinion, however, seems to favour his being derived from Uan, one of the seven wise teacher-guides sent out by Ea to give wisdom and knowledge to humanity. These seven sages were called the Abgallu in Sumerian — from *ab* meaning *water*, *gal* meaning *great*, and *lu* meaning *man*. These intellectual heroes of early civilization were traditionally closely associated with the city of Eridu, generally reckoned to be the oldest in Sumer.

Another intriguing theory suggests that the Abgallu came by ship, bringing with them great learning from some older, more technologically developed culture — such as the one that existed along the valley of the Indus. But it is equally likely that the Abgallu came over the sea from ancient Africa — wise followers of Behanzin. It has even been suggested that the wisdom of the Abgallu was so profound that they might have been survivors from Atlantis. Another strand of the Abgallu-as-sea-voyagers-from-afar theory is the possibility that Oannes was described as being fishlike because he was wearing disc mail or chain mail. To observers who had never seen such link, or disc, armour before, it would have suggested the scales of a fish. The human mind normally attempts to describe the unknown in terms of the known.

There are significant links between *water* and modern Santeria, Obeah, Voodoo, and similar mysterious religions. It is almost as if their ancient connections with sea gods, river gods, water gods, and fish gods were still preserved in their contemporary practices. There is, for example, an *eau magique,* described as sacred Voodoo water, available from practitioners in New Orleans.

In the Plaine du Nord in Haiti, worshippers gather at the Pool of St. Jacques, where they perform elaborate water rituals and pray to the *Loas* — their family spirits, or household gods. There are also services and ritual celebrations at Le Saut d'Eau — a French phrase meaning *the waterfall.* Worshippers here take what is referred to as a "fortune bath" involving the use of herbal medicines and fragrances. Saint Philomene, sometimes spelled Philomena, is also invoked both here and in the northern town of Limonade. She is associated both with water and with Africa, and the legend of her martyrdom is a tragic and sensational one. Said to have been the daughter of Greek royalty, she met the Roman Emperor Diocletian, who was overwhelmed by her beauty and asked her to marry him. When she declined, saying that she wished to remain a Christian virgin, she was imprisoned, tortured, stripped, tied to a whipping post, and flogged unmercifully. Lacerated all over, she was finally thrown back into her cell, where angels visited her with miraculous healing balm.

Tied to an anchor and hurled into the sea, Philomena was again saved by the miraculous intervention of angels, who snapped the anchor rope and returned her safely to land. Her persecutors then fired arrows at her, but these came back like boomerangs and killed the executioners. An enraged mob finally accused her of witchcraft — because of her miracles — and decapitated her.

Her miraculous healings and rescues are not without their parallels in Santeria, Obeah, and Voodoo, and the story of Philomena's sufferings would appeal strongly to eighteenth- and nineteenth-century slaves who lived in a savage and brutal world of captivity where flogging was their daily reality.

The ancient African snake god Danh of Dahomey is a total contrast to the water rituals of Haiti involving prayers to Philomena. Like the Midgard Serpent, Jormangund, also known as Midgardsorm, Danh has his tail in his mouth. But unlike the evil and antagonistic Jormangund, Danh is benign and beautiful — a rainbow serpent who symbolizes all that is good and complete. He is an ancient African religious symbol of peace and unification.

Ochumare of the Yoruba peoples is very important in this context, because she is the Santeria goddess of the rainbow. Like Danh, she is good as well as beautiful.

The equally benign and munificent Enkai, also referred to as Parsai by his faithful Maasai adherents, was associated with Danh insofar as Enkai was the god of the rain that often accompanied the beautiful rainbow serpent. Another rain god, famous throughout West Africa, particularly

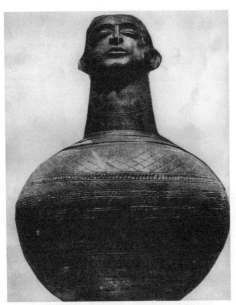

African pottery water or beer holder.

Zaire and Uganda, was Alur, sometimes called Jok Odudu, or just Jok. Traditionally, he demanded sacrifices in return for exercising his rainmaking powers, and black goats were usually offered to him.

Parsai, unlike Jok who demanded sacrifices, was a god of processes, a god who followed things through to benefit his people. The rain he sent made the grass grow, and grass became an important component of his rituals. He was also regarded as a beneficent deity of vegetation in general, and he delighted in blessing his grateful people.

The goddess Mbaba Mwana Waresa was worshipped by the Zulu peoples of Natal in connection with her powers over Danh, the rainbow, and over the rain. She is also an overseer of cultivation and crops — but her singular responsibility is beer. The Zulu peoples are expert beer makers, and they are also renowned for their superb basketry. They traditionally create very attractive beer baskets, known as *ukhamba*, for carrying containers of their favourite local brew.

For Enkai's faithful worshippers, this good work with the harvest and with fertility in general was reinforced by a tortoise-shelled goddess named Ison, who was also known as Ibibio and Ekoi. This concept of a goddess protected by a tortoise shell may be considered alongside the idea of Oannes, the fish–god. If he was a visitor from a more advanced culture, wearing chain mail, was Ibibio a similar visitor wearing either body armour *or a space suit?*

Fa of Dahomey had something in common with Akuj, the god of divination and soothsaying referred to earlier, but although Fa shared Akuj's concern with the future, he did more than predict it: he was a god of destiny, like Fate, Chance, or Lady Luck. Fa was the god who made things happen.

Where Fa was neutral, and brought both good and evil fortune, Guruhi of Gambia was a bringer of death and destruction. He had to be bought off, or avoided if at all possible. Meteors were regarded as a sinister sign of his evil presence, and he gave his adherents the power to kill their enemies.

The African moon goddesses, Ngami and Mawu, had many equally ancient parallels throughout the world, including the Greek moon goddess, Artemis, and her Aztec equivalent, Coyolauhqui, meaning *Golden Bells*, who was sister to the sun god, Huitzilopochtli. A similar brother-sister god and goddess relationship can be traced within the old Roman pantheon, where Luna (referred to as Selene by the Greeks) was regarded as the sister of Helios, the sun god.

In ancient China, the moon goddess, Heng-O, was the mother of twelve moons and ten suns. Her male counterpart in Japan was Tsuki-Yomi, who formed part of the Shinto religion. Khons, the Egyptian moon god, was the son of Amen and his consort, Mut. Sin, also known as Nanna, was a moon goddess of the old Sumerian civilization, and Soma — a male moon deity like Khons — was part of the Hindu pantheon.

Wherever a lunar deity was included among the catalogue of ancient gods and goddesses throughout the world, that deity was thought to have certain prominent characteristics. Lunar deities were frequently concerned with sexual attraction, and the mystery of the deeper, more powerful romantic love that transcended sexual desire but did not replace it. These deities were also associated with beauty, art, and profound wisdom. In countries where owls existed, they were often associated with lunar deities. These moon gods and goddesses were also the divine powers that governed changes and journeying — an idea that would seem to be logically associated with the phases of the moon. Another aspect attributed to some of the lunar deities was their power to affect the human mind. The word *lunacy* itself is rooted in this concept: the power of the lunar deity was thought to be the cause of human mental changes and disintegration.

The Nuer of South Sudan had a totally benign deity named Kwoth. In their eyes he was in charge of nature and had all the powers associated with natural things. Over and above this, Kwoth was venerated for his sense of justice, his unlimited mercy and compassion, and his willingness to help humanity — both collectively and individually.

Nzambi, an extremely powerful goddess of the Bakongo peoples of Angola and the Congo, has an important role in tracing modern Santeria, Obeah, Voodoo, and similar religions back to their ancient African origins. Towards the end of the fifteenth century, the Portuguese arrived in the area and fought a series of wars against the Bakongo peoples until the area became a Portuguese colony in 1885. During this period attempts were made to convert the indigenous peoples to Portuguese-style Christianity. Adherence to their own ancient religion became a symbol of the Bakongo struggle against their Portuguese conquerors. This traditional African faith emphasized the importance of prophecy and attempts at foretelling the future in various ways, worshipping ancestral spirits, and using *nksi* — small figurines that gave protection against evil, illness, and injury. Their widespread use throughout the Bakongo culture extended to their political institutions, medical practices, agriculture, and warfare.

The most powerful of the fetish dolls used in their magic were known as *nkondi*. These were carved from wood and then covered with small blades or nails. The *nkondi* were hollow and were able to contain hair, fingernails, and teeth. It was believed that these enclosures would strengthen, direct, and focus the magic. There is a strong connection between these old African Bakongo *nkondi* and figurines associated with traditional medieval European witchcraft.

Oddudua, another Yoruba goddess, was of primary importance. In one of the legends concerning Oddudua, her brother-husband, Obatala, had been sent to earth by the supreme god Oludomare to create the human race. Unfortunately, Obatala landed in a coconut palm tree, drank some fermented coconut juice, and was inebriated when he began creating. Disappointed with Obatala's poor workmanship, Oludomare sent Oddudua to join him and put right his errors. This she did. When he recovered from the coconut juice alcohol, Obatala was unhappy because his sister-wife had done what he considered to be his work. In another version of the legend, when he came round from his alcoholic stupor, he helped her and they created the human race together.

In both versions of the legend, Oddudua is regarded as the ancestress of the Yoruba peoples and is venerated accordingly. There are clear connections between her and the primary earth mother goddess figure represented by the Venus of Willendorf. The most famous of these statuettes was discovered in 1908 in the Austrian village of Willendorf, not far from Krems. It is made from a type of oolitic limestone that is not found in that part of Austria, and the artist who fashioned it has decorated it with reddish ochre. According to the age of the strata in which she was found, the Venus of Willendorf is about 25,000 years old. Her exaggerated anatomy symbolizes fertility, but the unsolved mystery of her head covering has stimulated several very unusual and interesting theories — including the idea that she is an extraterrestrial alien humanoid wearing a space helmet. The statuette may be seen in the Naturhistorisches Museum in Vienna.

Ogun, revered by the Nago people as well as by the Yoruba of West Africa, is the equivalent of Hephaestus, blacksmith of the gods in the Greek pantheon, and Vulcan to the Romans. Ogun is the African god of war as well as the god of metal and technology. He is regarded as the deity who will come to the aid of his worshippers when they have difficulties that his skill can surmount.

Ruhanga of the Banyoro people is especially significant as a god who is concerned with death and rebirth — and the whole concept of reincarnation. Utixo, revered by the Hottentot peoples, is also a god who controls reincarnation.

Sakarabru is worshipped by the Agni peoples of Guinea. He has some connection with the moon but is not primarily a moon god. He is at his most powerful when the moon is waxing, and least effective when it is waning. This ties in with medieval European ideas concerning the advisability of planting certain crops when the moon is waxing and some of the old European healing magic that had to be applied when the moon was in a particular phase. Sakarabru is a god of healing, and it seems that when he is invoked at the time of the waxing moon, his patients are most likely to prosper and recover their health under his benign aegis.

The Nupe peoples of northern Nigeria credit their god Soko with power over magic and enchantments of various types, and with the ability to arrange communications with the dead.

Unkulunkulu is revered by the Amazulu peoples and by the Ndebele of Zimbabwe as their god of organization, effective administration, and good order.

Isaywa, also known as Wele, is a god of the stars and planets and all celestial phenomena. His role can also be associated with astrology because he is seen as a god of prosperity — so his control of stars, planets, and the zodiac may be thought of as the tools and instruments with which he brings prosperity to pass for his chosen devotees.

Undoubtedly, there was considerable movement of thought and ideas between Egypt and the rest of Africa — especially in the days before the Sahara became a desert. In consequence, there are clear theological parallels between the two religious systems. For the Egyptians, the supreme creator was Amun, Aten, Ptah, or Re. Hathor, Bat, and Horus were sky gods. Osiris was a god of the earth. Hapi was the Nile in flood. When things went wrong, the trouble was usually traced to Seth, the god of evil and destruction. Ma'at — the god of justice, truth, balance, order, and stability — put right again what Seth had disturbed. Thoth, alias Hermes Trismegistus and Melchizedek, was a god of wisdom who was also associated with the moon just as Re was associated with the sun.

The Egyptian gods were frequently localized. Amaunet, the female equivalent of Amon, was worshipped at Thebes, as were Amon and Mut. Amon was elevated to the role of king of the gods at Thebes, where he was also called Amon-Re. Anuket, the gazelle goddess, was revered at Elephantine. Hathor, the beautiful and sensuous goddess of wine, dancing, and lovemaking, was sometimes represented as a cow — and at Thebes she acquired the additional responsibility of being goddess of the dead. At Dendera, she was believed to be the partner of Horus. When she was worshipped in Byblos, she was closely associated with Isis. Isis, in turn, was worshipped at Philae and was the sister-consort of Osiris. She was linked with Astarte, Greek Αστάρτη, and identical to the goddess Ishtar of Mesopotamia. Normally portrayed as a beautiful, naked woman, Astarte was a goddess of fertility and sexuality. Worshipped in Tyre and Sidon, she was also known to the Greeks as Aphrodite, and Cyprus became one of her worship centres.

The shapes of the gods were ripe with symbolism. Horus, who was thought to be one of the earliest royal gods, was a falcon whose eyes were the sun and moon. Rather surprisingly for a falcon–god, he was also Khentekhtay — the divine crocodile. Sobek was another crocodile–god who was worshipped at the Faiyum. Khnum was conceived of as having a human body topped by a ram's head. His worship centres included Esna and Hypselis. Serapis was worshipped in Alexandria, and was regarded by his Greek adherents as being one and the same as Zeus, king of the gods. When the wise and benign Thoth was worshipped in Hermopolis, he was depicted as a baboon.

It would be possible to spend many years of research in Africa constantly discovering fresh facts about these ancient pantheons and the ways in which knowledge of them travelled westwards and northwards — not least, via the slave trade.

Chapter 3
THE SLAVE TRADE
AND ITS CONSEQUENCES

SLAVERY IS one of the oldest human institutions. Different forms of slavery seem to have existed since the earliest human societies and cultures came into existence. The exploitation of one human being by another goes back for many millennia. One of the oldest sets of laws available to historians and archeologists is the Code of Hammurabi, dating from about four thousand years ago in Mesopotamia. Even as long ago as that, it refers to slavery as being an established part of the social order.

Groups of proud, independent, and knowledgeable people, overwhelmed by enemies and sold into slavery, have nevertheless survived and retained their identity because of highly prized social, cultural, and religious beliefs. During their slavery in Egypt, and again during their captivity in Babylon, the Jewish people demonstrated just how potent such belief systems could be.

Jeremiah, chapter 52, verses 28–30, records three separate captivity events. In 597 BC, during the reign of the Jewish king Jehoiachin, prominent citizens were taken away into exile and the Jerusalem Temple was raided. During the reign of Zedekiah in 586 BC, Jerusalem was severely damaged and more of its citizens were taken as captives to Babylon. In 581 BC there was yet another captivity episode. However, when the Persians overcame the Babylonians, the good and humane Emperor Cyrus gave the Jews permission to return to Jerusalem in 537 BC. Throughout that long exile, the Jewish captives had maintained their national identity, and survived as a people, because of their religious beliefs.

When Africans were sold into slavery, those with the strongest cultural and religious beliefs were the ones who retained their true identity against all that they had to endure. They never gave up. They never gave in. Instead they welded their ancient African faiths onto the religions of

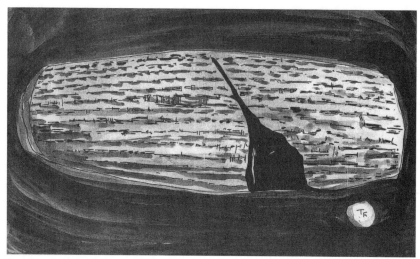

Scroll cylinder of Cyrus of Persia.

those who had enslaved them. From the fervid heat of that emotionally charged welding process came the power and mystery of Santeria, of Voodoo, of Obeah — and of many other similar magical religions.

Historians have long observed that when things are at their worst, heroes arise and lead their people to better times. Particular hardships seem to give people specific strengths that enable them to overcome their difficulties and endure their sufferings. A closer, more specific analysis of that generalization suggests that slavery can *create* indomitable conquerors. Spartacus provides an example. The proverbial iron enters the soul. The whips, chains, and branding irons of their overseers can change vulnerable and oppressed slaves into free and independent men and women whom nothing can stop.

The mysterious, magical religions of the Caribbean, of Cuba, Haiti, and Barbados, and of New Orleans and South America are all inextricably intertwined with the slave trade from Africa dating from the sixteenth century to the nineteenth. As early as the end of the fourteenth century, wealthy and powerful Europeans began buying slaves in Africa and taking them to Europe. In those days, the captives were mainly set to work as domestic servants or as agricultural workers.

Religion was a prominent part of the picture at this stage, and the excuse of the Europeans who took Africans as slaves was that they wanted to give them a chance to become Christians. The logic here was as hypocritical and perverted as the logic of the Holy Inquisition. Heretics were tortured and then burnt alive on the grounds that the Inquisition was giving them just a little temporary pain in this world to save them from the everlasting fires of hell in the next. In the same way, these earliest slave exploiters argued that taking Africans away from their homelands and families in order to make them Christians was perfectly justified. It was greatly to the Church's discredit that it wholly approved of and encouraged these practices.

Spanish and Portuguese sea captains would sometimes take their black slaves with them as servants on their voyages, and the amazing career of Estevanico demonstrates how far such adventures could lead. Also known as Esteban the Moor and Little Stephen, Estevanico was a North African Berber, born in 1503 in Azamor, which was then a Portuguese stronghold on the Atlantic coast of Morocco. Enslaved by the Portuguese, Estevanico was sold to a wealthy Spanish nobleman, Andrés Dorantes de Carranza. After many adventures by land and sea in the New World, he reached what is now Arizona and New Mexico. The details of the end of his life are not clear, but according to one persistent tradition, he escaped in 1539 from the indigenous American village of Hawikuh, in what is now New Mexico, and made his way to Rio Mayo. Here he settled with the Mayo people, acquired a small harem, and had a number of children. One of Estevanico's sons, named Aboray, was said still to be living there in 1622.

The indigenous Cubans, led by their fearless and formidable chief, Hatuey, put up a tremendous struggle against the European invaders but were eventually defeated by superior Spanish weapon technology. One demographic estimate suggests that there were well over a million people in Cuba before the Europeans arrived. A quarter of a century later, that population was down to two thousand. Starvation and disease killed many of them. Some died of overwork in the mines. Others ended their own lives out of sheer desperation. Indigenous populations on many of the Caribbean islands fell in much the same way. This created a problem for the mine owners, plantation owners, and other slave users: without adequate manpower there was no profit to be made. They turned to importing slaves from Africa. By the middle of the sixteenth century, as many as ten thousand slaves were being brought in from Africa each year.

British involvement led to prison fortresses being built along the African coasts so that slaves could be held there until the next slaving ship arrived. Initially, slaves were obtained from victorious local chieftains selling off their prisoners of war. As the demand increased inexorably, raiding parties went out with the sole intention of capturing slaves who would be exchanged profitably for the prestigious European goods that the victorious chieftains wanted.

What is often referred to as the Atlantic slave trade consisted of the capture, enslavement, and shipping of perhaps as many as 40 million victims from West Africa and Central Africa across the Atlantic to the Caribbean islands and the Americas. Contemporary specialist historians, however, estimate the number to be less than half the earlier estimates. Academic African-American experts use the term *Maafa* for this wholesale tragedy. *Maafa* is a Kishwali word that translates as "major disaster" or "cataclysmic event." The economic stimulus behind all this human suffering was known as the Triangular Trade — it affected millions of slaves, it lasted four centuries, and its impact affected four continents.

In South Carolina, New England, and Virginia, the colonists were struggling to survive against hostility from the indigenous American peoples nearby. The colonists therefore needed to make treaties and alliances with them. Such treaties precluded attempting to take any of the indigenous peoples as slaves. That meant importing slaves from somewhere else.

One side of the notorious Atlantic Triangle was the trading of goods from Europe to Africa in exchange for slaves, and it needs to be remembered that much of this trading was coercive. The African customers for European goods were only too well aware that if they failed to provide the slaves that the European traders wanted, there was a very real danger that they and their people would themselves end up chained in the hold of a European slaving ship.

There were eight principal areas from which slaves were taken across the Atlantic to the New World on this second instalment of the triangular run. Victims were embarked in Mozambique and Madagascar; they also came from Gabon, Angola, and the Congo, while other dispatch points were Senegal, the Gambia, and Guinea-Bissau. The Côte d'Ivoire and Ghana were used, as were Benin and Biafra.

Having acquired the African slaves whom they wanted, the slavers set off for North and South America and the Caribbean Islands. Two out of every five slaves came from the region of West Central Africa. One in five came from Benin, and one in ten from the Gold Coast. Each of the other regions was responsible for approximately one slave out of every twenty.

Academic analysis of the ethnic groups to which the African slaves belonged indicates that there were between forty and fifty distinct groups represented among them. Of these forty-plus groups the Chamba, Yoruba, and Igbo peoples of Nigeria were prominently represented, as were the Wolof of Senegal and the Makua of Mozambique. The Yoruba are especially significant here because of their powerful, ancient African religious traditions. Much of their ancient faith survives in Santeria.

There are records of what were euphemistically termed "training camps" or "seasoning camps" for newly arrived slaves. The luckier slaves went straight to their new work on the plantations. Those who were put through the seasoning camps frequently died during their so-called training. In the minds of those who ran the camps, the new slaves needed to be broken in — like horses — and for the slaves this meant savage torture to ensure their future docility and obedience.

Once the slaves were auctioned off in the New World, to start their processing in the conditioning camps, the ships were loaded with tobacco, rum, molasses, sugar, and cotton from the slave plantations and then headed back to Europe to complete the triangle. As soon as the goods were sold in European markets, the whole sordid business began again with yet another voyage to Africa to collect fresh slaves.

Analysis of the underlying economics indicates that many of the products of the New World that were wanted in Europe simply could not be grown there. Other commodities could be grown far more cheaply in the Caribbean and the Americas than they could in Europe. The problem for the New World producers was that their harvests were very labour intensive. This labour problem was aggravated and prolonged because there were vast amounts of inexpensive land available in the Americas. When free workers arrived from Europe, they were soon able to acquire land for themselves and needed workers to develop it.

The tragedy for Africans captured as prisoners of war or abducted on slaving raids was that if they had been allowed to remain in Africa instead of being sold to Europeans, they would have had a reasonable chance of escape. They might well have been liberated and repatriated if their own people had regained a military advantage over their opponents. In any case, the traditions associated with internal African slavery were less rigorous than those that applied in the New World. African slaves who remained in Africa were often paid a small wage and could hope eventually to buy their freedom.

Inhabitants of the Niger valley, when captured by slavers, would be taken to the coast and sold to Europeans or exchanged for alcohol, cloth fabrics, and weapons such as muskets that would enable the African slave dealers to acquire more prisoners. It also became common practice to punish criminals by selling them as slaves, who then ended up abroad.

One strange and interesting example of the consequences of the African slave trade and its mysterious religious impact on the New World can be traced back to Oistins, near Christchurch in Barbados, and the unsolved mystery of the Chase Elliott tomb. Excavated prior to 1724 from the coral stone of which Barbados is formed, and built of sturdy coral stone blocks above-ground, the tomb had been intended to house the body of James Waldron, a wealthy Barbadian planter. Whether he was ever buried there is a matter of conjecture, because the tomb was empty when the first of the Chase Elliott family was laid to rest there in 1807. Over the next few years, right up until 1819, the previously buried coffins were found to have been disturbed between interments.

Every time a burial party entered to carry out a fresh interment, they would find the previously interred coffins in a state of chaotic disorder. Precautions were taken to ensure that there were no secret passages leading into the tomb through which intruders might have entered to carry out the desecrations. Sand was sprinkled on the floor to detect any footprints, flood marks, or drag marks. The big blue Devonshire marble slab that covered the tomb entrance was sealed, and on the penultimate

The Chase Elliott vault on Barbados.

occasion, in 1819, the governor of Barbados, Lord Combermere himself, was present and placed his official seal into the soft cement — as did a number of reputable leading citizens.

A few months later, when the tomb was reopened on Combermere's orders, the seals were all intact, and there were no marks in the sand, but the coffins were again in disorder — one of them was even reported to have been found halfway up the coral stone steps that led down from the vault.

That was enough even for Combermere — a seasoned cavalry commander from the Peninsula Wars, where he had served with the Duke of Wellington. With the agreement of the vicar, the Reverend Doctor Thomas Orderson, all the coffins were reinterred in separate graves in the Christchurch cemetery.

The sinister tomb has stood empty for close on two centuries — as it was when we examined it thoroughly as part of a BBC documentary we were making on location in Barbados.

Among the varied theories that researchers have put forward to account for the mystery of the moving coffins — several of which were lead-covered and extremely heavy — was that some form of powerful religious magic was involved: Voodoo, Santeria, Obeah, or one of the others.

Lionel
holding a
small stone
from the
Chase vault
in Barbados.

Among those who lay in the Chase Elliott vault was Samuel Brewster, a relative of the Chase family, who had been killed during a slave revolt in Barbados. Another corpse that lay inside the vault in a wooden coffin with a lead covering was that of the notorious Colonel Chase, who had been hated and feared by his family, his servants, and his slaves alike. Very powerful emotions like the ones he aroused are believed to play a significant role in the spells, charms, prayers, and incantations of the magical mystery religions such as Santeria, Obeah, and Voodoo. There was no shortage of negative emotion between sugar planters and slaves on Barbados at the time when the coffins moved in the Chase Elliott vault. The risk of a slave revolt was high on the island because there was little or no hope of escape for slaves on Barbados.

By contrast, for slaves who were sold to American mainland plantations some faint hope still survived. For them there was the Underground Railway — a secret system of hiding and transporting fugitives — that helped escaped slaves from the south to reach the north.

Perhaps the best known episode of this era was John Brown's capture of Harper's Ferry. It was on October 16, 1859, that John Brown's handful of men — barely twenty of them — captured the arsenal at Harper's Ferry. Already deeply committed to the abolitionist cause, Brown and his men knew that weapons and ammunition would be of crucial importance if they were to succeed in what they regarded as their war against slavery. When President Washington had originally chosen Harper's Ferry as the site of the arsenal and armoury, he had had in mind the importance of waterpower for manufacturing — and Harper's Ferry was close to both the Shenandoah and the Potomac Rivers. Part of the armoury became known as John Brown's Fort during the bitter fighting that ensued before Brown and his surviving abolitionists were killed or captured, tried, and subsequently executed. Brown's raid on Harper's Ferry became a memorably charismatic event in the war against slavery.

Abolitionists offered the shelter of their homes, along with refreshments and money, to fugitives who were making a break for freedom. Fourteen northern states and Canada were involved in the Underground Railway, and by the middle of the nineteenth century more than three thousand freedom lovers were working to help escaped slaves. After slavery had been abolished in Canada, and the 1850 Fugitive Slave Act became part of legislation in the U.S.A., it was naturally to Canada that escaped slaves headed from the southern plantation states of America. The 1850 Fugitive Slave Act gave bounty hunters the right to pursue runaway slaves into free areas and to abduct them back into slavery. It is greatly to the credit of Canadian captains and seamen on many of the nineteenth-century Great Lakes ships such as *Phoebus*, *Forest Queen*, and *Morning Star* that they would pick up fugitive slaves and take them to the safety of the Canadian side without asking for a fare.

It is also greatly to the credit of Canadian members of the Society of Friends that they founded the Wilberforce Settlement: they bought nearly one thousand acres of land on which escaped slaves could settle. In 1851 Henry Bibb and Josiah Henson worked together to establish the Refugees' Home Colony for escaped slaves who had managed to reach Canada.

For this in-depth study of Santeria, Obeah, Voodoo, and the other mysterious, syncretized religions associated with them, there are seven significant points to analyze from the African slave trade from the sixteenth to nineteenth centuries and its consequences today.

The first factor is that until European, Arabian, and Asian ingressions into Africa, most Africans who found themselves enslaved remained in their own vast continent. Even if escape or repatriation did not occur for them, most of them were still within their own familiar climatic and cultural environment. Although the religious beliefs of one African group might differ significantly from those of another, there was far more in common between the range of ancient African faiths than there was between any of those old indigenous religious systems and Islam or Christianity — and yet, like Islam and Christianity, the ancient African belief systems acknowledged the existence of one supreme god. Africans enslaved by a neighbouring African power had no particular reason to change their religion. One of the most important consequences of their being sold across the Atlantic was that they were under strong pressure to change — or to appear to change.

The second point is that during slavery and its consequential hardships — often very prolonged ones — religion was a vital factor in psychological survival. Holding on to the belief that their gods would help, support, sustain, and perhaps miraculously liberate them often enabled enslaved peoples to endure their deplorable living conditions. If their ancient, traditional religions were forbidden, if mentioning an Orisha's name in the hearing of an overseer would invite the lash or the branding iron, then the old gods in whom they still believed had to be effectively camouflaged.

How could a traditional, ancient African god be disguised in a western Christian culture? African slaves in contact with Christianity — especially with Catholicism — soon became acquainted with an alphabet of saints, both historical and legendary. This vast array of holy men and women included Abban the hermit, Barnabas, Callistus of catacomb fame, Dagobert, Edward, Florentius, Thomas Garnet, Helen, Ignatius, Joachim, Kenelm, Laudus, Matthew, Nectan, Odilo, Philomena, Quentin, Radegund, Sexburga, Thomas, Ulric, Valentine, Withburga, Ythamar, and Zeno.

There were, therefore, Christian saints to spare who could serve as disguises — or alter egos — for the ancient African deities that filled the memories of the slaves. These ancient gods included Elegua, Obatala, Shango, Bumba, Abassi, Eshu, Oloron, Anansi, and Yemaya — a list almost as long as the catalogue of saints. A slave beside a Cuban waterfall ostensibly praying to Saint Philomena or to Saint Jacques was in reality praying to an Orisha, or to one of his Loas, or household gods.

Saints identified as Orishas.

The third factor is the way that the old African religious ideas were so widely disseminated as a result of the transatlantic slave trade. Caribbean slaves brought their African religion with them. Slaves in South America and the southern states of the U.S.A. brought it with them. When the Underground Railway got them out of slavery and up to Canada and the free northern states of the U.S.A. their ancient African religion travelled with them.

The fourth point is that all human ideas — including religious ideas — are affected by travel and exposure to other cultures. Even without the necessity to pretend to belong to a new religion while secretly holding fast to the old one, traditional belief in the gods of ancient Africa was unavoidably modified to a greater or lesser extent because the believers found themselves in a totally different environment. Different demands were placed on them by that environment, and those varied demands led to changes in their prayers and supplications to the old African gods.

The fifth factor is the inbuilt human desire for newness, for change, for innovation. Tradition and stability have their appeal — but so does the craving for change. Scientists and inventors make new observations and they then produce new theories and technologies that harmonize with those new observations. Theologians, philosophers, and religious leaders do the same thing. Saint Paul's theology as he travelled widely among Greeks and Romans during the first century differed significantly from the teachings and practices of Saint James and the early Jerusalem Christians. Religious leaders among the African slaves were just as dynamic and innovative in their thinking as any other theologians. Some began to question the old ways. They looked for new and different explanations for what was happening to them and to the world.

The sixth point is the heredity factor. Although family life was cruelly broken and disrupted for many of the slaves, there were nevertheless a few families that were relatively stable despite the worst that their owners could do to them. There were warmly loving slave husbands and wives, with loyal and affectionate sons and daughters to whom the old African religious ideas and traditions could safely be passed on. Down from father to son and from mother to daughter went the names and characteristics of the old African gods, and the traditional techniques of invoking their aid by prayer, worship, and sacrifice. Some escaped slaves also found loving partners from other ethnic backgrounds and in their combined families the old African beliefs tended to blend with the partner's different faith and cultural background.

The seventh factor — perhaps the most potent of all — is the universal human need to cope with life's difficulties: poverty, illness, injury, unsatisfied ambition, and the deep need for purpose and self-fulfillment. For those who mingled with African slaves and their descendants, and were prepared to listen to them, there were opportunities to learn about the ways that the old African gods helped and supported their worshippers. Stories of divine intervention to bring about a desired marriage, to make crops grow, to cause rain to fall, to make the sun shine, to escape from dangerous wild beasts — or from human enemies — these all spread from their African originators to those who were prepared to listen to them. History shows repeatedly that when people are desperate enough they will try any remedy rather than no remedy. As the syncretism between Christianity and the old African faiths grew into Obeah, Santeria, and Voodoo, so increasing numbers of *people with needs* began to approach priests and priestesses for help.

From this interface between Christianity and the ancient African belief systems that took place during the turbulent centuries of the American and Caribbean slave era grew the mysterious syncretism that underpins Santeria, Voodoo, Obeah, and other quasi-magical religions.

Chapter 4

CHRISTIANITY ENCOUNTERS
THE OLD AFRICAN RELIGIONS

CHRISTIANITY has always been an adventurous, challenging, and exploratory religion. For traditional Christians, the core teachings of the faith are about a supreme father god whose nature is infinite love personified, allied with omnipotence, omniscience, and omnipresence. Involved alongside God in the mystery of the Holy Trinity are Jesus Christ, his son, the saviour of the world, referred to by Saint John the Evangelist as the *logos* or *word* of God; and the Holy Spirit, the comforter, the strengthener, the inspirer and helper of Christian believers.

For traditional Christians, God is the creator and sustainer of the entire cosmos — of all that ever was, of all that is now, and of all that can ever be. It is the loving will of God that all who seek Him will find Him, and that all who find Him will enjoy eternal and abundant life with Him and with one another.

For traditional Christians, the life of Jesus begins with his miraculous birth to Mary the Virgin, wife of Joseph the carpenter from Nazareth. At the start of his earthly ministry, during the episodes known as the temptations, Jesus decides what sort of Messiah he is going to be and how he will accomplish his mission of salvation. He teaches sublime truths about love, mercy, and forgiveness, and he announces that the Kingdom of God is at hand. He performs miracles of healing, and challenges the humbug and hypocrisy of the contemporary religious leaders who promptly plot to have him killed. Following his agonizing death by crucifixion at the hands of the Roman occupiers of the Holy Land, he is resurrected. He appears to his overjoyed disciples on numerous occasions and then ascends to Heaven.

For traditional Christians, the world will end when he returns in power and glory to judge it.

Saint Mary
the Virgin.

Traditional Christianity also includes a belief in angels, in Satan — otherwise called Lucifer — and in fallen angels, or demons, who follow him and cause the suffering, misery, and evil that spoil our world and our lives. Many Christians believe that as well as angels, there are saints and other holy beings who have conquered evil in this world and are now in Heaven with God. A majority of Christians believe these saints listen to our prayers and pass them on to God — and generally protect and assist us.

Mainstream Christianity promotes an ethical system that is rooted in loving and serving God and treating our fellow human beings as we would like them to treat us. There are more specific moral teachings about the desirability of faithful, monogamous marriage, and some Christians question the ethical foundations of same-sex relationships, genetic therapy, abortion, and euthanasia.

Different Christian groups have their own ideas about the nature and meaning of baptism and the sources of religious authority. Some church organizations are centralized, hierarchical, and bureaucratic. Others are largely free, autonomous, and independent.

One group looks to its priests, bishops, archbishops, cardinals, and the papacy. For them, authority is vested in the Church and the hierarchy controlling it. Questions of doctrine and ethics, creeds and moral behaviour are referred to its leaders to decide. For another group of Christians, the inspiration of the Holy Spirit is authoritative. Believers in this group look inside themselves for God's guidance as the occasion demands. They observe a situation and pray about it before deciding what God wants them as Christians to do about that specific situation. Many of these Christians follow what they describe as the principle of *situational ethics* rather than any system of prescribed and definitive ethics for all occasions. On principle, such autonomous moral thinkers do not say *never* or *always* in a religious context. Their loyalty to the underlying Christian principle of love is the background against which their decisions are made — but there is great flexibility in their decision making. Reason and logic blend with spirituality and religious commitment. They trust their own decisions — not those of any hierarchical, bureaucratic, ecclesiastical establishment.

A third group of Christians relies upon scripture. For them the ultimate authority is the Christian Bible, which they regard as the inviolate and infallible Word of God.

Today's academic Christian theologians — independent progressives, modernists, and liberals — question the authority of the Church hierarchy on the grounds that those who occupy its ranks are neither more nor less qualified than anyone else to make religious pronouncements. These progressive Christians also question the absolute authority of Scripture — however ancient and sacrosanct — on much the same grounds. They would argue that those who had set down their religious thoughts and opinions in writing millennia ago, often in the honest belief that they had been inspired to do so, might be just as right — or just as wrong — as any twenty-first-century religious thinker putting his or her thoughts on paper for posterity to read. Modernists argue that the Bible, by which fundamentalists set such great store, is a miscellaneous collection of very different books, written by authors from divergent cultures. Those scriptural writers lived in different centuries and, unsurprisingly, focused on dissimilar priorities.

The book of Genesis serves as a useful example. The oldest available Masoretic (Hebrew) texts are the Aleppo Codex from approximately AD 900 and the Westminster Leningrad Codex from around AD 1000. Fragments of Genesis were also found among the Dead Sea Scrolls, which could be from as early as 200 BC. Modern academics have identified several separate texts comprising Genesis as we have it today. There is the E text, so named because it uses the word *Elohim* when referring to God. This E text was probably composed in the Northern Kingdom of Israel a little later than 922 BC, which was when the united Kingdom of Israel and Judah that had been ruled by David and then Solomon broke up. It was almost certainly written by a priest — or a group of priests — in the holy place at Shiloh prior to 722 BC when the Assyrians overran and destroyed the Northern Kingdom of Israel. In this E document Jacob's all-important birthright is bestowed upon Joseph, who had all the adventures in Egypt and became the ancestor of the tribe of Ephraim. The Northern Kingdom's royalty were members of the tribe of Ephraim. The E document identifies Shechem as the northern capital and describes it as the burial place of Joseph. Judah, whose name is later applied to the whole of the Southern Kingdom, doesn't get a mention at all in the E document.

Genesis also contains a document named the J text because it refers to God as *JHWH* in German, or *YHWH* in English. The J document is about the same age as the E document but seems to have been written by a group of priests in the Temple in Jerusalem. It stresses the importance of the royal family of Rehoboam, a son of Solomon who founded the Southern Kingdom after the country split. Another identifiable text within Genesis is called the JE strand because it has been created by welding the J and E documents together.

Further literary analysis reveals the P text, a priestly document composed during the reign of King Hezekiah (715–687 BC). The P text is concerned with deeply ethical and religious matters rather than with the petty rivalries of the monarchs of the Northern and Southern Kingdoms. It was also written with the less righteous intention of elevating the power and authority of the Aaronite priests who ran the Jerusalem Temple and had a vested interest in concentrating worship there exclusively via the sacrifices that they alone could carry out. The P documents made no reference to direct contact with God via dreams. Neither does P mention angels. It also omits the curious phenomenon of the serpent in Eden that had the ability to speak. Another interesting aspect of this P document is its omission of references to any prophets who preceded Aaron himself.

Moving on beyond Genesis, scholars can detect the existence of a D document, which seems to have been written during the reign of King Josiah (640–609 BC). Further complications arise with the detection of yet another thread known as the R text. This is the work of a redactor, or editor, who seems to have welded D, E, J, and P together into the Jewish Torah. There is also evidence that an earlier book than Genesis once existed, which appears to have been called the Book of Generations. Some scholars suggest that it was an independent work not connected with the writings and editings of D, E, J, and P.

But this questioning of both hierarchical, ecclesiastical bureaucrats and sacrosanct scriptures by progressive modernists had not yet modified the inflexible, old-style *traditional* Christianity that confronted the African slaves.

Broadly, they had their own general African beliefs in a supreme god surrounded and assisted by benign Orishas and Loas, but what *precise* religious ideas did the different groups of African slaves actually hold? What did they fall back on as *authority* for their religious beliefs and actions? How far was African religious thought influenced by the ideas of ancient Egypt? Or did religious ideas flow in *both* directions?

It is highly probable that there was a dynamic two-way traffic between the religious ideas of Egypt and the rest of Africa. Egypt also had contact with states that lay to its north and east: Babylon, Assyria, Persia, and the Empire of Solomon. Religious thought from those territories could also have reached Africa — and African religious ideas could have reached them as well.

There are tantalizing biblical references to Solomon's prolifically productive gold mines at a site named Ophir, regarded by a number of serious religious historians as being somewhere in Africa. Certainly vast quantities of gold were reaching Egypt and Solomon's Empire, and Africa seems to be one of the most likely adjacent sources.

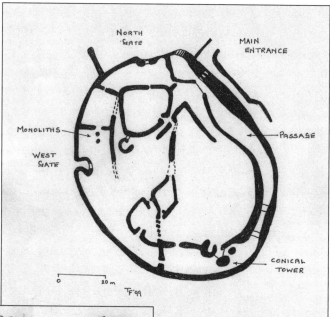

Above: Zimbabwe plan.

Left: Zimbabwe ruins.

The tomb of Pharaoh Tutankhamen provides germane evidence of the quantities of gold involved. When it was opened by Lord Carnarvon and Howard Carter in 1922, it was found to be packed with priceless golden objects. In considering the magnitude of Egyptian gold, it must be remembered that Tutankhamen was only a relatively minor and unimportant pharaoh compared to someone like the great Rameses II. If there was so much gold in such an insignificant tomb as Tutankhamen's, how much more must there have been in ancient Egypt as a whole — and *where did it come from?*

Moses led the Hebrews out of their Egyptian slavery during the reign of Rameses II, which ended circa 1225 BC. Approximately forty years later, under Joshua's powerful and effective leadership, the Israelites were established in Palestine. After some two centuries of being ruled on an ad hoc basis by leaders referred to as judges, the Israelites appointed Saul as their first king. He was followed by his son-in-law, David, one of whose later wives was the famous but mysterious Bathsheba. She became the mother of the wise and powerful Emperor Solomon, but Bathsheba's own origins and ancestry are shrouded in mystery. Her name literally means *daughter of Sheba*. Does that suggest that she originated in that strange, semi-legendary country, whose beautiful Queen Makeda later visited Solomon? If the controversial land of Sheba lay in Africa, did it also house the elusive gold mines of Ophir?

There is significant evidence suggesting that present-day Ethiopia was once the ancient land of Sheba. One of its early rulers, Menelik, was also called Ibn al-Hakim. Traditionally, this Menelik was the son of Queen Makeda and King Solomon, and his name meant *Son of the Wise Man*. Could he have been conceived when the famous queen visited Solomon? The biblical book called the Song of Songs, or in some versions the Song of Solomon, is a long and sensuous poem describing the passionate relationship of a beautiful black girl and her adoring lover. Does that elegantly written love poem refer to the relationship between Solomon and Makeda, the exquisite black Queen of Sheba?

Tutankhamen is also relevant to the analytical study of Santeria, Voodoo, and Obeah because of the curse associated with the violation of his tomb. Lord Carnarvon, Carter's financial backer, died of something similar to blood poisoning following an insect bite. The curse on the tomb supposedly read, "Death shall come on swift wings to him who desecrates my tomb." Whether the curse was intended literally or metaphorically is a matter of conjecture — but it seems likely that a bite from an infected flying insect caused Lord Carnarvon's death. He was only fifty-seven years old. Howard Carter lived on until 1939, dying of natural causes in England at the age of sixty-four. His remains lie in Putney Vale Cemetery in West London.

Although the curse is dismissed by skeptics and cynics, there are some significant statistics connected with it that are worth a closer look. Within seven years of Tutankhamen's tomb being entered, eleven people connected with it had died in questionable circumstances. Two of them were members of Carnarvon's family, another was Carter's secretary. Richard Bethell and his father, Lord Westbury, were also among the eleven. Within the next seven years the total of deaths *possibly* connected with Tutankhamen's curse had risen to twenty-one.

A sensible, pragmatic, psychological theory connected with investigations into alleged maledictions suggests, however, that so-called curses *can only affect those who believe in them.* It has been argued that *knowledge* of the existence of a curse can perhaps work at a subconscious level to persuade credulous victims to harm themselves. The external curse itself is totally innocuous. According to this theory, a dismissive disregard for curses — however convincing and blood-curdling they may seem — is the best defence against them. Positive, confident, optimistic thinking is armour plating that curses cannot penetrate. The defensive, therapeutic powers of the mind have yet to be definitively demonstrated, explored, and developed — but they are undoubtedly potent. Confidence in the strength and efficiency of our own mental, spiritual, and psychic immune systems — as well as our physical ones — can powerfully reinforce all three. A healthy mind and a healthy body invariably give each other mutual support.

A sense of humour can also provide an invaluable defence. Even the solemn and serious-minded Martin Luther (1483–1546) taught his followers to laugh at the devil in order to get rid of him: "The best way to drive out the devil, if he will not yield to texts of Scripture, is to jeer and flout him, for he cannot bear scorn."

Ancient magical traditions associated with Solomon make him a powerful controller of beings like Orishas, Loas, djinn, and other paranormal entities. They were in awe of him and his great seal, which could effectively imprison any who disobeyed him. Biblical evidence links him closely with the Egypt of antiquity and its sophisticated religious culture: "And Solomon made affinity with Pharaoh, King of Egypt, and took Pharaoh's daughter, and brought her into the city of David, until he had made an end of building his own house, and the house of the Lord, and the wall of Jerusalem round about" (I Kings 3:1).

There were literally tons of gold in those palaces and in the Jerusalem Temple. Just as with the gold in Tutankhamen's tomb — where did it all come from? *Where was Ophir?* If it was not in Ethiopia, could it have been in Zimbabwe? Although the famous Zimbabwe stone ruins are thought to go back no more than 1,200 years, Stone Age tools and weapons, pottery, and Khoisan cave paintings reveal that the area must have been inhabited for many millennia before that. It is certainly possible that both Solomon and the ancient Egyptians obtained their vast supplies of gold from Zimbabwe.

Thomé Lopes sailed with Vasco da Gama (1460–1524) on their epic voyage to India in 1502. Thomé thought that Sofala in Mozambique and the land around it was Ophir — and the home of the Queen of Sheba.

One important link between ancient African peoples and Egypt — and the empires like Solomon's that lay beyond Egypt — is forged from the gold of Ophir. There are other links, too, one of which is an overwhelming similarity between the Hebrew Song of Solomon and the tender sensitivity of ancient Egyptian love lyrics like this one:

> Oh, you beautiful one! The desire of my heart is
> To be your caring, protective husband, and to bring
> your food for you,
> My arm resting upon yours because your love has
> changed me.

Early African religion and culture differed from area to area and from one group of people to another. Some early Christian missionaries were unimaginative, inflexible, dogmatic, and unsympathetic towards other faiths. When they encountered rites and sacrifices that they could not understand among the indigenous Africans, they tended to regard the local religion as paganism at best and as Satanism at worst.

There were, however, broad compartments of thought into which the African religions that Christians encountered during the centuries of the slave trade could conveniently be divided.

Ubiquitous throughout the ancient African religions was a belief in One Supreme God. There was also a widespread belief in subordinate deities — Orishas and Loas. The third widely shared traditional African belief was in spirits. They could be the spirits of trees, of rocks and mountains, of fire and water.

Then there was also a widespread belief in the continuing existence of ancestors. These might be relatively impotent, like the shades that drifted forlornly in the Greek Hades and could only gather strength to speak to the living when they were given a blood sacrifice to sustain their ethereal forms. Some ancestors, however, like those of great chieftains and warriors, might yet be powerful in the physical world. If your grandfather had been an awesome hero and slain a hundred enemies in battle, it would seem reasonable to expect that he could be summoned from the spirit world to help you when you were in need. Invisible he might be — but powerless he was not.

Although Africans believed in making contact with dead ancestors, these ancestors were not worshipped. Families tended to treat dead forebears as if they were still alive and with them here on earth. It was customary for the Swazi people, for example, to address their departed ancestors in the same way that they spoke to the living. This is reminiscent of the thought expressed by the late Canon Harry Scott Holland of St. Paul's Cathedral in London in his "Death is nothing at all" essay, which brings a great deal of comfort to the bereaved when it is included in funeral services: "Speak to me in the easy way that you always used … let my name be the household word that it always was … laugh, as we always laughed, at the little jokes we enjoyed together."

Another interesting aspect of African religion was the belief in a kind of guardian spirit, like a double or doppelgänger. To the Yoruba peoples this was known as a person's *ori*. The Igbo called it a person's *chi*.

The idea of such a doppelgänger is well known throughout Europe as well. In Viking legends, for example, there was a creature known as a *vardøgr* that went ahead of the person whose double it was and did what he or she was about to do.

Just as in vampire folklore, the doppelgänger has no shadow and is unable to create a reflection in a mirror. Nevertheless, there have been notable accounts of doppelgänger reflections. In July of 1822, the brilliant young poet Percy Bysshe Shelley was drowned near Lerici. A letter from his widow, Mary, to her friend Maria Gisborne gave details of Percy's sighting of his own doppelgänger. Another famous doppelgänger case involved the metaphysical poet John Donne, who was said to have seen his wife's doppelgänger in Paris in 1612. The reflected doppelgänger case that went against the folklore tradition that doppelgängers do not have reflections concerned President Abraham Lincoln. In 1860 it was recorded that the President had seen his reflection in a mirror in the lounge of his home. There were two reflections of his face, and one was considerably paler than the other. His wife, Mary, said that she thought it meant that he would be elected for a second term *but would not survive it*. The account comes from Noah Brooks in his book *Washington in Lincoln's Time*, which was published in 1895. Brooks was adamant that he had heard the account from Lincoln himself.

Another famous and well-documented case of a doppelgänger being seen on several occasions relates to Emilie Sagée, a French teacher (1845–46) at the Pensionat von Neuwelcke, near Wolmar in Latvia. Julie von Güldenstubbe was a thirteen-year-old student at the school at the time and gave a full account of Emilie's doppelgänger appearances to Robert Dale Owen (1801–1877). Son of the great Welsh reformer Robert Owen, Dale was a famous anti-slavery campaigner and Democratic politician in the U.S.A. He served in the Indiana House of Representatives and later in the federal House of Representatives. The town of Dale in Indiana is named after him.

In our context of slavery in the U.S.A. and its bringing together of the old African religions and Christianity, it was Robert Dale Owen who wrote to President Lincoln on September 7, 1862, urging him to bring an end to slavery for ethical reasons.

A further important part of the ancient African faith was a belief in the potency of magical, therapeutic herbs. There were other forms of

An array of healing medicines.

healing medicines that could also be used: magic words and movements, spells, chants, dances, incantations, and enchantments.

Shape-shifting and other forms of lycanthropy had a place in many traditional African belief systems. The Bouda peoples were thought to have the power to transform themselves into were-beasts — especially were-hyenas, which were singularly rapacious and dangerous. By a widespread process of linguistic transposition, the term *bouda* began to be used for any were-beast — irrespective of whether it was associated with the Bouda peoples or with some other group in a different part of Africa. In the ancient kingdom of Kaffa, now part of Ethiopia, the were-beasts were called *qora*. Witches belonging to the Makanga peoples of central Africa were believed to be able to transform themselves into crocodiles.

When legends of were-leopards and were-lions are examined, the stories are often embellished by the concept of a leopard–god or –goddess assuming anthropoid form and mating with a normal human being. These hybrid offspring then grow up to be were-beasts, or to have other magical powers.

Were-lions in particular tend to be associated with royalty or with those who have the gift of leadership. The lions in Tsavo (an area of Kenya where the River Tsavo meets the River Athi) were believed to be inhabited by the spirits of warrior kings and chieftains. When the Uganda Railway was being extended by a bridge over the river, lions attacked the construction crew, and it was thought by some that they were were-lions obstructing the European bridge builders.

Every region of the world has its own local legends of were-beasts. Tales of were-bears are found in mountainous areas where real bears are a danger. Stories of werewolves come from dark and sinister European forests where wolf packs pose a threat. When the authors were carrying out research into unsolved mysteries in Hawaii, they came across stories of were-sharks that came out of the sea, assumed attractive male human form, married, and produced offspring. Their sons then grew up to have their father's appetites and powers of transformation.

What is the connection between these legends of were-beasts and the strange animal-headed gods of ancient Egypt? The jackal-god Anubis was the guardian of the dead. Knum was a ram-god — could Knum have been the ancient African forerunner of the myths and legends associated with the famous Derby Ram in England? Sekhmet was a lioness-goddess. The cat-goddess was known as Bartet. The first possibility is that a mutual interchange of ideas took place between Egyptian and African travellers, and that the fundamental concept of animal-human hybrids led to traditions of animal-headed gods at one extreme and were-beasts at the other. The second possibility is that deep, abstract philosophical and theological concepts were identified with the characteristics traditionally associated with a particular animal (e.g., the gentle parenting skills of a cow with a calf, the ferocity and courage of the lion). Each of these abstract characteristics could be personified as a hybrid creature having the head of the relevant animal surmounting a human torso.

The ancient African religions that formed part of the slave culture contained elements from Egyptian, Babylonian, Assyrian, Canaanite, and Hebrew beliefs. The traditional Christianity of the five slave centuries aimed at simplistic conversion rather than tolerance and understanding. There were three distinct results from the encounter between this type of Christianity and the old African religions: conversion, syncretism, or mutual opposition.

The first scenario was straightforward conversion: the African slave abandoned his old faith and became a Christian of his own accord. A nineteenth-century example is provided by the autobiography of Padre Petro Kilekwa, entitled *Slave Boy to Priest.* This very interesting account of Petro's early life as a slave was translated from the original Chinyanja language by K.H. Nixon Smith and published by the Universities' Mission to Central Africa in 1937.

Born in the middle of the nineteenth century as a member of the Mbisa people in the area around Lake Bangweolo, in what was then Northern Rhodesia, young Kilekwa was captured by the Maviti and sold as a slave.

He was only a very young child at the time of his capture and enslavement. It happened because he and some other young children had got up early to play in the shallow ponds a few hundred metres from their village. They particularly enjoyed playing games with the frogs that lived in and around those ponds. When they came back to the village later in the day, they saw a group of strangers walking through it. The children were too young to understand their danger and merely assumed that the strangers were ordinary visitors.

They were, in fact, slavers. The rest of the villagers had seen them coming and fled. Kilekwa and the other children were captured and later sold. After some years, he was rescued by the British navy while on board a dhow filled with slaves and their owners. Kilekwa describes vividly how the slave owners drew swords and guns to defend what they thought of as their property. The British naval officer in charge of the rescuers drew his cutlass and said grimly to the slavers, "Put your weapons down now — or we will kill you all." There was no doubt in the slavers' minds that he meant exactly what he said. Not long afterwards, Kilekwa served as a cabin boy under Admiral Lord Charles Scott. While Kilekwa was serving aboard HMS *Bachante* he learned that Queen Victoria's grandson, the future King George V, had also served there.

The next stage of Kilekwa's many life-changing experiences was to learn about Christianity at Kiungani College — also known as St.

Andrew's. This was where other boys rescued from slave dhows by the Royal Navy were taken to be educated. It was Kilekwa's time as a student at St. Andrew's that led him to train as a priest and to spend the rest of his life in the African Church.

Some African slaves in the U.S.A., South America, and the Caribbean underwent similar conversions and chose to become Christians.

The second scenario — syncretism — gave rise to one or more of the mysterious magical religions, including Voodoo, Santeria, and Obeah. There were aspects of Christianity that the African slaves found attractive and acceptable: the One Supreme God, miracles, healings, and companies of benign, paranormal beings such as saints and angels. Some African slaves reinforced and reinterpreted these acceptable ideas with their own ancient beliefs about Orishas and Loas, spells, incantations, rhythmic dancing, sacrifices, herbs, and magical potions.

The third scenario — defiant opposition — led to the determined preservation of ancient African religious ideas going back for thousands of years. It also led to the development of new and variant faiths that eschewed any form of syncretism with Christianity.

Chapter 5

STRANGE RELIGIOUS HYBRIDIZATION

WHERE THE solution of syncretism was selected — rather than conversion or opposition — numerous styles of hybrid worship came into being. The Yoruba slaves especially linked their own divine and semi-divine beings to various Catholic saints whom they learnt about in the Caribbean. In essence, there were three distinct levels in the religious hierarchy of the Yoruba slaves. Right at the top was their omnipotent creator god, referred to by several names, including Oludomare (spellings vary). He was identified with Jehovah, or Yahweh, God the Father of the Christian Trinity. The Yoruba Orishas and Loas became the archangels, angels, cherubim, seraphim, and messengers of God in general. There were, however, seven very high powered Orishas — equivalent to archangels — who were referred to as the *Siete Potencias*, meaning the Seven Powers. Many of the Orishas are identified with several Christian saints or angels, not just one.

The third and lowest level of the spiritual hierarchy was composed of ancestral spirits, who were also referred to in Yoruba culture as *eggun*.

Further detailed examination of the conflated Orisha-saint identities begins with the very powerful Orisha referred to as Eleggua or Elegua (spellings vary). Referred to as the cunning one, the trickster, the overcomer of obstacles, and the messenger, Eleggua has many of the qualities associated with Ulysses, the classical Greek hero who could always devise a cunning plan to overcome Sirens, Cyclops, Scylla, and Charibdis. An oppressed, enslaved people feel the need for such a leader whose subtle planning and benign trickery exercised on their behalf can help them to survive the hard labour, abuse, and cruel punishments associated with slavery. For many followers of the hybridized religion, Eleggua was identified with Saint Peter. The detailed account of Saint

Peter's escape from King Herod's prison in Act 12, verses 1–11, would have appealed strongly to African slaves who understood chains and imprisonment all too well from personal experience. Herod had just executed Saint James, the brother of Saint John, and when he realized that his persecution of the early Church was increasing his popularity, he gave orders for Peter to be arrested and incarcerated. Peter was accordingly chained between two soldiers, and, to further reduce any possibility of escape, additional soldiers guarded the door of the prison. During the night an angel appeared to Peter and his chains fell off miraculously. He followed the angel as instructed, and, after they had passed all the other guards, the great iron city gates opened of their own accord. The angel then vanished, leaving Peter free inside the city. This kind of magical power was attributed to Eleggua, the powerful Orisha, and he became identified with Saint Peter, among others.

Saint Martin of Tours, who is known as Saint Martin Caballero (Saint Martin the Horseman) in Latin America, is another saintly equivalent of Eleggua. Born a Hungarian during the declining years of the Roman Empire, Martin became a Centurion in the Roman army. One day he encountered a shivering beggar with barely enough rags to keep him alive. Martin paused, cut his cloak in half, and gave half to the beggar. During a dream that night, Martin saw Jesus wearing the half-cloak that had been given to the beggar. Martin left the army and became a monk, eventually becoming Bishop of Tours in France. He is regarded in Latin America as the patron saint of the poor who are desperate for life-sustaining gifts of food, clothes, or money. Impoverished shopkeepers in Mexico look to him for help. He is also a patron saint of lorry drivers, who regard their trucks as the equivalent of his horse. By another process of association — horses and lucky horseshoes — Martin is the patron saint of gamblers.

Saint Anthony of Padua is another of Eleggua's alter egos. Born in 1195 in Lisbon, Anthony became one of the most effective preachers of his day. His extraordinary communicative powers are seen as shared by Eleggua. Anthony became the patron saint of poor and oppressed people and those who travel. He is also the saint on whom believers call when anything is lost. It is said that when Anthony died at the age of only thirty-six, on June 13, 1231, in Arcella on his way back to Padua, children

Author Lionel Fanthorpe admires a lucky horseshoe talisman.

cried in the streets and angels came to earth to ring the church bells for him. These miracles associated with Anthony encouraged members of the syncretized religions to identify him with Eleggua.

In the early fifteenth century, when the Moors captured the little Spanish town of Atocha, prisoners were desperate for food and water. Every day a boy, dressed as a pilgrim of the period, arrived with food and water for them. The tide of battle eventually turned against the Moors and the prisoners were released. No one knew the identity of the young pilgrim who had undoubtedly saved their lives. Word began to spread that it must have been the young Jesus himself. From time to time the miraculous boy appeared again in Atocha helping to prevent kidnappings and other crimes. He became the patron saint of prisoners and those who needed help because of unjust legal proceedings. Eleggua is identified with El Nino de Atocha as well as with Peter, Martin Caballero, and Anthony of Padua.

Eleggua has another alter ego known as Saint Expedite. There are numerous light-hearted stories associated with Expedite and his origins.

One tells how the early priests of the Chapel of Our Lady of Guadalupe in New Orleans sent for a statue of Mary the Virgin from a religious sculptor in Spain. (From 1763 until 1803 New Orleans was a Spanish settlement.) The statue duly arrived by ship a few months later accompanied by another large crate. The priests opened the crate containing the statue of Mary that they expected, and they were very pleased with the sculptor's work. They then examined the second crate, which bore the single word *Expedite.* When they opened it, they found the statue of a handsome young Roman centurion — which they had definitely not ordered. Uncertain, they eventually decided to erect it in the church, where they labelled it *Saint Expedite.* Being ignorant of shipping procedures, the priests had not understood that the lettering on the centurion's crate was simply an instruction to get on with it, as in "Expedite this order."

Statues of Expedite show him holding a cross with the word *hodie* (Latin for *today*) written on it. He also has a crow trapped under his sandalled foot, and the Latin word *Cras* is coming from its beak — whereas the English word for a crow's note is "Caw." The Latin *cras* means *tomorrow* and forms one syllable of procrastinate — meaning the bad habit of putting off until tomorrow things that need to be done today. Candles burned in honour of Saint Expedite are red and covered in what Santerians would describe as quick-luck oil. Prayers and candles tend to be offered to Expedite on Wednesdays — the day associated with Greek Hermes (Roman Mercury), the god of speedy messages. According to Santeria traditions, Expedite should be rewarded with a gift of flowers and cake if he answers a worshipper's prayers. He also appreciates having an entry placed in the papers thanking him for his help.

The most elevated of all Eleggua's alter egos is the Archangel Michael. He is the most powerful and warlike of all the angels and is thought of as the commander-in-chief of God's armies. In one of the mystical visions of Daniel, it is Michael who assists Gabriel in his contest with a Persian angel. There is considerable detail about Michael in the *Book of Enoch*. He is also seen alongside Saint George the dragon killer as a patron saint of warriors. Michael is especially revered by paratroopers and police officers. Throughout the dedications of early Christian shrines and sacred sites, it was regarded as traditional to rename an old pagan holy place after Saint Michael, or after Saint Michael and all the angels, as an indication that the great warrior archangel had conquered whatever pagan entity had once been worshipped there. St. Michael's Mount is a case in point. The similarity between the militant Saint Michael the all-conquering archangel and the leading Orisha Eleggua was one that appealed strongly to followers of Santeria and similar religions.

Another great Orisha was known as Obatala, or Obatalia, and regarded as the parent of humanity. Obatala's main attributes were harmony, peace, and love — consequently in the minds of Santeria believers Obatala was associated with two great manifestations of Christian holiness: Our Lady of Mount Carmel and Our Lady of Mercy.

Oya, the Orisha who combines the qualities of a female warrior with the power of the storm and the strength of magic, is linked in Santerian syncretism with Saint Catherine and Saint Theresa. Catherine was a virgin martyr who was brilliantly intelligent and eloquent, and who defeated the finest minds that the Emperor Gaius Julius Verus Maximinus could marshal against her. He was emperor only from AD 235 to 238. As unintelligent as he was ruthless, Maximinus was supported by the Praetorian Guard, who overawed a very reluctant senate to accept him as emperor. When Maximinus failed to defeat Catherine, his fury knew no bounds. Like Philomena, Catherine was savagely flogged and sentenced to die on the wheel that still bears her name. According to the saintly legend, the torture wheel was miraculously destroyed. Maximinus had Catherine beheaded, whereupon angels carried her body to Mount Sinai where a church was built in her honour. Her appeal to the Santerian African slaves was as great as Philomena's — largely because both brave young martyrs had suffered as the slaves did.

Oya was also closely associated with Saint Teresa of Avila (1515–1582). Teresa was a renowned Spanish mystic. Like Catherine, Teresa was brilliantly intelligent and was officially recognized as one of the thirty-three Doctors of the Church — only three of whom are female.

For devout Roman Catholics, Stella Maris is Our Lady, Star of the Sea, the patroness of all who sail the world's seas and oceans. But as well as protecting them, she is also understood as the guide and protector of those who metaphorically sail the stormy waters of life.

Saint Bonaventure said of her that she guides those who sail the ship of innocence and penance through this troubled and difficult world to the safety and peace of the heavenly harbour. Santerians associate her with Yemaya, the Orisha of motherhood, the moon, and the sea. In one or two of the Brazilian religions such as Umbanda and Candomblé, her name is Yemanjá, or Lemanjá, and it is customary to honour her with gifts of flowers, perfume, decorative combs, mirrors, and jewellery. These gifts are thrown into the sea for her, and although she is regarded as normally benign and helpful, it is considered very rash and hazardous to pick up any offerings that were intended for her.

There is a vast annual event on December 31 when many of these votive offerings for Yemanjá are thrown into the sea by a huge crowd who wade into the water from Copacabana Beach in Rio de Janeiro.

It is essential to protect the identity of the central character of the following event, but rigorously accurate records of it are kept in the archives of the Society for Psychical Research in London. An SPR investigator was working in Brazil a few years ago when these facts came to his attention. The central character is referred to throughout as "Belinda" in order to protect her anonymity. She had studied psychology at the University of São Paulo, which had given her an objective, scientific attitude to life.

One day, when she was with her family on the beach at Santos, which is less than one hundred kilometres from São Paulo, she discovered a small statuette of Yemanjá that had apparently been thrown up by the sea — and was almost certainly a votive offering from Copacabana Beach. Very little paint remained on the figurine after having been in the sea for so long. The paint that was left became highly significant when considered in the light of later developments. The jaw and neck retained some pigment, as did the arms. There was a little more between the shoulder blades. One eye still retained its bright blue colour.

Despite the warnings of the more superstitious members of her family, Belinda took the statuette home with her. Within a few days, she became so ill that she was taken to hospital with suspected tuberculosis. X-rays revealed that there was a TB lesion on her right lung — *corresponding to the spot of paint on the statuette.* After her successful treatment, the doctors ordered her to rest and she stayed with her parents for several months in their home a long way from São Paulo. Nothing untoward befell her while she was there. Some researchers into the mystery wondered whether she was too far from the statuette for it to have any effect on her.

As soon as she returned home, however, her pressure cooker exploded, badly scalding her arms, face, and neck *in precisely the same areas on which the figurine still had pigment.* Her gas oven then exploded just as inexplicably as her pressure cooker had done, and she began to feel very depressed and suicidal.

Her scientific training and attitude did not help her, and, very reluctantly, she visited an Umbanda centre and obtained advice from their leaders. They told her to take the statuette back to where she had found it, which she did.

From that moment on, the depression lifted, and she settled down to a safe, normal, routine existence.

The episode is hard to reconcile with the normally benign nature of Yemanjá, otherwise known as Yemaya. If there was any mysterious, negative power in the figurine, was it some sort of evil, vengeful influence emanating from those who had *made* the statuette and given it to Yemanjá rather than from the benign Orisha herself?

Yemaya is also identified with Our Lady of Regla, meaning Our Lady of the Rule. A church associated with her is situated in the town of Opon on Mactan Island, separated from the city of Cebu in the Philippines by a narrow causeway. In 1735, Father Avalle, who was an Augustinian monk, showed a picture of the Virgin de la Regla to his parishioners. The original image of her was venerated by Augustine in the fifth century, but when the Vandals arrived in AD 433, the monks took it with them to Spain. Centuries passed and the sacred likeness was all but forgotten, then King Ferdinand, who had reconquered Spain, dedicated the cathedral in León to Our Lady of Regla.

An Augustinian priest in León then had a vision of her and was sent to find the lost painting. After a very long journey, the priest was sleeping under a tree when he heard a voice saying that he had now found the place. He prayed for further guidance and a ball of fire from heaven struck the tree without harming it. Amazed by what they had seen, local villagers came to help the priest. They dug into the ground beside the tree and encountered a large rock. When that was lifted it revealed the entrance to a subterranean cave where a lamp burned miraculously in front of a protective wooden case. A statue of Our Lady of Regla — not just a painted image of her — was found inside the case. A shrine to her was constructed over the cave. A large portrait of her was completed in 1735 and according to local tradition miracles began to happen when her help was invoked. These miracles associated with Our Lady of Regla fit in harmoniously with the Santerian ideas about their benign Yemaya.

Cachita, Our Lady of Charity, also known as Our Lady of Caridad del Cobre, is closely associated with the Santerian Orisha known as Ochun, Oshun, or Ochum (spellings vary), who is in turn connected with love, beauty, and femininity. Maintaining pure, fresh water is another of her divine responsibilities.

The story of Cachita's discovery goes back to the start of the seventeenth century, when Juan and Rodrigo de Hoyos were travelling in a canoe with a young slave boy named Juan Moreno. They had to fetch salt urgently to preserve meat from the slaughterhouse at what was then called Santiago del Prado and is now El Cobre. This meat provided essential food for the workers.

A terrifying storm made them seek shelter for the night, but next morning the sea was as calm as a millpond and they set out again to find the vital salt. A white bundle floated towards them, and they thought at first that it was a large seagull resting on the placid water. As it got closer they thought it looked more like a small girl swimming gently in their direction. When it reached them, they saw that it was a statuette of the Virgin Mary, standing on a representation of the moon among silver clouds in which three angels spread wings of gold. It was attached to a floating board on which was written "I am the Virgin of Charity." Miraculously, in view of the storm that had driven the canoeists to seek shelter the night before, the statuette and her clothes were perfectly dry. The syncretized Cachita-Ochun became a central figure in local religion and is the divine entity associated with womanhood, happiness, love, gentleness, and fresh water.

The names of the Orishas frequently present problems for researchers because of the different spellings that are encountered for the same mysterious entity. Sango, Chango, Shango and Xango, for example, are one and the same being. Historically, Shango was the fourth king of the Yoruba, but he was transformed in Santerian thought into their powerful and warlike god of thunder. He is, therefore, an African equivalent of the Celtic Taranis, the Norse Thor, the Babylonian Marduk, the Chinese Lei Gong, and the Japanese Tenjin. He is the counterpart of the Hindu Indra; he is Zeus for the Greeks and Jupiter for the Romans. In the strange religious hybridization that linked slave-centuries Christianity with ancient African traditions, Shango became united with Saint Barbara and Saint Jerome.

According to her legend, Barbara lived around AD 300 and was the daughter of Dioscorus, a rich pagan merchant from Nicomedia in Asia Minor. Because of Barbara's great beauty, her jealous father confined her to a tower. While he was away on a business trip, Barbara became a Christian, and she altered his plans for a new bathhouse so that it would have three windows to symbolize the Holy Trinity. When he returned, he was furiously angry about her conversion and the alteration of his bathhouse design. He brought her before the local Roman prefect, who sentenced her to be tortured first and then beheaded. Dioscorus himself did the decapitation. Very soon afterwards he was struck by lightning that totally consumed his body. In consequence, Barbara became the protective patron saint from thunder, lightning, storms, and fires. After the invention of gunpowder and the development of primitive artillery, she also became the protective patron saint of artillerymen, who were frequently killed or severely injured when an artillery piece exploded instead of firing its missile at the enemy.

While it is easy to see the thunder and lightning connection between Barbara and Shango, his connection with the peaceful, ascetic, and scholarly Saint Jerome (AD 342–419) is less obvious. His main achievement was the translation of Greek and Hebrew texts into the Latin version of the Bible referred to as the *Vulgate*. It is probably for his skills as an interpreter and translator that he is venerated by Santerians and ranked alongside Shango. For newly arrived African slaves, a sympathetic and kindly interpreter would have been a very welcome asset.

Another important senior Orisha was known as Ogun, sometimes spelled Ogum, who was a warlord and a master of minerals, metals, tools, and implements. He can be seen as the African equivalent of Hephaestus or Vulcan in the Greek and Roman pantheons. Ogun's powers also extended to animals and birds. The Christian saints with whom he was largely identified were Saint George the heroic dragon slayer and Saint John the Baptist — the fierce, uncompromising, Elijah-style prophet who criticized Herod Antipas for marrying his brother Philip's wife, Herodias. The links between Ogun and both saints are logical and rational ones. The fearless warrior George, risking his life to slay a dragon to rescue a princess, is clearly a model of courageous self-sacrifice — a noble parallel for Ogun the African warlord. George is traditionally portrayed in armour, and Ogun, master of metals and workshop tools, can clearly be seen as a divine blacksmith and armourer. The equally great, outspoken, moral courage of John the Baptist is also a fitting attribute for a warlord such as Ogun.

Another important Orisha is Orunmila, sometimes shortened to Orula. Orula is bonded with Saint Francis of Assisi in Santerian thinking. He is regarded as a teacher and prophet by his worshippers, as well as a healer. Working with him is Osain, the Orisha of healing plants and herbal remedies. Orula is also thought of as the guardian and interpreter of the mysteries contained in a Santerian book of baffling prophecies. He is thought of as controlling secret wisdom and divination — in these respects he is similar to Melchizedek, Thoth, or Hermes Trismegistus, keeper

and reader of the inexplicable Emerald Tablets. In Santerian eyes, Orula is also identified with Saint John the Evangelist. As John is recorded in early Church history as the teacher of Papias, one of the Church fathers, John's identification with Orula as a teacher becomes understandable.

Dives and Lazarus are the central characters in a parable

Saint Francis.

that Jesus told concerning a very wealthy man and a sick beggar lying outside the gate of the rich man's house and living on the scraps that fell from the rich man's table. Both die and the poor beggar goes to eternal comfort and joy in a paradise referred to as "Abraham's bosom." The rich man finds himself in a burning hell. Although intended only as a fictional character in the parable, Lazarus becomes venerated as a saint with especial responsibilities for helping the poor and the sick. In Santerian religious thought he becomes identified with Babaluaye, or Babalu Aye, the Orisha who provides money and healing for the sick poor. He is particularly associated with healing smallpox and, more recently, AIDS. His colourful robes are red, white, purple, and blue.

Religious syncretism also needs to be analyzed in other ways over and above the identification of various leading African Orishas with Christian saints. Modes of address and prayers are remarkably similar. A familiar prayer to Saint Anne, mother of Mary the Virgin, contains these words:

> Dear St. Anne,
> I wish to honour you
> In your images and statues.
> They are the representations
> Of the mysteries of divine love
> That were brought about in you.
> Oh, good and great Saint Anne,
> Pray for me and for all my brothers and sisters.
> Hear my special prayer
> For the sick and injured,
> For the hungry and for those in need.
> Obtain for all men and women the gift
> Of love for one another in God
> And grant peace to God's world.

A Santerian prayer that is frequently recited by *santeros* (Santerian priests) contains these words:

Hail to Oya, our Orisha, with her crown of light.
Here is Oya, lady of the wind and rain.
Hail to her as she travels over the forests and hills.
All praise to her, for she is the mother of nine.
Earthly winds, bring us health.
Heavenly winds, bring us great fortune.
Our lady of the winds is wonderful.
Amen — so let it be — amen.
Our lady of the sunset,
You paint for us the leaves of autumn.
We hear your song at dusk and dawn.

The frequent, symbolic use of candles in Christian worship is a reminder to Christians that for them Jesus is the light of the world. Lighting a candle and carrying it into a place of Christian worship symbolizes that Jesus is there with his worshippers. When two candles are placed on a Christian altar, it signifies that for Christians Jesus is both man and God. When the candle is carried out again after worship it symbolizes the presence of Jesus in the outside world, the whole of the earth. Before the invention of gas and electric lighting, the candles in Christian churches provided light as well as acting as symbols of God's presence in the place of worship. Votive candles can be lit to accompany prayers. In Orthodox churches, where icons are revered, candles may be lit in front of an icon. In some churches a paschal candle is lit at Easter, and then kindled again for special services such as baptisms and funerals. It is also customary in certain churches to observe Candlemas at the end of Epiphany, and at these ceremonies the priest blesses the candle that will be used throughout the remainder of the year. Candles were used on Christmas trees before electrical tree lights became available. In Scandinavian churches on December 13 (St. Lucia's Day) it is customary to present a young girl with a crown of candles.

Candles also feature prominently in the syncretized Santerian ceremonies and festivities — but they feature most significantly of all in Santerian spells and enchantments, where the behaviour of a candle is used as a monitor by the wizard who is performing the spell.

Different Santerian authorities in different countries may interpret candle behaviour in different ways, but there is nevertheless broad, general agreement.

If a candle refuses to light, or goes out almost immediately after being lit, it signifies to the Santerian wizard that spiritual cleansing has to be carried out before the enchantment will work. This cleansing may require the use of holy water — blessed either by a Santerian priest or a Christian priest. If the candle burns, but produces only a small flame, it indicates opposition to the spell currently being used. Suppose, for example, that it is a love spell: the low flame suggests that another spell, cast by a rival wizard, is weakening the attractive power of this particular magic charm. The man or woman at whom the love spell is being directed may already be under the influence of this opposing enchantment. When a Santerian sorcerer or enchantress is faced with a low flame indicator, he or she will augment the ineffective spell with two or three reinforcing spells. A high and vigorous flame naturally indicates the opposite of a low flame. It means that the incantation is working powerfully and swiftly, and that the healing, protection, or prosperity at which the benign spell is aimed will be rapidly achieved.

An exploding candle is an ambiguous symbol. In some Santerian schools of thought it means that something very powerful and negative has been directed against the wizard's client, but the equally powerful defence spell that the wizard is using has neutralized it. Conversely, if the enchanter has been working on a benign spell to increase the client's power and wealth, an exploding candle can mean that negative forces have neutralized his attempts to improve the situation. The accepted formula is to repeat the incantation and then light a candle of exactly the same kind as the one that exploded.

The behaviour of the candle and its flame are regarded by santeros as momentous portents, but attention is also paid to the behaviour and colour of the smoke. There is a parallel here with the papal election process. When the ballot papers for the new pope have been counted, they are burnt in a special oven in the Sistine Chapel. *Fumata nera*, black smoke, means that no one has yet been elected. *Fumata bianca*, white smoke, means that there has been a successful ballot for the new pope.

Candle spell indicators.

Candle smoke.

In Santerian magic, if a candle gives off white smoke, it's a good omen — it means that the prayer being offered on the client's behalf will be answered. If the candle gives off black smoke it suggests that negative influences are being defeated — and the client will succeed after a time.

Very often, the sorcerer's indicator candle is lit inside a protective glass cylinder. Santeros believe that if that cylinder is blackened from top to bottom, it means that the spell being performed on the client's behalf has met with very powerful opposition. Reinforcing spells should be used, and another, identical candle should be lit in a different glass. If only the lower part of the protective glass cylinder is blackened, santeros believe that a benign spell employed on their behalf for improved health or prosperity has been weakened by negative forces directed against them. If, conversely, only the upper part of the glass is blackened, it signifies that there was opposition at first, but the client's spell has conquered. Blackening on one side of the glass indicates that a spell was only partly effective and needs to be repeated. If the glass actually cracks during the performance of the spell, it suggests that the wizard has broken the dark forces that were being sent against him and his client.

Should the flame separate into two or more distinct flames, then the major flame represents the person for whom the wizard or sorcerer is working the Santerian magic, and each of the other flames — of various sizes — represents a rival in love, an opponent, or an enemy. Additional spells may be needed to overcome this opposition. A flickering flame is indicative of spirit presences in the room. They may be assisting the spell — or hindering it.

The direction in which smoke moves is also important. Santerian enchanters believe that if the smoke drifts towards the client for whom the enchantment is being performed, the prayers are answered or the benign and positive spell has worked satisfactorily. If the smoke moves away from the client, the spell will still work, but there are difficulties ahead and perseverance will be needed to gain the victory. If the smoke moves away to the right, the subject will need to think hard about the problem connected with the spell to find a way through the difficulties. Patience and pure reason will be the best allies. Smoke that drifts to the left is less auspicious than smoke that drifts to the right. Left-drifting smoke suggests that the subject is too emotionally involved in the problem at which the spell is directed. These overreactive emotions are preventing the spell from working. The magician's advice to his client is to relax and be calm.

Traditional Christianity and the ancient African religions are to some extent syncretized in Santeria, Obeah, Voodoo, Umbanda, and the other quasi-magical religions that form one significant part of the legacy of slavery. There are specific areas that can be analyzed *within* that syncretism. Some important underlying beliefs are common to the conjoined faiths; then there is the conflation of Christian saints and African Orishas. There are similarities in the modes of addressing the saints or Orishas and in the styles of prayers to them. Christian candle symbolism can also be observed alongside Santerian candle symbolism. Having established the essentially syncretized nature of the mysterious beliefs and practices of Voodoo, Obeah, Santeria, and similar religious systems, it is possible to explore and examine their fundamental principles.

Chapter 6

THE PRINCIPLES OF SANTERIA, VOODOO, OBEAH, AND SIMILAR RELIGIONS

THERE MAY be a few written accounts of what Santeria and the other mysterious Afro-Christian syncretized religions are, but they have no official, centrally authoritative book, such as the Zend Avesta of the Zoroastrians, the Analects of Confucius, the Book of Mormon, the Christian Bible, or the Holy Koran.

Santeria, Voodoo, Obeah, and the other mysterious syncretized faiths have been — and are still — passed along by oral tradition. Because practices and beliefs vary considerably from one worshipping group to another, such few informal, written records as do exist are mainly in the form of eyewitness accounts of ceremonies and the personal recollections of initiates and practitioners.

An act of Santerian worship is presided over by a *Babalawo* (high priest) or an *Iyalocha* (high priestess). The religious leader conducting the service begins by taking a mouthful of *aguardiente* and spraying it over the congregation. *Aguardiente* literally means *firewater* or *burning water* and is usually about 50 percent proof alcohol. In Colombia and Mexico it is made from sugar cane. In Chile it is brewed from the stems, pulp, and seeds left over after the grapes are pressed. Another variety is flavoured with sun-dried cherries and called *enguindado*. *Aguardiente* is by any standards a truly formidable beverage.

The members of the congregation are all dressed in the colours appertaining to their own special Orishas. They may have their Orisha's sacred, magical number embroidered on their religious garments. Orishas also favour certain foods, and the worshippers bring these to the ceremony. For example, the number seven identifies Ogun, the Orisha of iron and war, and his favourite colours are black and green. Oshosi, another military Orisha, favours blue and yellow. Obatala combines all the colours of the rainbow into a brilliant white, but sometimes adds red and purple as trimmings to his all-encompassing white robes. Oya favours maroon and wears it in patterns of flowers. Famous as "The Mother of Nine," she can also be represented by nine different colours. Oshun wears yellow and gold, and five is her magical number. Yemaya dresses in blue and white — like white foam on blue waves — and her number seven reminds her worshippers of the seven seas. Shango recognizes the numbers four and six. Numerologists add four and six to make ten, then add one and zero to make one. Shango's colours are white and red, whereas Orunmila has green and yellow as his distinguishing colours.

The altar occupies a central place during Santerian ceremonies, and an image of Christ is displayed prominently. Pictures or statues of Saint Barbara, Saint Philomena, Saint Teresa, and other dual Orisha-saint characters are placed on it or close to it.

Santeria and most similar religions believe in *ache* — which can best be understood as a form of spiritual energy. It can also be thought of as psychic power or mental strength. The ache of the Orishas themselves can be concentrated in stones of various kinds — just as the ache of Thoth, Hermes Trismegistus, and Melchizedek was thought to be concentrated in the sacred Emerald Tablets. These sacred power stones associated with the various Orisha-saints are known as *otanes*. Because the beautiful and sensuous Orisha Ochun is associated with rivers and streams, her otanes are gathered from the beds of clear, fast-flowing, fresh water. Yemaya — an Orisha of the sea — has otanes that are gathered from the seabed.

The otanes of Ochossi — an Orisha similar in several ways to the English concept of Herne the Hunter — are gathered from deep forests and wild land associated with hunting. In one of the legends attached to the English Herne, he was thought to have been a loyal and valiant servant of King Richard II, who reigned from 1377 to 1399. When a large stag attacked the young king, Herne intervened and saved the monarch but was mortally wounded himself. A wizard restored him to life — but with the stag's antlers attached to his head.

There are many more Wild Hunt legends throughout Europe and Scandinavia, and some may well have originated in Africa and made their way to Europe via traders or African soldiers in the Roman army. A

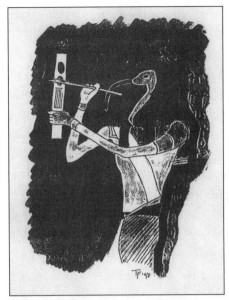

Hermes Trismegistus, also known as Thoth and Melchizedek.

significant percentage of Roman legionaries and gladiators were African, and some early legends of wild, paranormal hunters could well have crossed the Mediterranean with them.

The Wild Hunt and its fearsome leader — sometimes headless, sometimes with antlers — is known as Wutan's Army in parts of Germany, and as Odensjakt in Sweden and Denmark. For the Danes, its leader is King Waldemar. In other English versions of the legend the Chief Huntsman becomes a Saxon rebel named Wild Edric. The French claim that he is one of their great heroes: Charlemagne, Roland, or Oliver. A version of the legend that may possibly link the European Wild Hunt and its mysterious leader with Ochossi and the African Orishas is the story of Herla, King of the Britons.

In this early Wild Hunt narrative, Herla met a mysterious King of the Dwarves, who was riding a goat (an important symbol in Santeria). They made a solemn pact that each would attend the other's wedding. Soon afterwards, Herla married. The name of his bride varies, but in this narrative we refer to her as Adyna, a beautiful young Celtic princess. Herla was passionately in love with her, and they began an idyllic life together. As arranged, the dwarf had duly attended their wedding and bestowed generous gifts on the royal couple. A year after their marriage, the dwarf king returned to announce his forthcoming nuptials and reminded Herla of his promise to attend the dwarfish wedding. Reluctantly, Herla took leave of his exquisite young queen, as one of them had to remain behind in charge of their joint kingdom while he and his men attended the dwarf king's wedding. Bearing generous gifts, Herla's party followed the uncanny dwarf and his riders to the sheer face of a sinister cliff. It opened at the dwarf's bidding, and closed again behind them.

Herla and his party were entertained and honoured by the dwarves for three days. Before they left they were given magical horses and a mysterious enchanted hound, which rode on Herla's saddle. The dwarves warned them that the hound must alight first whenever they stopped. They were then escorted back to the cliff that opened again at the dwarf king's bidding and sealed itself once more behind Herla and his men.

The first person they met was an elderly shepherd, who had great difficulty in understanding what Herla was asking him.

"You speak a very old language, which I have not heard for many years," explained the old man apologetically. Herla's first question was about his beloved Adyna. Was all well with his queen and their kingdom? The old shepherd scratched his head for a few minutes and then said slowly, "Before my great-grandfather's time, there was talk of a good queen by that name, who ruled our land justly and well for many years — *after the king vanished.* It was said that her great beauty attracted many suitors, but she refused them all … she watched and waited faithfully for him until her death."

After listening to the old shepherd's story, one of Herla's men alighted to give the old man a few coins — but as his feet touched the ground, the generous nobleman turned to dust. They realized then that the enchanted hound was still in the saddle with Herla *and until it leapt down, they were eternally trapped.*

The legend tells how they ride until the world's end, looking in vain for the enchanted portal in the cliff that leads to the dwarf king's domain. This quality of being a cunning trickster — like the dwarf king — forms part of what might sometimes be considered the negative side of the characters of some Orishas. Eleggua in particular has this Odysseus-like quality, while Ochossi, the wild hunter Orisha, rides like Herne.

The otanes associated with Shango and his awesome thunder and lightning are meteorites. As these are very rare and hard to find, stones in his honour are brought down from the tops of mountains where Santerians believe that the powers of thunder and lightning are greatest. Once the otanes of an Orisha have been properly collected by worshippers

Herne the Hunter, the demigod with antlers.

and brought to the ceremony, they are duly sanctified and blessed by the priests and priestesses.

Ownership of the otanes may be the privilege of one individual worshipper, the family of that man or woman, or the whole community gathered at the ceremony. According to Santerian belief, the spiritual energy of the Orisha associated with his or her particular otanes works *with* the spiritual energy of the worshipper and confers psychic power and protection on that worshipper.

The place from which the otanes were gathered is also thought of as a type of motherlode, and here too the power of the relevant Orisha is regarded as being extra potent. Parallels with traditional Christian beliefs can be seen again here. Certain holy places, shrines, and centres of pilgrimage are felt to be extra powerful sites from which prayers can be offered more effectively.

The otanes are kept in big, covered, ceramic dishes — not unlike soup tureens — and these are placed in front of the images of Christ and the saints who are associated with the Orishas. The cowry shells used in Santerian divinations are also kept in these tureens.

The first type of divination used at the ceremony is known as *dilogun*, and is performed with sixteen cowry shells. The shells are thrown onto a tray and careful note is taken of the pattern in which they land, and whether the shell's opening is upwards or downwards. By following a prescribed system known to Santerian priests and priestesses, the reader of the shells can decide what the worshipper's problem is and which of the Orishas can help to resolve it.

Ifa is a more complicated system that can be operated by a Babalawo or Iyalocha. It uses as many as 256 signs known as *odu*. For this more elaborate system, the cowry shells may be threaded onto necklaces, and several necklaces are thrown on the divining tray at the same time. This advanced technique is used for advising the worshipper on important life changes such as marriage and career moves.

There is another form of oracle known as Biague. This was the name of the first Babalawo who used the technique. In the ancient African traditions, Oludomare blessed the coconut palm tree and granted it a special gift: *You shall give food and oil to humanity — and through you they shall be able to divine what is to come.* The Biague oracle operates when four pieces of coconut shell are thrown to the ground. The Babalawo, inspired by the relevant Orisha, is thought to be able to divine the future from the pattern formed by the falling pieces of shell, which are called *obinu.* The Biague oracle can respond only with yes or no answers — as in the old English quiz game of twenty questions — so questions posed have to be simple and direct.

Another central part of the service is the sharing of *omiero.* The preparation of this liquid is very complex and elaborate. Holy water is solemnly mixed with rainwater, seawater, and river water. Then some very powerful aguardiente alcohol is stirred in. Pepper, eggshells, honey, butter, and herbs are also added. The most important part of the preparation, however, involves malanga — which is also known as yautia, tannia, or cocoyam — a plant belonging to the xanthosoma species. A large malanga leaf is wrapped around a live coal, which is then lowered into the mixture and left to brew for twenty-four hours.

The Babalawo or Iyalocha in charge of the service ceremonially presents the container of omiero north, south, east, and west, and pours out a little of the liquid at each cardinal point. The mixture is taken to the altar next and offered to the Orishas. After this the priest or priestess in charge pours a few drops on the floor next to the doorway of the room in which the service is being held. After the ritual at the door, omiero is spilt on the floor in the centre of the room three times. Most members of the congregation then take a few sips of the omiero.

The next stage is for the priest or priestess to take a small portion of soil from the roots of the plant associated with a particular Orisha, mix it with powdered eggshell, and use the mixture to make patterns on the floor. The symbols drawn there are duly blessed and sprinkled with corn flour. Just as with European magical services involving pentagrams, candles are lit and placed at strategic points around these Santerian designs. They are then regarded as sacrosanct, and the worshippers take great care not to step over them or inadvertently to walk on them.

If any new candidates for initiation are present at the ceremony, they reverence the Orishas, then turn away from the altar, looking towards the Santerians who have sponsored them for membership. Their sponsors then reverence the Orishas on the new candidates' behalf, and the sacred drumming starts.

Just as members of the congregation can find themselves overwhelmed at a charismatic, evangelical Christian service, so members of the Santerian gathering may now feel that powerful, spiritual force possess them. In this possessed state, the Santerian shivers, shakes, experiences convulsions, and may even collapse inert on the floor.

When bodily functions are restored, it is part of Santerian belief that the man or woman who has been influenced so dramatically by the Orisha becomes the steed that the Orisha rides and controls. The technical term for the supposedly possessed person is *montado* or *caballo* during this part of the proceedings. Santerians believe that the Orisha has taken over the person completely — the possessed individual's voice and mannerisms undergo dramatic changes. The original personality of the montado is no longer observable: the phenomenon is very similar to the condition that psychiatrists would describe as multiple personality disorder. It is also comparable with the dual personalities of Dr. Jekyll and Mr. Hyde in Robert Louis Stevenson's immortal classic — except that the personality demonstrated by the Orisha is simply *different:* not evil as Hyde's was. Each Orisha has a particular drum rhythm by which he or she can be recognized, and one of these specific rhythms now takes over the previous percussion pattern.

The next stage of the Santerian initiation process takes place when Obatala, Shango, Yemaya, and Oshun take on the role of sacred *asentados*, which means "those who have taken their seats." Santerians believe that these first four very important Orishas have taken their places on the candidate, and he or she has now entered Santeria under their protection. After that, it is the other Orishas who select the candidate as *their* Santerian: candidates do not select their Orishas — the Orishas select them.

Orishan baptism — similar in many ways to full-immersion Christian baptism — is also an important element in the initiation service, as is the special ceremony of feeding an angelic being called an *eleda*. In the Santerian faith, an eleda is a personal guardian angel that is located inside the believer's head. If it is neglected, it will leave, and the Santerian will consequently have less intelligence and less protection against evil entities than before. Some researchers into the mystery of the crystal skulls have suggested that they may be intended to symbolize the dwelling places of these eleda.

The principles of Santeria include animal sacrifices — which are similar in many ways to the sacrifices (burnt offerings, sin offerings, and peace offerings) that were carried out as part of Judaism in Old Testament times. Santerians defend the practice by saying that the priests and priestesses who carry out these bird and animal sacrifices on behalf of their worshippers are trained to do it in a swift and humane manner. They also argue that the meat is eaten by the worshippers so that nothing is wasted and only the blood is sacrificed to the Orishas. It is also customary to offer trees to an Orisha. Music, dancing, and drumming are prominent in Santerian worship and are regarded as equivalents to prayer.

The principles of Santeria do not include good versus evil dualism like the Christian idea of God versus the devil. For Santerians, the universe is subject to opposing forces such as *expansion* and *contraction*, which are not of themselves good or evil. They believe everything in the universe

Fairy as eleda.

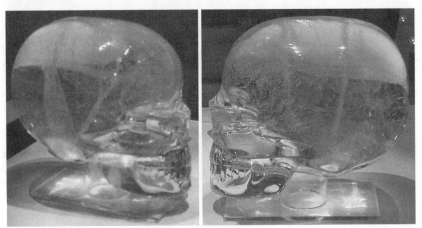

Crystal skulls — dwelling places for the eleda.

has positive attributes that are referred to as *Iré* and negative attributes that are described as *Ibi*. Positive elements are thought of as constructive, while negative elements are thought of as destructive. There is also an important sense that the formation of right character is an integral part of Santerian faith. Good character in the Santerian belief system is called *Iwapele* and consists of doing good deeds and striving to be a good person. It also consists of a particular motivation as the dynamic for being good and for doing good. Iwapele requires a Santerian to choose to do good simply because it is good. Santerian morality and ethics are not based on rewards for good behaviour or punishment for bad behaviour: they focus on the importance of doing right simply because it is right.

There are significant differences between the mysterious syncretized religions in the group that contains Santeria, Voodoo, Obeah, and similar faiths. *Voodoo* has several variant spellings — including *Vodou, Vudun, Vodoun,* and *Vodun* — depending upon the language of the culture where it is recognized. The most familiar form of the word, *Voodoo,* is the one used frequently in the New Orleans area of the U.S.A. *Vodou* is the name employed in Haiti. *Vudun, Vodoun,* and *Vodun* are the variants used by worshippers in Brazil. *Vodun* is also an old Fon word that simply means *spirit.*

However it is spelled, Voodoo can be thought of as traditionally West African — like Santeria. The heart of Voodoo's religious, theological, metaphysical, and philosophical thinking is close to the core of most major world religions: an attempt to understand and explain the universe and the vast forces within it, to control or influence those forces, and to influence human thought and behaviour. Like Santeria, Voodoo and its derivatives were carried by the slave trade to the Caribbean, the Philippines, and the Americas.

Very similar to Santeria in many ways, Voodoo theology begins with the concept of a supreme creator god who is called Nana Buluku and who is responsible for the entire universe together with everything it contains. The religious traditions of the Fon people of Dahomey include the idea that Nana Buluku generated the moon god and sun god, whom they refer to as Mawu and Lisa. In another variation of the ancient African belief systems, Nana Buluku can be identified with Yemaja, described by some theologians as the *female thought* of the male creator god, whom they then refer to in that context as Ashe. This concept is then pursued along the lines that as Yemaja — the female thought — Nana Buluku became the dynamic process behind all later creation.

A development of this Voodoo idea of Nana Buluku as the original creative force is the existence of the voduns — superhuman divinities who work for God or act for God. They are practically equivalent to the Orishas and are understood to be the children of Mawu and Lisa, the grandchildren of Nana Buluku. Voodoo is also deeply concerned with ancestral spirits, and different African families have their own highly trained and specialized priests and priestesses. These roles can be hereditary.

It is important to make a clear distinction between the role of a genuinely religious Voodoo priest or priestess and that of the *bokor*, meaning a wizard, an enchanter, or a magician. The use of poppets, or Voodoo dolls, is part of the Hoodoo derivative of Voodoo, rather than having a central place in Voodoo religion as such. Again, in any paranormal use of such dolls — as a form of very ancient sympathetic magic — the bokor would be more relevant than a legitimate priest or priestess. These pinned dolls also have centuries-old counterparts in medieval European witchcraft, and it is certainly possible that the idea came from Africa to Europe during Roman times — or even earlier.

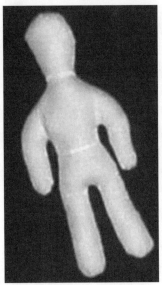

For oppressed and abused slaves in the Caribbean and the Americas who had almost no defence against the cruelties of their owners, the idea of a *magical* defence might have had considerable appeal. In tropical climates where a healthy plantation owner could succumb to infection, sicken, and die within a week, superstitious neighbours might wonder whether a slave-sorcerer had killed his owner with pins in a magical poppet.

A Voodoo doll or poppet.

Misunderstandings of the real meaning and purpose of these strange dolls might also have arisen because they were at one time used as psychic messengers — almost in the way that a human medium might be considered to act as a bridge between the invisible world of spirits and the physical world of the living. Haitian Voodoo custom included nailing poppets — and discarded shoes — on trees near burial grounds. Another, and very different, practice was to build the poppets into altars or sacred objects intended to honour and venerate voduns, Orishas, and distinguished ancestors.

In popular literature and folklore, Voodoo has been seen as very close to Satanism, or similar types of devil worship, but this is not borne out by the facts. In order to draw the clear and necessary demarcation lines separating Satanism from Voodoo, Santeria, Obeah, and the other syncretized religions, it needs to be understood that Satanism — like the Hydra of classical mythology — has several heads!

At one extreme there is what may be described as theistic Satanism, in which the devil is considered to be a real and powerful psychic entity, with certain objectives as far as he and his worshippers are concerned. At the other extreme is the philosophical atheist, who believes in no psychic entities of any kind whatsoever but feels that his or her instincts are being suppressed and inhibited by the law, order, and culture that protect society. There are other Satanists who try to trace their religion back to the worship of Set in ancient Egypt. For them Setianism (rather than Satanism) is a hedonistic religion of pure, wild, uninhibited, totally selfish pleasure.

Sensationalized, melodramatic portrayals of Satanism usually include primitive mockeries of Christianity, particularly the so-called black mass ceremony. The philosophical ideas of good and evil put God's unselfish love for humanity and His will that human beings should love, care for, help, and protect one another very clearly on one side of the moral and ethical conflict. The various forms of Satanism, despite their wide divergence from one another — and whether they worship human instincts or some real or imaginary evil psychic entity — broadly advocate the selfish pursuit of individual pleasure at the expense of anyone weaker who gets in the way. The followers of Voodoo are not dualists — they believe in one benign Supreme Being. They ask help from that Supreme Being's assistants: the Orishas and the voduns. There is no perspective from which Voodoo worship can be seen as a form of Satanism. Some Orishas and voduns have negative as well as positive aspects — but Voodoo worshippers accept that all human beings have similar negative and positive aspects. It may conflict strongly with the popular concepts of Santeria, Obeah, Voodoo, and the other syncretized religions — but the followers of these religions strive as hard as any human being can to reach what they describe as a state of Iwapele: a state of being a good person who strives after goodness for its own sake.

Obeah is more magic-orientated than either Voodoo or Santeria, but like them its origins can be traced to ancient Africa. Slaves who came from the Ashanti peoples would refer to their religious leaders as *Myal* men and to the magic that their leaders worked as *Obi* or *Obeah*. The meaning of the word extended so that it also came to refer to a talisman, a spell, a magician's wand, or any other piece of magical equipment. There was a darker side to Obeah as well, so that anything used for harmful magical purposes was referred to as Obeah. Yet it was also used in positive and benign ways to bring good luck, to heal its followers when they were sick or injured, and to solve problems connected with money. Many Obeah spells also related to love and marriage.

One of the most useful research sources into late eighteenth and early nineteenth century Obeah is William Earle's novel entitled *Obi, or the History of Three-Fingered Jack*. The story was published in 1800 and formed the basis of several popular melodramas in London theatres. The hero is the real-life escaped slave, freedom fighter, and Jamaican folk hero Jack Mansong. In this quasi-historical account of his adventures, Man-

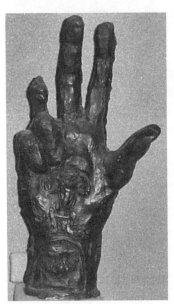

song is described as a skilled practitioner of Obi (Obeah), from which he gained his superpowers. Further fiction with a strong factual basis, *Hamel the Obeah Man*, was published in 1827. These literary insights into Obeah were reinforced by the dramatic interpretations of celestial phenomena that are found not only in astrology but in many religions — the star that led the eastern Magi to Bethlehem is a case in point.

The comet called Schwassmann-Wachmann 1 has an orbital period of about

Is this the hand of Three-Fingered Jack?

fifteen years and a more circular orbit than the usual cometary ellipse. Its brightness also changes dramatically from time to time. This comet, or one very similar to it, made some spectacular nineteenth-century appearances over the Caribbean and caused massive religious disquiet in Jamaica.

Spiritualism was in fashion then, and there were numerous outbreaks of end-of-the-world religious enthusiasm among a number of fundamentalist Christian groups. During this socially disturbed period, Myal men and Obeah practitioners frequently confronted one another. The Myal men claimed that they were on the side of the angels, and that their opponents, the Obeah men, were carrying out evil enchantments of all types — including stealing people's shadows. The Myal men naturally offered to recover the stolen shadows.

Nomenclature is one of the major problems for researchers exploring the mysteries of the syncretized religions. Some of the important distinctions separating Santeria, Obeah, and Voodoo have already been examined, but Candomblé — sometimes called Batuque and Macumba in different regions — also needs to be analyzed. It is practised mainly in Brazil, where it arrived with African slaves in the middle of the sixteenth century. Some of these captives were actually high-ranking Candomblé priests, and others were devout followers of the religion.

Candomblé can be described as a spiritual religion in the sense that its worshippers revere one supreme god. This supreme deity is Nana Buluku to the Fon, but the Bantu peoples use the name Zambi, or Zambi-apongo. There are also demigods and spirits of various kinds. The Bantu call these Candombléan demigods *nkisis*, and they are more or less the equivalents of the Orishas and voduns.

Modern nkisis are sometimes described as "power statues" and are thought of as embodying, or otherwise encapsulating, magical energy. They are used for divination, healing, and promoting success. Practitioners believe that their little nkisis statuettes are in contact with paranormal forces. They are thought of as magical devices — something like the psychic equivalents of radio or TV receivers — through which very strong signals from the spirit world can reach the Candomblé believer.

These Candomblé entities — like the different Orishas, or the Kami of Japanese Shintoism — all have specific powers that are associated with a wide range of different natural phenomena. Although each specific entity is thought of as having a particular location as well as individual powers, they can be guests in one another's domains. A Candomblé family who are the people of one Orisha-type spirit can, therefore, invite another powerful psychic being to come to their aid when his or her powers are more relevant for their needs at a particular time.

Just as was the case with Santeria, a syncretizing interface occurred between Candomblé and Christianity, and crucifixes were often displayed on the altars in Candombléan temples and in worshippers' homes. Candombléan ritual dances were often said to be in honour of various Christian saints rather the Candombléan deities at whom they were really directed. There was, however, a certain one-sidedness to the toleration and inclusiveness manifested in this syncretized religion. Christians would not accept the demigod status of the Orishas, or orixas, as they were also known; whereas Candombléans were more than happy to regard Jesus and Christian angels and saints as very powerful and benign psychic entities.

A Holy Christian icon.

The Candombléans were also willing to reverence the local gods, goddesses, and powerful spirit beings of South America. These included Amana, a creator goddess associated with the sea, and her two sons, Tamus and Tamula. When Amana created the sun, she did not realize how powerful its heat would be, so she dips it into the sea each night to prevent it from damaging the earth. Tamus helps her by working through the day and cutting off the sun's radiant heat-serpents. He throws them into the air where they burn out harmlessly as meteors and comets. Does this South American folk belief connect in any way with the panic in Jamaica when the very bright comet appeared?

Tamula takes over from his brother after Amana has dipped the sun into the ocean. His job is to keep dark covers over the sun throughout the night, until his serpent-cutting brother takes over again at dawn. Amana, like many of the Orishas, is associated with a mystic number. Hers is 1468. Numerologists analyze this as $1 + 4 + 6 + 8 = 19$ and then $1 + 9 = 10$ followed by $1 + 0 = 1$.

The number one is of special significance in numerological analysis. It denotes massive strength, willpower, and creativity. It is a particularly relevant number for a god, a goddess, a demigod, or an Orisha.

Other gods of South American cultures, such as the mysterious Aztecs, also found their way into Candombléan religious thought. Some legendary accounts of Aztec origins suggest that they arrived from the north and occupied the Anahuac valley close to Lake Texcoco. Other accounts suggest that they came from Chicomostoc, which means "the place where seven caves are situated." There are theories that this links with the classical Roman tradition that the great city was built on seven hills *and that the seven Aztec caves of Chicomostoc are a coded reference to Rome.* When the Huns, Goths, and Vandals descended on Rome, did a group of prudent Romans sail past the Pillars of Hercules (Gibraltar) and away across the South Atlantic? This unusual theory of Aztec origins finds support in the ancient Aztec beliefs concerning "white gods" who would one day return from across the sea. Could those "white gods" have been powerful and wealthy Roman aristocrats with their soldiers and servants? Was it their semi-legendary knowledge of *Roman* gold that gave the Aztecs their desire to locate, mine, and store it in vast quantities? Other legends of Aztec origins place them in Tamonachan, but Tamonachan was simply a place like the Garden of Eden — or even the Olduvai Gorge — that was recognized as the starting point of all civilizations. Was it a *notional* location rather than a geographical one?

There were numerous Aztec gods for the Candombléans to learn about and perhaps to absorb alongside the other indigenous South and Central American gods and goddesses such as Amana, Tamus, and Tamula. These deities included the underworld god Acolmiztli and the god of lakes and rivers, Amimtl. There was also Camaxtli, the god of fire, warfare, and hunting; and Chantico, the goddess of hearth and home as well as volcanoes. Ehecatl was a wind god who helped to support the sky in a similar way to the Greek Atlas. His breath was powerful enough to affect the position of the sun and to move the rain. Most importantly, he possessed good and positive emotions and consequently fell in love with Mayahuel, a human girl. In this respect, Ehecatl resembled Zeus, head of the Greek pantheon, whose continual love affairs with human girls aroused the formidable anger of his jealous goddess wife, Hera. The beneficent Ehecatl bestowed the ability to love on humanity in general so that Mayahuel could return his love for her.

Another benign member of the Aztec pantheon was Ixtlilton — their god of healing, games, dancing, celebrations, and festivals. He would have appealed strongly to Candombléans, for whom rhythmic dancing was an essential component of religion.

At one time, Candomblé, Santeria, Umbanda, and Quimbanda were grouped with some of the shamanic faiths and included under the general category of spiritist religions. It was Allan Kardec (1804–1869) who claimed to have coined the word *spiritism* as the name of his religious system, but traditional and fundamentalist Christians used the word disparagingly to show their prejudice against any religion that encouraged, accepted, or tolerated mediumship.

There is an important but subtle distinction between Kardec's precise use of the term *spiritism* and the nineteenth and early twentieth centuries' English use of *spiritualism*, although there is also a significant overlap between the two sets of ideas. Nicolas Camille Flammarion (1842–1925) combined professional astronomy with authorship and was sympathetic towards Kardec's spiritism system, as was Arthur Conan Doyle. Flammarion's most famous comment on the subject was this: "It is by the scientific method alone that we may make progress in the search for truth. Religious belief must not take the place of impartial analysis. We must be constantly on our guard against illusions" ("Death and its Mystery," 1921). And when he spoke at Kardec's funeral, Flammarion made the point that "spiritism is not a religion but a science." Despite Flammarion's phrasing, however, he and Doyle were equally interested in what was more generally referred to in their day as spiritualism.

The particular variety of syncretistic religion referred to as Umbanda derives its name from the Hindu term *aum-gandha,* which translates broadly as "godly or celestial rule or principle." It contains ideas about the spirit world and psychic healing that can be traced back to African, Hindu, and Buddhist concepts. Umbanda can be condensed to three fundamental principles. The first is that human beings possess a spiritual body as well as a physical one. The second is that spiritual beings of all types are in contact with our ordinary, everyday, physical world. The third is that it is possible for human beings to contact these psychic, ethereal entities, to learn from them, and to be healed by them when necessary.

Quimbanda, on the other hand, while still belonging to what might be termed the spiritist group in general, has what some researchers think of as negative associations. The Umbandistas (followers of Umbanda)

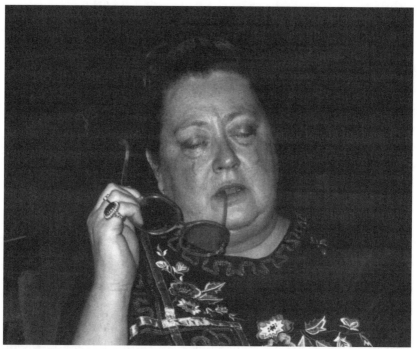

Bremna Howells, medium and psychometrist.

take a very positive view of the psychic world. They do not believe that any psychic entities are evil but acknowledge that some can be very mischievous. Umbandistas believe that these "naughty" or "mischievous" spirits need only to be re-educated. Quimbandistas, however, set out to exploit these mischievous ethereal entities and to take power from them for their own personal use — which makes it easy to understand why the Quimbandistas are sometimes referred to as witches, wizards, enchanters, or sorcerers employing black magic.

The word *Quimbanda* came originally from the Angolan Kimbundu language, where it had the connotation of a seer, a prophet, a soothsayer, or a healer. Quimbanda rituals focus on necromancy — which can be defined as the practice of seeking advice and information from the spirits of the dead. The biblical Witch of Endor provides a prime example when she contacted the spirit of Samuel on behalf of King Saul, although the Book of Deuteronomy (chapter 18, verses 9–12) warns against it. Ancient Persians, Chaldeans, Etrurians, and Babylonians all included necromancy in their belief systems. The *Odyssey* records how Odysseus visited Hades using a form of necromancy that Circe had revealed to him.

Bringing together — as far as is possible — the principles of the various syncretized religions reveals a significant common core. The most ancient of their roots go back to very early African beliefs. There are also elements of ancient Babylonian, Chaldean, Egyptian, Greek, and Roman concepts. The idea of one supreme god is common to all of them, and this primal creator deity is assisted by numerous demigods and spiritual entities of various kinds, each with explicit powers and areas of responsibility. There are specific numbers, colours, and identifying items such as sacred stones that are associated with these individual Orishas and similar paranormal power-beings.

One of the most challenging questions concerning the mystery of Santeria and similar syncretized belief systems is whether these paranormal entities have any real and objective existence. Belief systems tend to persist and expand where they produce psychological and sociological benefits for their adherents — irrespective of whether those belief systems are true or real in any objective scientific sense. One such motivational benefit in medieval Christendom, for example, was the avoidance of persecution, torture, and death for heresy. In tyrannous, totalitarian dictatorships, empowered by ruthless secret police and close surveillance, there are very powerful incentives to pay lip service to the dictator — irrespective of the validity of what the dictator proclaims.

It can also be argued that belief systems tend to persist and expand where evidence does support — or may *seem* to support — their truth and reality. If enough people over enough time have witnessed phenomena involving the apparent intervention of Orishas and similar entities, belief in such beings will tend to persist and expand. It cannot be denied that such phenomena have been reported persistently over very long periods: but the question of their true *causality* remains open. It is very much to the credit of the mysterious syncretized religions that they encourage goodness, morality, and ethical behaviour. They also encourage spells, charms, talismans, enchantments, and various types of magic. Drumming and dancing feature prominently during the rituals and ceremonies, and there are altered states of consciousness and trance experiences that have something in common with hypnotism — either self-induced or induced by the priest or priestess.

The power of the human mind, when properly focused and directed, is capable of achieving far more than is generally recognized. Evidence suggests that the release of mind-power is triggered at a subconscious or semiconscious level. Hypnotized subjects have been shown to be capable of remarkable feats that are not apparently achievable during their normal, conscious state. Is this one of the great secrets at the back of Santeria and similar religions?

Wizards often possessed hypnotic powers.

Chapter 7
HYPNOTIC LITURGIES
AND RITUALS

ALTHOUGH modern scientific and medical hypnotherapy may be only two or three centuries old, hypnotism itself dates back for millennia. Ancient Egypt and classical Greece were aware of hypnotism, and it was certainly practised successfully in the Temples of Sleep used by the early Hindus. The ancient Sanskrit Law of Manu recognized different levels of hypnotically induced sleep in India millennia ago. Differences between ecstasy-sleep, dream-sleep, and waking-sleep were noted even in those early days.

Although not named as such, some elements of hypnosis are indistinguishable from certain trancelike states induced during ancient religious ceremonies involving rhythmic drumming, chanting, or deep meditation.

Paracelsus (allegedly 1493–1541, but he probably lived much longer) was an alchemist, a magician, a doctor of medicine, and, in the opinion of some researchers, possibly a time traveller as well! He discovered the usefulness of mercury as a means of allaying and ameliorating some of the symptoms of syphilis, and his innovative medical skills included stroking a patient's body with a natural magnet — a lodestone. This stroking technique seems to have been closely allied to an early form of proto-hypnosis, in which healing suggestions accompanied the moving magnet. The stroking with a magnet technique was continued and developed by "The Great Irish Stroker," whose real name was Valentine Greatrakes (1628–1682). He actually worked with the pioneering scientist Robert Boyle (1627–1691), who carefully noted Greatrakes's method of magnetic stroking. The technique, as Boyle observed it, consisted of drawing the pain from the afflicted part towards the end of the limb and then out of the body altogether.

Many years ago, we worked with a hypnotherapist named Louis Dorey who was also a skilled puppeteer. Louis's technique was very similar to Greatrakes's method. For example, he encouraged the patient to move a headache into an elbow or knee, along the limb and then *out of the body altogether.*

Father Johann Joseph Gassner (1727–1779) was a Catholic priest at Klosterle and later at Pondorf, now part of Winklarn in Bavaria. He firmly believed that illness was caused by what he called demons, devils, and evil spirits. Working as an exorcist, Father Johann cured patients by a process that he believed involved driving out the evil spirits responsible for their illnesses. If his work is considered within the context of hypnotism and suggestion, however, it might be argued that his patients benefited from being *told* that the cause of their illness was being driven away.

One of the most famous names in the history of hypnotism is Franz Anton Mesmer (1734–1815). He studied under Father Maximilian Hell (1720–1792), who, despite his surname, was a Jesuit. Maximilian's healing methods consisted of applying magnetized steel plates to the patient's body. In 1774, Mesmer gave one of his patients a dose of "medicine" that contained a significant quantity of iron. He then ran magnets over her body, and the patient described her strange feelings. She said it was as if tides, or streams, of fluid energy were running through her body and she reported that she felt much better for several hours afterwards.

Mesmer was not convinced that the magnets were solely responsible for her improvement. He developed a theory of "animal magnetism" that involved healing power flowing from him to the patient. Later experts on hypnotism felt that processes other than what Mesmer called "animal magnetism" were the real causative factors.

Armand-Marie-Jacques de Chastenet, Marquis of Puységur (1751–1825), was an enthusiastic follower of Mesmer's ideas and methods. His brother, Antoine-Hyacinthe, the Count of Chastenet, had taught him about mesmerism. One of their first patients was an employee named Victor Race who went into a state of what Puységur called "artificial somnambulism." It was not until 1842 that James Braid referred to it by its familiar, contemporary name — *hypnosis.*

As far back as 1785, however, Puységur was already teaching hypnotherapy — although he was still calling it animal magnetism out of deference to his much-admired Mesmer. Part of Puységur's course included the words "I believe that I have a power within myself … and my will is to exert it. The whole doctrine can be expressed in two words … *believe* and *want* … I *believe* that I have this power and I *want* to use it … on behalf of my fellows … If you also *believe* and *want* you will be able to do as much as I can do…"

This pioneer hypnotist's thinking has much in common with the fundamental ideas of Santeria, Voodoo, Obeah, and the other syncretized religions. If their magic and sorcery is to succeed, the priests, priestesses, and practitioners of Candomblé, Umbanda, and Quimbanda need to *believe* that the Orishas and other psychic entities exist and that they have the power to intervene in human life and the natural environment. The would-be workers of magic also need to believe in their own ability to communicate with the powerful psychic entities, to use them, and to be used by them. Just as the element of *belief* is an integral part of syncretistic religious magic, so is the element of *wanting*. The magicians and their clients *want* health, material prosperity, and success in love. Most of their magic is aimed towards these goals.

Another pioneering hypnotist was a Scottish surgeon named James Esdaile (1808–1859). He worked in India where he performed more than two thousand operations using a form of hypnosis to anesthetize his patients while the surgical processes were being carried out.

Not all medical experts and experienced practitioners of hypnosis would agree, but hypnosis can be defined as a state of increased suggestibility during which ideas and instructions become readily acceptable to the subconscious mind. Hypnosis can "cure" (eradicate and replace) long-established habits and attitudes that the patient wishes to change. Expressed in its most basic form, and focusing on the powers of practitioners of Obeah, Voodoo, Candomblé, and the other syncretized religions, hypnosis opens a ready channel of communication between the subconscious, conscious, and superconscious minds. Once that channel is open and fully established, the unfathomable powers of the subconscious and superconscious are accessible to our desires, ambitions, and aspirations. The sky becomes the limit.

Examples of the power that mind can exert over matter include the amazing feats of Francisco Rodriguez, better known as Pipin Ferreras (Spanish nickname meaning "The Iron Man"), whose outstanding exploits were featured on co-author Lionel's widely acclaimed TV series *Fortean TV* on UK Channel 4. Francisco, who was born in Cuba on January 1, 1962, had a degree of mind-over-body control that enabled him to get down to depths of over five hundred feet under free-diving conditions.

On Sunday, July 15, 2007, Lewis Pugh, using mind-power alone, super-heated his body until he was sweating and then plunged into sub-zero water close to the North Pole and swam over half a mile.

These examples of mind control to overcome water pressure and very low temperatures are outstanding, but the mind control exercised by a yoga master named Haridas in 1835 is even more sensational. The whole story was recorded in the *Calcutta Medical Times* for that year. Haridas, a fakir and advanced yoga practitioner, had developed his powers of mind over matter to a point where he claimed that he could be buried alive for a period of forty days.

Preparations for Haridas's feat included severing the muscles below his tongue so that it could be rolled back to seal off the airways in his throat. Prior to being buried alive, he went to great lengths to cleanse his alimentary canal. These purging techniques included swallowing ninety feet of linen bandage and then slowly regurgitating it. Haridas also sealed his nose and ears with wax as a precaution against predatory insects while he was underground. The doctors who were examining him found that his pulse was practically undetectable as he was placed inside a large chest that was then padlocked shut. The Maharaja of Lahore, who was a well-educated, thoughtful, and objective thinker, was in charge of the experiment and had the chest sealed with his own personal seal. It was then buried, and a wall was built around it. The Maharaja posted guards at the site and ordered barley to be sown over the fakir's grave.

On the fortieth day, the Maharaja and the other witnesses arrived at the site to reopen the grave. The barley plants had grown undisturbed. The chest was still sealed and padlocked. When it was opened, the fakir was in his original position and apparently lifeless. Sir Charles Wade, an unimpeachable witness, reported that Haridas looked like a corpse. His limbs seemed to be shrunken and rigid; his head rested on his shoulder. There was no detectable pulse. The doctors in attendance removed the wax from his ears and nose, extracted his tongue from the position where it was blocking his airways, and massaged him for several minutes. Then they reinflated his lungs using bellows: *within an hour he was back to normal.* The delighted Maharaja gave him a handful of diamonds.

In the light of men such as Ferreras, Pugh, and Haridas, it is relevant to ask how much is known about the real power and function of the subconscious and superconscious minds. How close are their strange powers to what adherents of the mysterious syncretistic religions would speak of as *magic* and *sorcery*?

Colin Wilson, in his outstandingly interesting foreword to the edition of the *Necronomicon* that George Hay edited so effectively, says this about the relationship of the superconscious, conscious, and subconscious minds: "Does it have an upstairs above the ground floor of consciousness as well as a garbage-littered basement beneath? ... cases of remarkable genius seem to suggest that man possesses a 'super-consciousness' as well as an 'unconscious' mind ... and it is equally alien to the everyday personality..."

The subconscious is the reservoir of memories and the control room of habits — including those that are the products of addictions. Compulsive behaviours are also directed from the subconscious mind, and yet it is not without a simple sense of humour. A.P. Herbert (1890–1971) had a keenly perceptive insight into what a sense of humour really is. He is credited with describing it as the apperception of the juxtaposition of the incongruous. The subconscious mind is certainly crammed with enough incongruities to make a sense of humour essential for its survival. There is a childlike simplicity in the subconscious and there are occasions when even the most solemn psychologist would regard it as having a childlike capacity for play as well. There is nothing more pleasing to the subconscious than order, routine, and methodical processes. This seems to be associated with its next characteristic, which is *repetition*. When the conscious mind goes over the same things repeatedly, the subconscious mind absorbs them and makes them part of itself. This ties in closely with the repetition of liturgies and rituals, rhythmic chanting, music, and drumming patterns, which are integral components of Obeah and similar religions.

There is another important aspect of the subconscious, which can be thought of as *automatism*. Once it has been programmed or conditioned, the subconscious mind responds swiftly and automatically in accordance with what it has learned. In this respect it behaves rather like a programmed computer. Hypnotism is the keyboard and mouse that enable the conscious mind — the computer operator — to input the commands and instructions that will make the computer function as required.

A more complex approach to what links mind processes of the hypnotic type to the mysteries of the syncretistic religions is neuro-linguistic programming, or NLP. It goes a step further than basic hypnotism by suggestion that *linguistics* is involved in character changing and improvement of human performance. NLP considers that body, mind, and language interact to give an individual his or her perception of the environment. According to NLP theory, what a person *thinks* about the world will influence the way that he or she *reacts* to it. NLP theory also suggests that changed perceptions lead to changed behaviours, and one of the characteristic NLP techniques is referred to as "modelling." In its most rudimentary form, this involves studying the behaviour and speech patterns of successful individuals, and then emulating them. It also involves studying their belief systems — particularly the ways in which they see themselves relative to the world around them. Modelling has been defined as "the study of excellence and how to reproduce it."

The similarity of NLP theory to the processes that take place in syncretistic religions becomes distinct when the relationship of the Orishas and their worshippers is viewed as a form of what NLP calls modelling. Powerful spiritual entities are seen by their worshippers as possessing excellence in the NLP sense. Devout believers want to emulate their Orishas, their saints, and their gods in order to achieve that excellence for themselves.

NLP also makes reference to the "meta-model," which consists of language patterns and questions that are designed to help the NLP practitioner to widen his or her perception of the environment. Working with a meta-model is believed to help an individual to discover any restrictive, limiting thoughts he or she may have concerning the way that the environment is perceived: things like "I cannot do this because…" and "I cannot achieve this highly desirable goal because…" By finding these mental restrictions and inhibitions — what some writers refer to as a glass wall — the individual working with NLP is enabled to break through the obstacles and succeed. This meta-modelling technique also has its parallels within the syncretistic religions. An Obeah follower may begin by believing that certain goals and achievements are hopelessly out of reach. By its very nature, this restrictive thought makes those goals seem unattainable. Once the person can become at one with a powerful Orisha, however, the inhibitory, restrictive thoughts melt away and the Obeah worshipper breaks through the barriers that formerly separated him or her from the desired success and achievement.

Another NLP technique is referred to as the "Milton model" because it is based on the work of Milton Erickson (1901–1980). Erickson was a brilliant pioneering psychiatrist who specialized in medical hypnosis and became the founding president of the American Society for Clinical Hypnosis. Erickson believed that the subconscious mind was largely separate from the conscious mind and very different from it. In his view, it had its own awareness and its own interests. He regarded it as a place where solutions to problems were generated and he also saw it as a creative and positive entity.

When Erickson's ideas about the subconscious are held up against the Obeah concepts of Orishas and saints as entities that solve worshippers' problems, a number of significant similarities begin to appear.

The Milton model in NLP can be regarded as a special way of using language to help to produce and maintain a sufficient level of trance to enable the conscious, subconscious, and superconscious minds to communicate effectively with one another. There were three aspects of the Milton model. First, the language used helped to build and maintain a trancelike condition that opened portals between the different minds. Second, the language was intended to distract and occupy the conscious mind so that the subconscious could communicate more effectively. The third aspect was the most intriguing of the three: the special language used in the Milton model was packed with meaningful stories, parallel ideas, analogies, and metaphors through which Erickson's therapeutic suggestions could be expressed.

The mysterious syncretistic religions — Obeah, Voodoo, Candomblé, and the others — are all rich in allegories, fables, metaphors, and similes. At many ceremonies, the high priest or high priestess will teach the worshippers in this way. While waiting for the ceremony to begin, worshippers will often regale one another with ancient African myths and legends or with stories of the sufferings and deaths of the Christian saints and martyrs whom they identify with their Orishas.

Some of these fables and allegories refer to fireflies, or *nimitas* as they are known in the Dominican Republic. They are said to be the souls of the dead shining their lights to watch and guard the loved ones they have left behind on Earth.

The tortoise of a thousand tricks.

Another of these stories with a meaning comes from an ancient Yoruba tradition. A certain African king had a daughter named Bola who was unable to speak. A cunning tortoise — a paranormal entity that was known as the tortoise of a thousand tricks — went to the king and offered to heal the girl. The king promised to give the tortoise half of his house if he could cure Bola of her muteness. The tortoise accepted the king's offer and found Bola asleep beside a large bush outside the village. He placed a container of honey nearby without her seeing him and then concealed himself where he could watch her. Bola awoke, looked around,

African girl who might be Bola.

and saw the honey. She put her hand on the container and the tortoise shouted, "Bola has stolen my honey!"

"I haven't stolen it!" cried Bola — speaking for the first time in her life.

The tortoise tied her wrists and led her back to the village singing, "Bola is a shameless thief." Bola protested her innocence and sang her denials in response to the tortoise's accusations.

When they reached the village, the king and the villagers rejoiced that she could now speak and the grateful king rewarded the cunning tortoise with half of the royal house. Underneath that simple story are some deep and interesting concepts concerning the nature of psychosomatic illnesses and inabilities — and the tortoise's use of shock therapy.

Another teaching legend concerns the Ciguapa, which has the appearance of an exquisitely beautiful dark-eyed girl but is cruel, deceitful, and dangerous. Her shining black hair reaches to her ankles and is her only clothing. Victims of her fatal beauty follow her into deep, dark forests and are never seen again. In some versions of her legend, the Ciguapa is the personification of Death — a more attractive one than is the old man with the scythe. Another part of her legend warns prospective victims that if they stand by the shore and call out for her a huge wave will rise and draw them out to sea.

Yet another cautionary legend from the Dominican Republic refers to *Los Indios de las Augas*, which translates as "The Water Indians." These strange beings — if they are anything more than myth or legend — might even be connected with the old traditions of Atlantis. They are believed to live in deep caves, near rivers and lakes, and on the coast. As with the

Ciguapa, their women are exquisitely beautiful and are said to come out of their caves at night looking for men. A man who accompanies a Water Indian girl back to her cave, however, is never seen again.

In other versions of the legend, the Water Indians are kind and generous people who are powerful magicians and healers. They generously help human beings and teach people about therapeutic herbs.

Another strange story — a very popular mystery with those who live near it — is a hill that appears to defy gravity. It is situated on the Cabral-Polo road between Auyamas and Polo in the Dominican Republic. The hill in question is known as *La Cueva*, meaning "The Cave." Witnesses report that cars left out of gear appear to run up the hill, and a football or cylindrical tin will also appear to roll upwards against gravity. This provides exactly the kind of story-with-a-meaning that leaders of the syncretized mystery religions can employ — all types of metaphors and allegories can be drawn from it. It would have had special appeal to runaway slaves and others who chose to go against what society expected of them. Watching and waiting beside the road as object after object appears to defy gravity also has trance-inducing properties — of the type used in religious services for millennia.

Egyptologists who have made specialized studies of trance practices in ancient Egyptian religion and therapy refer to "therapeutic dreaming." Patients could visit some of the ancient Egyptian temples, where, in a separate area, the priestly hypnotherapist would induce a trance by lighting an oil lamp to aid the patient's concentration. This would be accompanied by quiet, gentle, repetitive droning chants.

Other Egyptologists examine the mysterious and all-embracing concept of Neter in this context. Neter can be interpreted to mean the Supreme Creative Power, very similar to the idea of the One Supreme God at the head of Voodoo, Obeah, Candomblé, and Santeria. Other Egyptologists suggest that the word *Neter* carries the sense of continuous renewal, renovation, and re-creation rather than a once-and-forever process. This aspect of Neter makes the One Supreme God the sustainer of the cosmos as well as its creator. Other linguistic scholars regard Neter as referring to that which is divine, holy, and separate from creation. Some translators link it with the full and original meaning of the Latin *natura*, which personifies the entire natural existence and function of the universe as a totality — cosmic creation followed by rhythmic renewal.

In other versions of this ancient Egyptian therapeutic trance ceremony, the seeker went into the dream chamber alone, carrying the hypnotic lamp. Herbs and spices were burned and the enquirer gazed at the flame and inhaled the aromatic fragrances until the trance state was achieved. The Neter was then said to appear and the enquirer would lie down and continue drifting deeper and deeper into a strange, trancelike sleep. The Neter's purpose was to provide healing and give messages to the self-hypnotized sleeper.

Just as the word *Neter* could refer to the One Supreme Creator-Sustainer of the universe, so the term *Neteru* referred to the lesser gods of ancient Egypt whose statues filled the various temples. The Neteru can, therefore, be considered the ancient Egyptian equivalent of the Orishas.

A number of researchers into these ancient Egyptian mysteries have reached the conclusion that where accounts exist of Neteru statues apparently coming to life while their worshippers sat staring at them in

Amenhotep III, who was the ninth pharaoh of Egypt's Eighteenth Dynasty, succeeded his father, Thutmose IV, during the fourteenth century BC.

their half-lit temples, the worshippers had slipped into trance states in which the statues *appeared* to them to become animated.

Something very similar seems to have occurred in the ancient temples of Tarxien on Malta. Researchers believe that there were dream chambers within these prehistoric temples in which aromatic herbs were burned to encourage the trance process.

These temple complexes at Tarxien have been described as the cathedrals of Stone Age culture — and it is not difficult to access Malta from Egypt or other parts of North Africa. Dream chambers in ancient Egypt could have been inspired by the dream chambers of Tarxien, or vice versa. Alternatively, both could have come from a third more ancient and more technically advanced civilization with its roots far to the west beyond Gibraltar.

In 1915, Sir Temi Zammit, an outstanding Maltese archaeologist, began work on the Tarxien temples after their accidental discovery by stonemasons the previous year. (If these craftsmen were members of one of the ancient Masonic Orders — as seems likely — their discovery may not have been entirely accidental.) Following Zammit's expert work, the partial remains of a large statue of the Earth Mother goddess revealed that this temple complex was dedicated to her and that the majority — if not all — of her worshippers here would probably have been women and girls. This Maltese goddess could be the Tarxien counterpart of the Orisha Yemaja, or perhaps of Oshun, Orisha of love and fertility. She is also understood to be a patron of art, and the Tarxien temple complex is very beautifully decorated with scrolls and spiral patterns.

Statues of a bull — representing masculine strength and potency — and a sow with her piglets — representing fertility — are also prominent in the Tarxien temple complex. The bull might possibly represent the Orisha Shango, a potent male god of thunder.

The sounds of religious liturgies can also become trance-inducing. Just as focusing on a small light source — such as a lamp or candle flame — can influence those areas of the brain that deal with visual stimuli via the optic nerve, so those areas of the brain that process sound stimuli can respond to certain pitches, volumes, and persistent repetitions. In broad terms, concentration on a single light source, especially one that is moving rhythmically, has the effect of encouraging trance. In much the same way, concentration on a prolonged sound, especially one that is rising and falling rhythmically, has the effect of encouraging trance. When carefully analyzed, most religious liturgies have this quality. The liturgical chanting used in Voodoo, Obeah, Santeria, Candomblé, and similar religions is particularly trance-inducing. Their rituals also involve repetitive rhythmic movements aligned with the chanting and these movements also encourage the trance state. When aimed in the same direction, light, sound, and movement act effectively together to induce trance.

For religions such as Santeria, aimed at producing magical or supernatural effects via the Orishas, the trance state is of prime importance. A survey of hypnotism and hypnotherapy indicates that there is enormous power in the subconscious, and that some of this power can be released, directed, and used when the subject is in the trance state. Whether the power comes from the subject's mind or from an external psychic entity such as an Orisha, a saint, or an angel does not detract from its effectiveness. Light can do its job whether it comes from the main electrical supply, a battery, or a hand-operated dynamo. A devout Santerian may believe that the archangel Michael, St. Catherine, or Shango the Orisha has miraculously restored his health. The observable, objective, scientific fact is that he really has been healed. If it is the patient's own subconscious mind-power that has done it, via his belief in benign paranormal entities, that does not lessen the healing effect by one iota. It is also worth considering the possibility that the benign psychic entities are perfectly real and objective phenomena and that they perform their healing miracles by enabling the human subject to activate the therapeutic powers in his or her own subconscious or superconscious mind.

When entire groups are participating in hypnotic rhythmic movement in Santerian and similar ceremonies, it is useful to compare the phenomena with what has been described medically as mass hysteria. This has three major components: mimicry, contagion, and loss of mental and physical control. Those affected by it seem to imitate the movements of those around them, and the behaviour spreads as if it were a contagious disease — yet no viruses or bacteria so far discovered have been able to spread at this rate.

An unfortunate French priest named Urbain Grandier was burnt at the stake on August 18, 1634, in connection with an outbreak of mass hysteria at the Ursuline convent of Loudun in Poitou. Although acquitted at his first trial, Grandier made the fatal mistake of criticizing Cardinal Richelieu and was subsequently tortured before being burned at the stake.

A similar outbreak of mass hysteria in Salem, Massachusetts, in 1692 led to the deaths of twenty people and the imprisonment of another two hundred, five of whom died in prison. The tragedy began with the dramatically hysterical behaviour of two girls who said that they were bewitched.

An even stranger series of phenomena was associated with a Jansenist deacon named François de Paris who was buried in the cemetery of Saint-Medard in Paris in 1727. Miracles of healing were reported from his tomb, and in the presence of many witnesses, those suffering from deafness, arthritis, rheumatism, blindness, tumours, fevers, and ulcerous sores were all healed. One of the most famous cases concerned the niece of Pascal, the pioneering mathematician. She had a severe eye ulcer that was cured by a Jansenist miracle.

Following these healing miracles came strange convulsions and weird distortions of the human body that would have been impossible in the normal conscious state. Some of the strangest aspects of these supernormal happenings were cases of apparent invulnerability. A member of the then Paris Parliament, Louis-Basile Carre de Montgeron, gave a detailed account of one of the convulsionaires, as they are called, a twenty-year-old girl, Jeanne Maulet, who was struck repeatedly in the stomach with a sledgehammer and seemingly took no harm from it whatsoever. In normal circumstances, a single blow would have been fatal. Other convulsionaires were attacked with swords, axes, knives, and drills — *which all failed to injure them.* Is it possible that the seemingly limitless power of the mind can really do all this? The witnesses were totally convinced — even those who had gone with the intention of proving that the Jansenists were frauds.

Although most western cultures seem to demonstrate a strong dislike — even fear — of the symptoms of mass hysteria, it is neither disliked nor feared by devotees of the ancient African religions. The tendency there is to regard it as a manifestation of possession by a divine power or psychic entity such as an Orisha. This attitude to individual or group manifestations of hysterical behaviour could lead to the appointment of an individual as a shaman, prophet, seer, Babalawo, or Iyalocha largely *because* he or she demonstrated hysterical behaviour or went into periodic trance states.

The head of an Orisha or a loa.

Contemporaries naturally assumed that the bizarre behaviour was the result of contact with the spirit world and that the seer could convey messages from the gods and from dead ancestors. These communications could include vital information about where game was located, how enemies could be defeated, and how injured or sick people could be healed.

In addition to the nexus between mass hysteria and trance states, there is also a theory that the induction of a very deep and permanent trance might account for the phenomenon generally categorized as zombiism. In contemporary Voodoo it is believed that the snake–deity, or python–god, is invoked to animate the zombie. The sorcerer, or enchanter, using the process is thought to have become the owner and master of the moving corpse. Ancient African religious and magical practices combine with equally old western occultism and certain aspects of traditional Catholicism to create the ceremony at which the zombie is reanimated and made subservient to the sorcerer.

Haitian Voodoo and zombiism are best understood within their historical context because they played a significant role in the successful slave revolution that ended French rule on the island. In 1791 France was in revolutionary turmoil and the Haitian slaves were being inspired to rebel by the mysterious sorcerer-priest Dutty Boukman. He led them into a secret rendezvous in the depths of the forest, accompanied by a terrifying storm that acted as a dramatic background to their proceedings. Here Boukman sacrificed a pig, and his revolutionaries drank its blood. They then stormed many of the plantations, and their owners — known as the plantocracy — were slaughtered. Boukman himself was captured by the French soon after the start of the rebellion that he had inspired. They decapitated him and displayed his head in the hope of quelling the legend of his invincibility — but it had the opposite effect and the rebellious slaves fought harder than ever for their freedom. It took a further twelve years for the revolutionaries to establish their new Republic of Haiti under the leadership of President Toussaint L'Ouverture.

The sorcerer or magician in charge of the zombie is known as a *bokor*. Traditionally, the bokor removes a newly dead corpse from its grave and uses spells to rekindle a spark of life within it. For those who believe in the existence of zombies, the resurrected corpse can eat, drink, excrete, hear, and speak. According to Voodoo folklore, the zombie does not know who it was prior to being zombified and has no memory at all of its earlier human life. It lurches from side to side as it walks, and the rest of its actions are clumsy, awkward, and robotic in character. The voice, when it speaks, is decidedly nasal, and this is thought to be due to the funeral custom of padding out the nostrils of the corpse with cotton wool.

Rational explanations of zombiism involve the use of drugs similar to the one that Father Laurence gave Juliet in Shakespeare's play so she would appear to be dead. According to this theory, the bokor administers such a drug to the victim who is destined to become a zombie and digs up the apparent corpse a few days later. Some partial antidote is administered, and the revived victim faces a life of mindless slavery to the bokor, or to some new owner to whom the bokor has sold that victim.

Another theory involves the use of hypnotism at a very profound level — so deep in fact that the bokor's victims never regain their original self-consciousness. Both methods could be combined so that the drugs

Expressionless face mask. Does it represent a zombie?

and hypnotism reinforced each other in producing the traditional zombie-state in the victim.

Fraud also needs to be considered as a possibility. There are accounts of a bokor — also referred to as a *hungan* — being caught out after opening a grave and apparently reviving the corpse lifted from it. The "corpse" turned out to be the bokor's accomplice, and a sharp-eyed examining magistrate found that an air tube had been connected to a hole in the coffin.

In Haiti again, back in 1937, a folklore researcher, Zora Hurston, came upon the case of a girl named Felicia Felix-Mentor. Felicia had officially died in 1907 when she was twenty-nine. Witnesses reported to Zora that they had seen Felicia wandering about in a zombielike state thirty years after her body had supposedly been laid to rest. Some of Zora's informants suggested that powerful drugs might have been responsible for zombifying a victim like Felicia.

Another account covers the story of a hungan who was strongly sexually attracted to a girl who wanted nothing to do with him. He promptly cursed her, and a few days later she became ill and died. Her grieving family bought a coffin, then found it was too short. They pulled her head down hard to one side so that her body would fit the inadequate coffin. During the family funeral party, a candle set fire to the lower end of the coffin lining and burned her left foot quite severely.

Several weeks after being buried, the "dead" girl was reported to have been seen with the bokor whom she had firmly rejected before her death. The family ignored these rumours and said that the hungan clearly liked girls of similar appearance and must have found a new one. Several years later, however, the girl's brother saw a woman who looked very much like her. When questioned, she had no idea who she was and no memory of any past life as his sister. She did, however, have a badly twisted neck and there were severe burn scars on her left foot. Taken home to what her brother believed was her family and his, she was loyally cared for until she died. During all this time, however, she failed to recall anything of her past life, and was able to exercise only the most limited mental functions.

The famous British anthropologist Francis Huxley reported a well-authenticated case of Haitian zombiism from the late 1950s. Huxley, a remarkable adventurer, had travelled thousands of miles in the Amazon basin studying the indigenous population and their religion. He was also a friend and colleague of the brilliant and dauntless Canadian medical research scientist Humphrey Osmond, who had immigrated to Saskatchewan in 1951 and done much to help patients at the Weyburn hospital.

A Catholic priest reported to Huxley in 1959 that what appeared to be a zombie had been found wandering in a Haitian village street and taken to the local police station. It seems that the police did not wish to take any action, but eventually the apparent zombie managed to mumble the name of a woman living in the village. When enquiries were made, she recognized him as her deceased nephew, *who had been buried four years ago in 1955.* The priest took a keen and sympathetic interest in the zombie, who — unusually — was able to name the bokor who had enslaved him. The priest duly informed the police, but they were still apparently very unwilling to confront and antagonize a powerful hungan. Instead, they sent him a message offering to return the stray zombie to him. Two days later the zombie was found dead — really and finally dead. The hungan was arrested but later released.

An equally impressive zombie report dating from the 1980s comes from the village of L'Estère in the Artibonite Valley in Haiti. A lurching, robotic figure with a blank facial expression and staring eyes crossed the market square and spoke to one of the local women, Angelina Narcisse. Suddenly she recognized him and gave out a terrified scream. She identified him as her brother, Clairvius Narcisse, whom they had buried nearly twenty years ago in 1962.

The head of the psychiatric centre in Port-au-Prince at the time was Dr. Lamarque Douyon, a gifted and rigorously professional Haitian psychiatrist who had trained in Canada. With proper professional scientific detachment, he had studied the phenomena associated with zombiism for over a quarter of a century. During the later stages, assistance came from his equally gifted colleague, E. Wade Davis, a botanist from Harvard.

When the case of Clairvius Narcisse was investigated in depth, it was found that he had been officially recorded as dead in the Schweitzer Hospital in Deschapelles in Haiti on May 3, 1962. Clairvius had arrived at the hospital three days earlier with a high fever and a body that ached all over. He was also spitting up a lot of blood. After the doctors officially pronounced him dead, he was placed in cold storage in the mortuary for a day before being handed over to his family for burial.

When giving an account of his grim experiences, Clairvius said that he remembered hearing the doctors announce that he had died. He also remembered his sister Angelina in tears beside his hospital bed when his death was pronounced. He was able to recall being buried, he said, because despite being conscious he was totally unable to move or cry out. As he listened to shovelfuls of earth landing on his casket lid, he had the strange feeling that he was hovering above the grave.

There was a scar on his right cheek, and he said that this had been caused by a nail driven through his coffin lid when he was being sealed in. He then vividly recalled how a bokor, or hungan, had taken him from his coffin, revived him, and transported him to a sugar plantation in the north of the island. Here, with a several other zombies, he had worked in slave conditions until their overseer had died. This provided the zombies with a chance of escape, and Clairvius had finally found his way back to L'Estère.

As Douyon's researches continued, he found that there was a socio-cultural factor in zombiism: in some areas it was regarded as a form of punishment for people who had contravened the social norms and mores of their community. From this perspective, it was apparent that Clairvius had appropriated land that was not legally his — at least its title was disputed. Had those who thought they had a better claim to it arranged for him to become a zombie?

Another apparent punishment zombie case concerned a woman named Francina Illeus, who was nicknamed Ti-Femme. She had allegedly been zombified for refusing to marry the man who had been selected for her, and for giving birth to the child of another man. Hospitalized with symptoms similar to Clairvius's but sent home again on February 23, 1976, she died there a few days later.

It was almost twenty years later that her mother recognized the female zombie walking uncertainly through the village as Francina because of her distinctive birthmark. Her coffin was exhumed but there were only stones inside it.

In the course of this chapter, an examination has been made of the nature of hypnotism, together with the use of hypnotic liturgies and rituals in Santeria, Obeah, Candomblé, Voodoo, and the other syncretistic mystery religions. In the light of research in these areas, it seems increasingly likely that the power of the human mind is far greater than is realized — *and has never yet been fully exerted.* In the next chapter a similar examination is made of the strange, magical powers inherent in music, drumming, and dancing.

Chapter 8
THE POWER OF RELIGIOUS MUSIC, DRUMMING, AND DANCING

THE POWER of music can be analyzed into two broad categories: pitch elements and time elements. The pitch elements include the timbre (sometimes called the *colour)* of the music, its melody, and its harmony. Melody is a succession of notes of different pitch and duration. Harmony is the combination of those notes, played simultaneously with other notes in a way that sounds pleasing to the listener. The time elements consist of rhythm, metre, and tempo: the way that sounds are repeated again and again in a recognizable pattern of beats, the way that those patterns can be identified by the number of beats that constitute a sequence, and the speed at which they are sounded.

The brilliant musician Daniel Barenboim gave the BBC Reith Lectures in 2006 during the course of which he said, "music has a power beyond mere words ... I would like to explore the power that music has over us." That mysterious power of music that Barenboim recognized so perceptively is an essential ingredient of Santeria, Obeah, and the other syncretistic religions.

Pythagoreans like Archytas (428–347 BC) discovered important insights into the power of music. He said that mathematics itself could be analyzed into four major sectors: arithmetic, astronomy, geometry, and music. Boethius (AD 480–524) wrote that the first three focused on rationality, but music involved human behaviour. He went on to quote Plato's famous comment: "The soul of the world is knit together by the harmony of music." There was a sense in which he saw music as "the fulcrum between the material world and the meta-reality of number." The Pythagoreans also observed that vibrating strings produced musical tones that were in harmony with one another provided that the ratios of the lengths of the strings were simple, whole numbers.

Pythagoras of Samos (560–480 BC) travelled extensively in Egypt and Babylonia, where his brilliantly fertile mind acquired and processed vast amounts of ancient wisdom. Long before it was generally understood and accepted, Pythagoreans believed that the Earth was moving. They also theorized about the music of the spheres, which they believed the planets generated.

In the Pythagorean schools in Crotona and Delphi, where music was studied in great depth, it was reported that certain sequences of notes and harmonious combinations of tones induced particular human responses. Pythagoreans understood that music could change human behaviour and reinforce the body's natural healing processes.

An essential part of this mysterious power that music possesses is its ability to stimulate human emotions. Once emotions have been aroused, they affect the way that a person perceives the world and the way that he or she responds to stimuli in the environment as seen through those coloured screens of the various emotions. Emotions dramatically affect behaviour. A soldier with fixed bayonet charging through battery smoke to kill the enemy gunners will charge faster and strike harder when inspired by loud, stirring, military music. A shopper on a limited budget will spend more than intended while the shop plays cheerful, encouraging background music. A fretful infant distressed by teething problems will settle down to sleep in mother's arms when she sings him a gentle lullaby. Santerian worshippers will lose themselves more deeply in their ceremonies as they dance and sing among the Orishas and saints they believe in.

There is an enormous range of human responses to music: clearly, different people will respond to the same music in different ways, but even the *same* person may respond differently on different occasions and in different circumstances. The First Book of Samuel, chapter 16, verse 23, relates how when King Saul was in a dark and dangerous mood "David would take his harp and play. Then relief would come to Saul; he would feel better, and the evil spirit would leave him."

Another way to analyze music as it reinforces Santeria, Obeah, and similar religions is to consider its role as a medium of communication as well as an influence over emotions. Not only does music stimulate, pac-

David with his harp.

ify, or quiet emotions: it can also carry messages. It says things that can be interpreted and understood. Some of these musical statements are as clear and simple as speech or writing, while others are deeper, more complex codes. They seem to bypass cognitive mind and thought and go directly to what poets and musicians would describe as the listener's heart and soul. Those who have experienced this musical fullness can only say that it cannot be thought about rationally; it has to be *felt*. It has a genuinely mystical quality.

There are times when it is the timbre, the melody, the harmony, or the rhythm acting alone that can carry the messages and stir the emotions; but there is also a *holistic* quality in the power of music. The whole really can be greater than the sum of the parts. There is also, perhaps, a sense in which the greatest power within music is its ability to lift the listener to *anticipate* something higher and greater.

This relates again to the idea of the subconscious, conscious, and superconscious minds being like a house with a superbly furnished upper floor and a lived-in ground floor as well as a cellar containing a powerful generator. The sublimity of music seems to suggest that the human mind can choose not only between "ordinariness" and "something lower" — no matter how potent the contents of the cellar may be — but between normal consciousness and an altogether higher and infinitely more powerful state of awareness and being.

To what extent does modern neurobiological research reveal *how* music affects the mind? There is evidence, for example, that areas in the right hemisphere of the brain can respond to melody more readily than they respond to language. It also appears that when a particular musical tone or sound pattern is associated with something significant to the listener — such as food, sex, or danger — the brain's response to that stimulus increases in line with the importance of the associated goal.

Other research findings have suggested that learning how to play an instrument has long–lasting beneficial effects on the brain. Cases have been recorded where Alzheimer's patients have retained their ability to play, long after other skills have been lost. There is also significant evidence that learning to play an instrument enhances brain function throughout life.

The indications are that the playing and singing that occur during Obeah and Santeria ceremonies are beneficial to the participants and have positive effects on brain function as well as influencing emotion and conveying messages.

The importance of rhythmic drumming during Santerian ceremonies, and those of similar religions, is extremely significant. Expert drum therapy practitioners maintain with some justification based on their case studies that drumming rhythms can promote self-expression and healing. The technique has been understood and used for millennia, especially in Africa. The ancient Egyptians were also experts in dancing to drum rhythms. According to expert percussion therapists, rhythmic drumming — especially when shared by groups of like-minded people — seems to accelerate healing and boost the immune system.

Academic studies have suggested that drum therapy can help disturbed children and teenagers, as well as Alzheimer's victims. Drumming has also been shown to be beneficial in reducing stress, hypertension, anxiety, and tiredness. It appears that participation in group drumming as practised in Santeria, Obeah, Voodoo, and similar syncretistic religions helps participants to relax. Blood pressure is lowered and this helps to prevent heart attacks and strokes. Other research has shown that percussion group therapy seems to help control pain and assists the body to produce endorphins. Defined scientifically, endorphins are endogenous opioid biochemical compounds that are manufactured in the pituitary gland and the hypothalamus. They con-

Egyptian dancing.

trol pain and produce feelings of happiness and well-being. In addition to these benefits it has been shown that being part of a drumming circle can stimulate and encourage the body's natural immune system. Dr. Barry Bittman of the Mind-Body Wellness Centre of the Meadville Medical Centre in Meadville, Pennsylvania, co-author of *Maze of Life* (TouchStar Productions, 2003), has said, "Group drumming tunes our biology, orchestrates our immunity, and enables healing to begin."

Other research has demonstrated that when rhythmic energy such as drum beating reaches the brain — via touch, vibration, or sound waves — the left and right hemispheres begin to work more closely together. Neuropsychology indicates that the left side of the brain is largely responsible for rational, cognitive thinking, while the right hemisphere is associated with emotion, instinctive behaviour, and intuition. In theory, then, when their ability to communicate and co-operate is enhanced by drumming, the brain's overall performance is vastly improved. It has also been theorized that rhythmic drumming enhances the communication between those basic areas of the brain that deal with non-verbal functions and the "higher" zones that process data and solve problems. This drum-facilitated communication could also be a source of insight and inspiration.

These neuropsychological ideas related to rhythmic drumming are germane to the analysis of what happens to the worshippers during Santerian and similar religious services. The repetitive drum rhythms enable their hearers to reach a higher state of consciousness in which the different areas of the brain are harmonized. Colourful religious imagery of saints and Orishas, and the worshippers' feelings of enhanced spiritual, mental, and physical power, can be better understood when considered in the light of the neuropsychology of drumming. However, when the music and rhythmic drumming are accompanied by dancing, their effects are reinforced still further.

Specialist dance historians have suggested that the simplest and most basic forms of dancing are probably as old as human beings. These earliest forms may have been stylized movements associated with the sympathetic magic paintings on ancient African cave walls, depicting hunters and their prey. These early dances may also have included simple mating rituals and courtship displays.

Drawings estimated to be at least nine thousand years old have been studied in the Bhimbetka rock shelters. These are approximately fifty kilometres south of Bhopal, close to the Vindhyachal Hills in Madhya Pradesh in India. Their geographical coordinates are 22° 55' N and 77° 35' E. They are named after Bhima, one of the sons of King Pandu and his two queens, Madri and Kunti. Even in these early times, the Indus Valley Civilization had a fully developed dance culture.

As time passed, dancing became inseparable from human culture and especially from rites of passage. In the sixth century BC, the Mahavamsa document records how King Vijaya reached Sri Lanka, listened to music, and watched the dancers at a wedding. Although much younger than the evidence from Bhimbetka, Sri Lankan dances are still among the earliest ever recorded. Known as Kandyan dances, they are accompanied by special cymbals referred to as *thalampataa* and recognized by characteristic rhythms called *tala*.

Homer also describes dancing in the *Odyssey*, and the many theories about where Odysseus really went on his long voyage home to Ithaca include the theory that he might even have ventured up into the Indian Ocean. Whether they found dancing in very distant lands like the Indus Valley and Sri Lanka, or whether it came to them from ancient African cultures south of the Mediterranean, the early Greeks were the ones who systematized it in their own characteristic way. For them, dancing became a method of expressing the full range of human thoughts and feelings.

In Greek theology, Mnemosyne and Zeus had nine daughters, who became the Muses, each of whom inspired a different form of art. Terpsichore was the muse of dancing and choral music. Aristotle was enthusiastic about both dancing and poetry, and could clearly see their rhythmic similarities. He noted the skill with which the best Greek dancers combined rhythm and gesture to express emotion. The Greek sculptors also knew this, and used the dancers as models for their best statues.

The ancient dance forms and styles from Africa are what choreographers would term *polycentric*. For exponents of genuine African dancing, the body is not regarded as an inflexible unit: it has numerous centres of movement. The feet, hands, legs, arms, shoulders, thorax, and pelvis — even the head — can move independently. It is as if the body were a formation team of independent dancers working in harmony — but not in unison. A talented and perceptive dancer also seems able to envisage a spheroid parameter inside which the different elements of the body are moving. It's as if the body became a miniature solar system inside which planets and satellites moved in different ways.

Like the ancient Greeks, gifted African dancers are able to express feelings — but with Santerian dancers there seems to be a two-way traffic of messages and emotions that use the dance movements as a medium.

Dancing within the labyrinth pattern.

Gifted dancers at an Obeah ceremony seem able to transmit and receive during the performance. The unanswered questions remain: Are they really communicating with saints/Orishas, who are objective, external, psychic entities? Are the powerful sensations of giving and receiving paranormal messages an expression of the dancers' communications with their own inner selves, their subconscious or superconscious minds? In the altered state of consciousness induced by rhythmic drumming, piquant melodies, and exquisite dance movements, are the dancers actually communicating with one another telepathically? Could it be that the priest or priestess conducting the ceremony is able to communicate mentally with the entire congregation simultaneously during the music, drumming, and dancing?

In addition to the harmonized dance movements of the various parts of an individual's body, there is also a collective unity in the dancers as a group. Biologists think in terms of muscle tissue, bone tissue, lung tissue, and the other specific tissues that make up an organ such as the heart or liver. They also talk of a group of organs such as the mouth, gullet, stomach, and other parts of the alimentary canal as systems in which several different organs co-operate to perform a specific biological function. Is there a parallel here with what goes on at an intellectual and spiritual level during Santerian group dances? Are the different sets and gestalts created by the dancers the psychic equivalent of organ systems in a biological organism?

In examining Santerian melody, harmony, drumming, and dancing, the same problems are posed that confronted the researchers in Chapter Seven. All three elements play an important role in Santerian religious experience, but is what takes place at the ceremony the opening of a portal through which internal powers are liberated? Or do the altered and enhanced mental states of the worshippers produce the remarkable psychic phenomena?

Once the trance takes effect, the magic of the music and the powerful rhythmic drumming and dancing all impinge upon the worshippers. Inexplicably strange things apparently happen during the ceremonies. The real origins of those uncanny Santerian phenomena are at the centre of the mystery that surrounds all of the bewildering syncretistic religions.

These strange Santerian ceremonies and sacrifices involving traditional Christian saints and ageless African Orishas are mixtures of hypnotic liturgies and rituals, which seem to reinforce and expand the minds of the worshippers, largely because of the neuropsychological effects of the music, drumming, and dancing.

Analyzing the probable *causes* of Santerian power, however, does not reveal the *extent* of the power. Knowing that a simple dynamo generates electrical energy does not reveal that the electricity so produced can save cardiac patients whose hearts have stopped, operate computers, generate surgical laser beams, produce images and sounds on television screens, and cook food or freeze it. Chapter Nine looks in depth at what can apparently be done with this enigmatic Santerian power during some strange ceremonies and sacrifices.

Chapter 9
STRANGE CEREMONIES
AND SACRIFICES

SO FAR, we have examined the underlying principles of Santeria and similar religions, together with the hypnotic elements of their liturgies and rituals. We have also looked at some of the effects of their music, drumming, and dancing. It is now possible to scrutinize their ceremonies and sacrifices per se and to look at the results that are claimed for them.

Historians and logicians are aware of the old *post hoc ergo propter hoc* fallacy that was always part of medieval university courses in logic. The Latin translates to "after this, therefore because of this." Common sense observations and everyday experience make it plain that an earlier event is not necessarily the cause of a later one simply because the two phenomena occurred one after the other.

The shaman or medicine man who puts on a cloak of blue and green feathers and then dances energetically in the centre of the village is unlikely to have *caused* the rain that falls as his dance ends. He may simply be a natural meteorologist who can discern the signs of approaching rain earlier than most of his peers. Then he dons his cloak and starts his dance conveniently just before the first drops fall.

It is not totally beyond the bounds of reason to suggest that there might be some strange, magical connection between his coloured cloak, the elaborate steps that he dances, and the precipitation that follows. It is highly improbable — but not impossible. The more we learn of science and of some of the least expected links between cause and effect, the more miraculous and mysterious our enigmatic universe becomes. Because there are no certainties, we have to calculate mathematical probabilities in a way that would have delighted the Pythagoreans.

Nevertheless, our *post hoc ergo propter hoc* fallacy is an essential guide and companion, an intellectual safety officer for those who study

Human sacrifice in ancient times.

what happens at Santerian ceremonies.

Because health and healing are of primary importance to everyone, it is natural to find that they are central to Santerian worship. The interaction between mind and body is indisputable. As in the Latin motto *mens sana in corpore sano*, physical and mental health are mutually reinforcing. Schwartz and Russek (1999) performed some very interesting research in this field, which produced strong evidence that there are transmissions of energy between people who are communicating with one another — in the way that psychic healers communicate with their patients.

Eric Kandel's earlier neural research work was referred to in an article in the *Scientific American* in 1979, reported by Lawrence (2001). Kandel concluded that when two people are in conversation with each other, "the neuronal machinery in one person's brain is capable of having a direct and long-lasting effect on the modifiable synaptic connections in the brain of the other." If Kandel's general findings in this area are focused specifically on healing techniques, it is possible to understand how healing can take place at Santerian meetings where many minds, raised to powerful emotional levels, can produce a definite benign and therapeutic effect on patients seeking healing.

This is reflected clearly in special Santerian healing ceremonies and at other more general types of Santerian services in which spiritual healing is not the primary focus — but nevertheless plays a significant supporting role.

Flowers, plants, and healing herbs are integral parts of Santerian healing. Peppermint (*menthae piperitae*), for example, is sometimes found among the worshippers, and may also be placed on the altar for the priest or priestess to use during the ceremony. The active ingredients of peppermint are generally reckoned to be the volatile vegetable oils, such as menthol.

The healing properties of volatile oils such as those found in peppermint are employed extensively in Santerian and similar religions' therapeutic ceremonies. This general use during Santerian healing is in accord with the alternative medical practice known in Canada, Europe, and the U.S.A. as aromatherapy. The term *essential oil* in this area of alternative medicine is simply a way of saying that the oil is an essence of the herb that gives it its name. It does not indicate that the oil is essential to good health, although many essential oils used in aromatherapy are beneficial and therapeutic. Essential oils have played their part in traditional folk medicines in Africa, Asia, Europe, the Middle East, and the New World for many centuries. Hippocrates, the ancient Greek medical expert who gave his name to the famous Hippocratic Oath, used a form of aromatherapy. The Ayurvedic medical techniques that have helped patients in India for more than three millennia also make use of aromatherapy.

Towards the close of the nineteenth century, three leading French medical researchers — Meunier, Chamberland, and Cadeac — worked on the properties of essential oils to destroy bacteria, and a few years later Rene Gattefosse made an important discovery by accident. Having burned his hand while working in the laboratory, Gattefosse instinctively reached for the nearest liquid he could find to cool his hand and ease the pain. It happened to be oil of lavender. To his surprise and delight, the burn healed quickly and with very little scarring. He then carried out valuable research on the medicinal uses of other essential oils. Jean Valnet, a French surgeon working through the traumatic years of the Second World War, took up Gattefosse's ideas and found that the antiseptic powers of essential oils were of great benefit to his patients. He also found that the aromas that came from the oils had a positive effect on his patients psychologically.

Modern pharmaceutical involvement with essential oils recognizes their time-honoured antiseptic qualities. The Good Samaritan in the New Testament parable, for example, applied oil and wine to the wounded man's injuries. It has also been suggested that just as music and rhythm can assist the mind to reach its optimum therapeutic function, so the aromas of certain fragrant oils can be equally beneficial — as Jean Valnet discovered. During some Santerian therapeutic ceremonies, therefore, the fragrance of the herbs and flowers associated with the benign Orishas who induce healing is very much in evidence.

The dog rose (*rosa canina*) produces rosehips that are rich in vitamin C and also contain significant amounts of vitamins A, D, and E. Rosehips also provide a worthwhile supply of antioxidant flavonoids. Rhodomel, an alcoholic beverage made from rosehips and honey, may sometimes be one of the drinks shared at Santerian healing ceremonies. Both its main ingredients are generally recognized as having healing properties. There is evidence that patients with rheumatoid arthritis may benefit considerably from taking rosehip preparations in various forms. Herbal healers prescribe rosehip medicines for patients with such widely differing problems as urinary tract infections, dizziness, and headaches.

It is particularly significant that rosehips were widely used therapeutically by the indigenous Americans, and when the enslaved African peoples came into contact with them it seems very likely that this indigenous American healing wisdom would have been incorporated into Santerian healing.

Safflower can also be seen among worshippers at Santerian healing ceremonies. Its use goes back to the most ancient African medicinal knowledge. Ancient Egyptian cloth has been found to contain dyes based on safflower, and wreaths of safflower were found in the tomb of Tutankhamen. There are also references to it in the ancient Linear B script.

Safflower provides excellent vegetable oil, which is extracted from the seeds. One type, oleic acid, is rich in monounsaturated fatty acid; another variety, linoleic acid, is an excellent source of polyunsaturated fatty acid. In 2007, it was reported that experiments with genetically engineered safflower enabled the researchers to produce insulin. These safflower oils have the same beneficial properties as olive oil. Ancient African herbal healing wisdom again seems to be justified by twenty-first-century Santerian healing practices.

Another plant that may be found during Santerian healing ceremonies is vervain. The contemporary English name came originally from two old Celtic words: *fer*, meaning to drive away, and *faen*, meaning stone. In olden times, the herb was used medicinally for patients with bladder stones. It was also thought of in olden times as a powerful aphrodisiac, when it was referred to as *herba veneris*. Some ancient Roman priests learned their secrets in Egypt and Africa and were familiar with vervain. To them it became *herba sacra*. Druids used it as an ingredient in their mysterious lustral water. This was usually kept in an aspersorium in which worshippers would dip their fingers, or from which the priest would draw water to sprinkle them. The oral spraying of the powerful alcoholic fluid at Santerian ceremonies is reminiscent of the use of lustral water in Egypt and Etruria and was also part of Druidic practices. Sorcerers and magicians of various types frequently used vervain in their spells and potions. Vervain was also worn as a protection against evil and as a good luck charm.

From the point of view of a syncretistic religion such as Santeria, vervain was particularly relevant because in Christian legend it was found growing on the hill of Calvary and was used to staunch the wounds of Christ. Those who know this legend bless the plant and make the sign of the cross over it as they pick it. It is used medicinally to make poultices for wounds and to cure ulcers. Before the discovery of antibiotics, vervain was regarded as a better-than-nothing treatment and partial cure of syphilis.

Verbena Jamaicensis, a variety usually referred to as Jamaican vervain, is also found in Barbados and other Caribbean islands. Carefully diluted concoctions made from it are regarded as particularly good for the eyes.

Once a Santerian ceremony was in full swing, a number of potent healing techniques came together. The rhythmical music, drumming, and dancing, augmented by hypnosis and herbal remedies, were all working together to assist the patient. His or her own mind would then respond to the components of the ceremony that were uniting and harmonizing its neural mechanisms. This enabled the patient's subconscious, conscious,

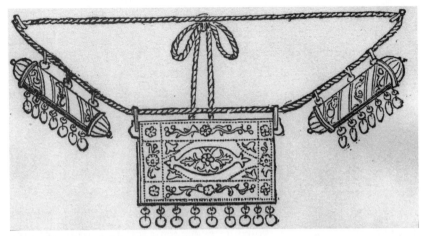

An amulet that could contain vervain.

and superconscious minds to work together to strengthen his or her immune system. What power the *group* mind of a room full of Santerian worshippers might have to aid the patient is still largely conjectural — but it could well make a significant contribution.

There is also the possibility that Orishas with healing powers *do* really exist as independent and very powerful psychic entities. Their presence at a Santerian healing ceremony would make a tremendous input into the healing process. There is one in particular, Osain, who is regarded as an Orishan doctor. He is also associated with Saint John and Saint Ambrose. In Santerian thought, Osain has all the medicinal plants and herbs under his aegis.

Colour is another extremely important factor in Santerian healing ceremonies. Colour therapists argue that colour can have a profound effect on human beings physically, spiritually, mentally, and emotionally. Colour affects and informs us in our everyday lives: red, green, and amber traffic lights; the ripeness or otherwise of fruits and vegetables; blues and greens that make us feel calm and relaxed; oranges and reds that are stimulating.

Scientifically, colour can be thought of as light operating at different frequencies and different wavelengths, and light itself is one of many forms of energy such as heat, sound, movement, and electricity. The universe contains a great many electromagnetic energy waves — light is only a small fraction of the total — and the different colours can be thought of as subdivisions of light. One of the strangest mysteries involving light and colour as human beings perceive them is that there are only three colours within our range. Scientists refer to these three as the *primary additives.* They are red, blue, and green. Mixtures of them create every other colour of which we can be aware. The rainbow reveals all the colours of the spectrum, from red to violet, and red has a high wavelength allied with a low frequency. Violet, at the other end, has a lower wavelength but a higher frequency than red. Because of these real, scientific differences that separate the colours, it might be reasonable to argue — as colour therapists suggest — that particular colours, or combinations of colours, can have therapeutic effects on different patients suffering from dissimilar ailments.

Red can create feelings of courage and leadership. It is the colour that inspires pioneers. Red strengthens the will and enhances the patient's confidence; it is associated with energy, determination, and spontaneity. Colour therapists would use red to help patients who are feeling tired or exhausted. The Orisha Oya — associated with various Christian saints, including Catherine, Teresa, and Barbara — is linked with the colour red. She is a fierce warrior who fights against injustice on behalf of her people. They wear red beads and red clothing in her honour.

Orange, which comes next to red in the spectrum, is regarded by colour therapists as very beneficial to the lungs and the whole breathing process. It is used to help patients with asthma. Colour therapists also recommend it for improving circulation and benefiting metabolism in general. Psychologically, it is regarded as the colour of joy and happiness, so colour therapists use it psychologically to combat depression. In Santerian thought, the colour orange is associated with the benign and generous Orisha named Oshun, their goddess of beauty, sensuality, love, and art.

In colour therapy, yellow is regarded as symbolizing the sun: it is the brightest of the colours that colour therapists use. They believe that it can benefit patients with glandular or lymphatic problems, and it is also thought to strengthen the nervous system. In Santeria, Orunmila, the Orisha of fortune-telling, prophecy, and divination, favours the colours yellow and green. This is interesting because they are adjacent on the spectrum.

Green, for a colour therapist, is the colour of healing and overcoming the passing years. Green is thought to be able to take a patient back to a time when he or she was younger, healthier, stronger, and more energetic. Green is regarded by colour therapists as particularly relevant to healing broken bones or other tissues that have been injured or damaged by illness.

In Santeria, black and green are associated with the Orisha named Oggun, who corresponds to Saint Peter in the syncretism of Orishas and saints. He is the Orisha of work and energy. Green is also sacred to Oshosi, known alternatively as Saint Norbert. Oshosi is regarded as a hunter god who lives in wild and lonely places.

Oggun, the Orisha of work and energy.

In colour therapy, blue represents serenity, peace, tranquility, and harmony. It is useful against fever because it is a cooling colour. It helps to reconstruct the patient mentally, physically, and spiritually. It is also thought of as a protective colour, guarding a patient against infection. In Santeria, blue and white are strongly associated with Yemayá, the prolific mother goddess of the sea. (The variant spellings of the Orishas' names means that Yemayá can also be written in many forms, including Yemoja, Yemonja, Yemana, and Imanja.)

Colour therapists maintain that indigo is one of the most dynamic and important of all the healing colours: they believe that its beneficial effects work on the mind and spirit as well as on the physical body. It improves the lymph system and glandular functions in general and reinforces the immune system. It is also thought to have valuable detoxifying properties and is believed to purify the blood and improve muscle tone. Colour therapists also believe that it can be used as an anesthetic, and that patients in an indigo environment can lose sensitivity to pain without losing consciousness. In Orishan tradition, Yemayá is the one who dyes cloth indigo.

Violet, easily confused with purple, is the last of the colours on the spectrum, and has a shorter wavelength than blue. Purple, technically, is not a colour of the spectrum but rather a mixture of red and blue light. In colour therapy, it is believed that purple is helpful for patients suffering with nerve disorders. Purple is also thought to help reduce pain, to benefit patients with rheumatism, and to help those who are suffering from epilepsy. In Santeria and the associated syncretistic religions, Nana is thought of as the mother of the Orishas. Purple is one of the colours linked with her worship.

During a Santerian healing ceremony, the worshippers wear the colours associated with their Orishas, and appropriately tinted cloths and ribbons will be swirled during the rhythmic dancing and the chanting of healing prayers.

In addition to healing ceremonies, Voodoo, Candomblé, Santeria, Lucumi, and the other mysterious, syncretistic religions are frequently concerned with prophecy, divination, and foretelling the future. These religions generally have an understood hierarchical structure for their religious leaders. A general term of respect for the priest in charge of an *ile* (or temple) is *Babalorisha*, meaning "father of the Orishas." The priestess in charge would be known equally respectfully as *Iyalorisha*, meaning "mother of the Orishas." The very special rank of *ifa* is awarded to those religious leaders who are believed to be in contact with Orunmila, the Orisha of prophecy and future knowledge. The title *Babalawo*, meaning "the father who has the secrets," is used as a term of respect for such an ifa priest.

Before investigating Santerian divination ceremonies in depth, it is essential to consider the underlying philosophical and theological principles behind *any* form of apparent prophecy. Belief in human freedom of choice, and the power of genuine decision-making, means that at any moment, any person can make a decision that will affect his or her future — and the future of others.

A kind-hearted, moral, and ethical person wins a huge sum of dollars on a lottery. That good person then *decides* to build orphanages and retirement homes, which in turn vastly improve the quality of life of their residents. Another person *decides* to try drugs and in time becomes an addict — so desperate now for the next fix that murder and robbery are used to pay for it. The addict's life and the lives of his victims are ruined. Human beings are free to make good or bad decisions. Every person has an infinite number of choices to make all the time, and those choices steer the future.

Divination makes sense only when there is a belief system that includes fate and predestation. Of course, as with many of the other great questions of metaphysics, philosophy, and theology, the argument between predestination and free will cannot be definitively resolved. A believer in human freedom will be quite certain that he or she has freely decided to buy a dog, go to the cinema, or take a holiday in Canada. The predestinationists will argue that God, fate, or destiny put it into the subject's head to take the particular course that he or she chose. For predestinationists, the apparent free choice is only an illusion. People merely deceive themselves into thinking that they made the decision.

Most Santerians would broadly accept that they have a preordained path to follow, and so it is important for them to find out how well they are following these paths — and to try to ascertain what is coming next along that path!

One of the most interesting and elaborate Santerian ways of doing this is by a technique known as *merindilogun* — a form of divination that uses sixteen cowry shells. This is a very ancient technique, and, in one form or another, may well have been used for millennia. In its modern Santerian form, it is governed by the Orisha Orunla, the keeper of memories, whose name can also be spelled Orunmila. Within Orunla's vast reservoir of knowledge, the destiny of every human life — past, present, and future — is stored. The Babalawo, acting for and with Orunla, can reveal an individual's path of destiny when certain Santerian ceremonies are correctly performed. Another Orisha involved in the sixteen-cowry–shell divination method is Eleggua, the messenger, the communicator, whose services facilitate the work of the other Orishas, the Babalawo, and the worshipper who has come to discover more about his or her destiny.

Some worshippers come seeking guidance because they feel that there is something missing in their lives: they think that perhaps they are not following their preordained paths as closely as they should. Other enquirers are concerned about money, health, and family relationships. In certain cases, worshippers claim to have received answers to questions that they did not ask but that were hidden below the surface questions that were asked. This is part of the deep understanding and trust that has to exist between the Santerian priest and the enquirer.

The process of using the cowry shells is also known as the *registro*, and has a great deal in common with the ancient and revered Chinese I-Ching system. Is it possible that ancient African cowry shell techniques were known and used in China? In which direction did the secrets move?

One I-Ching technique, for example, uses sixteen marbles or beads. These must all be of the same size and shape, but four different colours are used. It is not difficult to connect this sixteen-bead method with the Santerian registro; the colours on the Chinese marbles could link with the special colours allocated to the Orishas.

The Santerian obi divination system is also similar, but uses a coconut broken into four pieces instead of sixteen cowry shells.

The *Ukuele* is a method of divination reserved for those who have attained Babalawo ranks. A necklace of eight specially prepared coins, or eight pieces of carved and polished coconut shell, is dropped, and the divination is based on the patterns made by the eight concave-convex discs. The discs can produce 256 possible combinations. The Babalawo interprets these patterns in terms of folk tales, fables, and proverbs from the remote past. The way that the Orisha heroes overcame their problems in these stories guides the enquirers as to how they should deal with their own contemporary difficulties.

The most serious and solemn of the Santerian divinations is known as the table of *ifa*. It is a tray on which there are various writings and carvings, on which *yefa* powder is sprinkled. The original African yefa powder was apparently obtained from the residue left by termites chewing wood; it was duly sanctified and purified before being used for divination. Other varieties are obtained by drying and powdering roots.

Santerian spells and charms are in constant high demand. Many of these aim at attracting love, money, success, and fame. Those categories can be subdivided in various ways, but like the great majority of human beings, Santerian worshippers seek happiness, stable personal relationships, prosperity, admiration, respect, safety, and security.

All of these understandably desirable goals, towards which the "magical" element of the mysterious syncretistic religions is frequently directed, have *happiness* as a common denominator. Worshippers who request Santerian help to achieve strong, loyal, loving, and enjoyable human relationships seek such relationships because they bring great *happiness*. Seekers of wealth and prosperity want to use them to buy the luxuries and comforts that they think will increase their *happiness*. Social respect, admiration, and fame are also sought after as a path to *happiness*. The universe, of which our earth is a microscopically tiny part, is an extremely hazardous place. The security and safety that human beings crave are only additional routes to *happiness*. Therefore, pure and simple, it can be argued that *happiness* is the real objective of all types of enchantment.

How does Santeria set out to provide the happiness that its worshippers are looking for? Santeria demands high moral and ethical standards regarding a worshipper's attitude and behaviour towards other worshippers — and towards other people in general, whether they are Santerians or not. Because of this, Santeria is already well on the way to operating the basic formula for achieving happiness for its members. Psychologically, happiness and love both possess a real but paradoxical quality. When people seek genuinely and altruistically to give love and happiness to others, the love and happiness given rebound upon the giver in greater magnitude.

At the heart of Santerian faith is the basic ethical teaching that the one supreme, creating, sustaining God — and his powerful servants, the benign Orishas — want human beings to love one another and to do their best to promote one another's happiness. By teaching people to love one another in this way, Santeria is really teaching them to be happy themselves. This central truth is so close to the teachings of Jesus that it becomes easier to understand how Santeria, Obeah, and Candomblé developed as syncretistic faiths. The ancient Yoruba beliefs simply welded themselves to Christianity when African slaves confronted traditional European Catholicism from the sixteenth to nineteenth centuries.

Lucumi happiness spells work effectively during their ceremonies because those present really enjoy one another's company and genuinely want to make their brothers and sisters happy — both during shared worship and in the workaday world outside their temple.

One of the simple finance-as-a-path-to-happiness spells goes like this: Take gold, silver, or a note — say a $5 bill — and wrap it inside a clean, new, linen handkerchief, along with one, three, or seven small magnets. Put a few drops of holy oil — cedar wood oil is recommended — on the handkerchief. The package is then held up to a carving of Oshun — the Orisha of beauty, love, sex, sensuality, and *money* — that has been placed on the temple altar. The words of the spell are: "Oshun, good and powerful Orisha, grant your servant the blessing of wealth. By your power and kindness, let money come to me swiftly in my time of need."

This ceremony may be repeated to Saint Expedite, the Orisha who makes things happen quickly. Expedite, however, is not as uniformly benign and forgiving as Oshun. His image on the altar takes the form of a young and handsome Roman centurion. When Expedite answers a worshipper's request by providing money, the Santerian tradition says that it is essential to buy flowers for him and place them with a prayer of gratitude beside his image on the altar. He also likes publicity, and Santerians who have prayed to him and had those prayers answered place a notice in the local paper acknowledging Saint Expedite's power and thanking him for his help. Traditionally, those who forget to thank him are warned that there will be a death in the family if no praise and gratitude are forthcoming.

There are probably several thousand Santerian spells aimed at attracting not only wealth and money but good luck and prosperity in general. One expert recommends putting coins and candles in every corner of your house, and then doing the same at street corners and at crossroads. The reasoning behind this particular spell is that it will please Elegua, who will then put his power at the disposal of the spell worker. Another Santerian idea intended to attract good fortune is to make necklaces of jet and coral stones, wear them constantly, and wash them periodically in holy water and coconut water. An alligator's tooth is also believed to bring good luck if worn around the neck. Strangely, however, it should never be worn in a river, lake, or ocean, as this will weaken its powers.

A magical African model of a crocodile or alligator.

Co-author Lionel wearing a tooth talisman.

Just as the alligator's tooth magic is thought to be weakened by water, so some other good luck and prosperity charms are totally dependent on the spell maker's being immersed in water. One variation of this bath spell requires seven roses: a red, a white, and five yellows. The other ingredients are a red apple, a pint of milk — goat's milk if available — and seven fresh, crisp lettuce leaves. Other ingredients include honey, mint, lavender, cinnamon, almond oil, and patchouli oil. The ingredients are blended into a smooth paste, which is poured into a warm bath. The spell-worker lights a red candle and relaxes in the bath until it cools. The spell has to be repeated on seven consecutive days in order to be fully effective.

A far simpler good luck and prosperity ritual can be performed by using crushed laurel leaves in the bath — and that spell does not need seven repetitions.

For spell workers who are tired of the bathing spells and want something simpler and drier, there is a sleeping spell involving geranium leaves, lavender, and laurel, as well as pine needles and patchouli oil. The spell worker removes the stuffing from his or her pillow and replaces it with a mixture of the listed ingredients. Sleeping on this pillow every night is thought to bring good luck.

Another Santerian spell that is focused on bringing prosperity to the user involves the skin and leaves of oranges, generous quantities of natural sugar, and an all-important iron pot. The orange leaves and skin have to be dried so that they will burn easily. They are placed in the iron cauldron with the sugar — which can burn surprisingly well — and the compound is then ignited. After a few moments, put out the flames and leave the mixture smoking. While it smokes offer a prayer to Oshun requesting wealth.

Another wealth-attracting spell requires the use of a bowl of many colours — this is intended to please all of the Orishas, whatever colour each may prefer. The spell worker must also wear a multicoloured cloak for the same reason. Nine coins and a quantity of red ochre are also need-ed. Dust has to be brought from consecrated ground, such as a sanctified cemetery or churchyard, or from the blessed gardens in which a church or dedicated holy building stands. Pure fresh rainwater is needed, as well as a quantity of alum. The number nine is significant in performing this spell. The nine coins are placed in the multicoloured bowl and covered with alum crystals. Nine drops of oil are added, and nine pinches of red ochre are used — one pinch on each coin. The holy ground dust is added next and the rainwater goes in last to cover all the other ingredients completely. The enchanter then removes his or her multicoloured cloak and uses it to cover the bowl. During the temple ceremony, the whole is then laid rever-ently before the statuette of Oya on the altar. When the prayer is answered with money, the spell worker is required to buy a sacrifice for Oya.

Another significant aspect of Santerian worship is communication with the dead. Ancient African religious traditions seek to explain the role of ancestors and the importance of being able to communicate with them. This integrates well with traditional Christian ideas, and has biblical support in the account of Jesus speaking with Moses and Elijah on the Mount of Transfiguration (Matthew Ch. 17). The traditional Christian view of life after death also gains biblical support when Jesus speaks to the dying thief who is being crucified beside him: "And he said unto him, Verily I say unto thee, To-day shalt thou be with me in Paradise." The wise and perspicacious Canon Harry Scott Holland, who was at St. Paul's Cathedral in London a century ago, summed it up by saying, "There is absolutely unbroken continuity." Life goes on, so it should be possible to communicate with those who have gone before. Santerians not only believe in the possibility of communication — they practise it.

This communication takes two forms: requests for help, advice, prosperity, and protection, much as requests of these types are made to the Orishas — and normal, friendly, conversational communication of much the same kind that took place while the ancestors were still on earth.

In much the same way seances were conducted during the heyday of spiritualism in the nineteenth and early twentieth centuries in Europe, Canada, and the U.S.A., Santerian mediums, or channellers, believe that they are making themselves available to spirits of departed human beings or other paranormal entities. Having achieved the altered consciousness known as the trance state, the Santerian channeller may speak with several different voices that are unlike his or her familiar, normal voice. The channeller's facial expressions often change as well when the "other entities" are speaking. These phenomena are witnessed often enough — but what is really happening?

There are numerous theories concerning these manifestations. The apparent change of identity could be due to activity in the channeller's own subconscious: subordinate personalities are expressing themselves because the psychological security mechanisms that normally keep them in check cannot function effectively during the channeller's trance state.

Fundamentalist and traditionalist Christians tend to favour the view that when something speaks through a channeller, it is an evil spirit that has taken control. Accordingly, those who hold this theory deplore any form of channelling.

A third theory supports the view normally held by spiritualists that the channeller really is in contact with the immortal souls of human beings who once trod the earth. There is, therefore, nothing wrong with the practice at all, and if it brings comfort and consolation to the bereaved, it is positive and benign.

A fourth theory suggests that channellers are picking up messages from extraterrestrial intelligences, and during some research many years ago, the authors were present at a seance during which the channeller purported to give messages from such a being that called itself Sivas.

Other theories include the idea that the messages are coming from paranormal entities inhabiting other probability tracks, other dimensions, or other times. Subscribers to the hypothesis that *all* life is both intelligent and sentient — including the simplest plants and animals — have suggested that channellers may be passing on messages from flora or fauna.

Santerian ceremonies may also include bird and animal sacrifices that are intended as gifts, or thank-offerings, to the Orishas. It is part of a religious tradition that goes back for millennia, and it has to be acknowledged that these sacrificial offerings are killed swiftly and humanely, and then eaten.

All the Santerian ceremonies are led by priests and priestesses who exercise great power and influence over the worshipping community. In the next two chapters, their roles will be examined and analyzed.

Chapter 10

THE POWERS OF THE PRIEST

WHAT IS power? Although it's an everyday concept, it is not an easy one to describe or define. At its simplest and most basic, power can be defined as the ability to achieve what the power wielder desires. What power achieves for the person possessing it provides a scale of units against which relative degrees of power can be measured. From that starting point, it is possible to analyze and categorize the various forms and types of power.

First, there is emotional power: the strength of will and the degree of determination that an entity possesses. The famous historical example of King Bruce and the spider provides a clear case of determination changing the course of history. The depressed and defeated king watched a spider trying repeatedly to attach a strand of gossamer to the damp wall of the cave in which Bruce himself was hiding from his triumphant enemies. Again and again the spider failed — but it steadfastly refused to give in. Finally, it succeeded. Taking the spider's determination as his example, Bruce tried again — and won a kingdom. A more recent case from August 2007 tells how the Meng brothers, Chinese miners, dug their way through sixty feet of coal and rock to escape from a collapsed shaft. Pure willpower and determination drove them on and made the difference between death and survival.

Just as muscular strength and stamina can be improved by training in the gym, or by years of hard physical work, such as the Meng brothers had experienced as coal miners, so emotional strength and stamina, willpower and determination, can be improved by training the mind. Part of the mysterious power possessed by Santerian priests is the mental ability *to go on going on* against every setback and every disappointment. Their emotional reservoirs brim over with a mental power that disowns defeat. Their ancestors survived slavery and finally regained freedom. For them, failure was not an option. If the priest's ritual does not work the first time, he repeats it. If the charm, spell, incantation, or mysterious Santerian healing process does not function immediately, the healer-priest goes on trying.

In addition to emotional power, the priest possesses considerable cognitive power. In the ancient, pre-literate days of the complex Yoruba religions, there was so much to remember and to absorb as aspects of the oral tradition. Just as Druids among the ancient Celtic peoples committed vast amounts of knowledge to memory, so did the ancient African practitioners of what was eventually to grow into Santeria and the other mysterious syncretized religions. Their priests and leaders had to think sequentially, to work things out logically, to rationalize beliefs and the ways in which their beliefs fitted into the observed fabric of the world around them.

These emotive and cognitive powers of the priests' minds are distinct from another form of mental power that can best be described as religious charisma, a type of power that is shared by many Santerian leaders. Charisma is another quality, like power itself, that is extremely difficult to define and describe. We recognize it when we meet it, but it is far from easy to say what it is and how it works. It is an intoxicating mixture of attractiveness, style, transparent qualities of leadership, and an ability to inspire trust. The charismatic personality radiates confidence and convinces those who encounter it that the

Ancient priests in action.

confidence is not misplaced. It is possible that the charismatic power of a Santerian priest is an exciting and stimulating form of mental energy, powerful vibes, or neurological radiation. Serious scientific researchers into brain function might find that whatever force radiates from a charismatic mind, it could be *measurable* given the right instruments and location.

In Santeria, Voodoo, Macumba, and the other syncretized religions, absolute and infinite power belongs exclusively to Olurun, the name by which the One Supreme God of the universe is recognized. The name of Olurun may vary from language to language and from one syncretized religion to another, but by whatever name Olurun is known, Olurun represents infinite and absolute power.

Another way to calibrate power is to ask what an entity *cannot* do. There is nothing that Olurun cannot do.

Below Olurun in the relative power scales come a great many Orishas. Each of them can exercise power to a greater or lesser extent, but they are normally restricted to their own particular areas: sex and fertility, harvest, hunting, warfare, divination, prosperity, and love.

Priests and priestesses come below the Orishas.

Next in line after the lowest of the priest and priestess ranks are the spirits of dead ancestors. Their powers are far smaller than the powers of the Orishas — and they are to a great extent dependent upon the priests and priestesses who can summon or dismiss them — yet these ancestral spirits still exceed the powers of normal Santerian worshippers, ordinary men and women: mortal, terrestrial human beings.

Priests and priestesses in the Santerian religion are known as *santeros* (male) and *santera* (female). They may also be styled *omo-Orisha* — a Yoruba name meaning "children of an Orisha." There is a widely recognized hierarchy of priests and priestesses containing eleven or twelve grades. High priests of senior status are known as *Babalawos*. They carry out the sacrifices that take place during initiation ceremonies and they are called in to resolve arguments among ordinary worshippers or priests and priestesses of lower ranks.

Where does the Santerian priest's power come from? To believers in Santeria, the priest is able to call upon one or more of the Orishas to help a worshipper — or another priest — with a particular problem that falls within that Orisha's domain. The priest is also seen as having the power to offer prayers and sacrifices on a worshipper's behalf in order to persuade the relevant Orisha to help the worshipper overcome a problem or difficulty.

Santerian priestly power also stems from their expert knowledge of spells, charms, and talismans — and their access to them. Santeria and most of the other syncretistic religions are largely ethical, moral, and benign — but there is also a dark side to them, just as the Holy Inquisition's torture chambers and burnings at the stake were the dark side of Christianity. A tiny minority of practitioners desert the high moral principles of genuine Santeria and the other ethical, syncretistic religions and use their powers to do horrendous harm. One such example was the notorious Adolfo Constanzo (1962–1989), who was a leader of Palo Mayombe in Mexico, where he was known as "The Godfather of Matamoros."

Palo Mayombe, another of the syncretistic religions, is a mixture of ancient African beliefs from the Congo and from the Yoruba peoples welded to elements of Catholicism. The name comes from the Spanish term *palo*, meaning a piece of wood, a branch, a pole, or a stake. Practitioners, known as *paleros* or *mayomberos*, use wooden rods or wands to perform their enchantments.

Adolfo was born in Miami, where his fifteen-year-old Cuban immigrant mother, Delia Aurora Gonzalez del Valle, was already widowed. Delia soon married again and the new family moved away. While living in San Juan, Puerto Rico, young Adolfo was baptized as a Roman Catholic and grew up to serve as an altar boy. Delia, however, was a dedicated follower of Palo Mayombe — and this exerted a powerful influence over her young son.

The family went back to Miami in 1972, where Adolfo's stepfather died, leaving Delia well provided for. She married for a third time, but her new husband was involved in drug dealing and strange pseudo-occult practices. Adolfo and his Delia were drawn into petty crime — mainly theft and shoplifting — and were arrested more than once.

Shortly before the assassination attempt on President Ronald Reagan in 1981, Adolfo claimed that he had psychic abilities and had predicted the attack. Round about this period, Adolfo met a Haitian priest, a leader of Palo Mayombe, in which his mother was immersed. As far as can be ascertained, it was this priest who encouraged Adolfo to become a drug dealer, a confidence trickster, and worse. The priest's motto seems to have been "Follow evil and profit from it." It appears, from such evidence as is available, that the Palo Mayombe Orisha known as Kadiempembe, or Lukankasi, was thought of in some Palo cults as being the equivalent of the devil, Satan, or Lucifer, and it was to Kadiempembe that Adolfo was dedicated and committed.

It seems to have been Adolfo's visit to Mexico City in 1983, followed by his moving there full time in 1984, that turned him from being a criminal into something little short of a monster. He became a combination of cult-supremo, drug dealer, and priest-in-charge of expensive occult ceremonies. He and his cult members abducted victims for use as human sacrifices. They also systematically murdered rival drug dealers. It was part of their belief system that the sacrifice had to die with a maximum of pain in order to optimize the effectiveness of their magic. It is impossible to be certain about the number of victims who suffered at their hands, but there were at least dozens.

A young American tourist, Mark Kilroy, a student at the University of Texas, vanished while on holiday in Matamoros, and the Texan authorities from over the border used their very considerable weight and influence to ensure that the search for him was given top priority. The Mexican police swooped on the cult, discovered that they were responsible for Mark's murder, and closed in on Adolfo's hiding place on May 6, 1989. Rather than face arrest, Adolfo ordered one of his followers to shoot him, and he was dead when the police broke in. So deeply engrained were the cult's beliefs that one of them told the police, "Adolfo will not be dead long!"

Sara Maria Aldrete, his most powerful lieutenant in the movement, was later arrested and sentenced to serve more than sixty years in prison.

Power, then, as displayed by the priest of Santeria or any similar syncretized mystery religion, may be something *innate*. Certain genetic predispositions are likely to make a human being powerful. The environment and the belief systems within it can also help to create a powerful person. During the course of our lives, we learn from experience what the nature of personal power is and how to acquire it and exercise it. The power of the Santerian priest comes from these two sources: his genetic potential and the environmental, cultural belief system in which he has been raised.

The powers of the mysterious Orishas — if they really exist — must also be considered fairly and impartially. The Santerian priest who believes absolutely that the paranormal powers of the Orishas are inspiring, sustaining, and empowering him to heal and to perform magic and miracles may simply be enabling his own mind-power to do very remarkable things. If, however, the Orishas are *real* (whatever the elusive nature of *reality* may eventually turn out to be) then the Santerian priest's strange and mysterious powers may actually come from them.

This theory tends to be borne out by the African word *hourogun*, which stands for the elemental force — the Loa or Orisha — that believers think is the mysterious power that animates a hurricane. Given those beliefs as a premise, it is perfectly logical for the Santerian or Voodoo priests to attempt to redirect the hurricane by appealing to its controlling entity, an Orisha or a Loa.

How far have these traditions concerning Orishas, Loas, and their powers over nature travelled in the remote past?

There are traditions in Africa that credit Mechi, described as the African emperor of Mexico in 3100 BC, with establishing a kingdom there that incorporated the ancient African religious beliefs concerning Loas and Orishas. It is part of this same tradition that shamans from Africa were in Mexico nearly three thousand years ago, and that they carried the worship of Shango with them. If there is any historical basis to this tradition — and there may well be — it would indicate that the worship of the Orishas or Loas, and appeals to them to protect their people from hurricanes, was known in Mexico millennia before the Yoruba slaves arrived and established Santeria as a syncretism of Catholicism and Yoruban beliefs in the Loas and Orishas. Supporters of this tradition argue that the west coasts of Africa are relatively hurricane-free today because of the priests' successful appeals to the relevant Loas and Orishas.

The Santerian priest's power may then be thought to extend into the realms of weather control. Meteorologists will naturally find themselves at variance with this theory, but will, nevertheless, be among the first to accept that even when using the finest instruments and the most modern satellite weather technology, forecasts are never as accurate as might be wished, and the weather habitually springs one capricious surprise after another.

The theory that Loas or Orishas are able to take over the priest and work through him, or that dead ancestors of the worshippers can work through him, and be the source of his power finds a strange parallel in the life and work of the mysterious Francisco Candido Xavier (1910–2002). Popularly known as Chico Xavier, he was loved and admired by millions in Brazil as a great philanthropist, a remarkably perceptive and sensitive psychic medium, and the author of more than four hundred books — all written by psychography, the enigmatic process by which a gifted medium's hands do the actual writing that appears to come from external, psychic sources. Just as Santerian and Voodoo priests are possessed, or "ridden," by their Loas and Orishas, so Chico Xavier firmly believed that his spirit guide, Emmanuel, had once been the Roman Senator Publius Lentulus, was later reincarnated as Father Damian, and later still as a professor at a French university.

Chico always insisted that none of the many abilities he displayed throughout his long life were his: he regarded himself as a mere channel for the wisdom and creativity of the spirits whose writings came through him. The works that he created by psychography included some exceptionally good poetry and very advanced texts that seemed a long way beyond Chico's own educational level. He seems to present a definite example of spirit possession — and if departed writers and poets or other psychic forces could work through Chico, is it not equally possible that Orishas and Loas could work through their priests?

Another possible source of abnormal psychic energy is the theory of *group* mind power. When a number of people together have shared views and aspirations, can their combined mental power achieve things that a single individual — however intelligent and forceful — cannot do alone? Science fiction has often dealt imaginatively with the concept of a group mind, or *hive mind*, but is there more to the group mind hypothesis than ingenious fiction?

If mind, as dualists posit, is independent of the physical brain, is there some strange mechanism that brings individual minds together into a unity that is much greater than the sum of its parts? If gravity can bring tiny specks of cosmic dust together into a unity that becomes a blazing star, or a planet capable of sustaining life in its multitudinous forms, what can individual human minds achieve when they coalesce into group minds? Does the power of the Santerian priest consist partly of an ability to act as the cohesive force bonding the minds of the worshippers together into an entity that is able to achieve miracles of magic and healing?

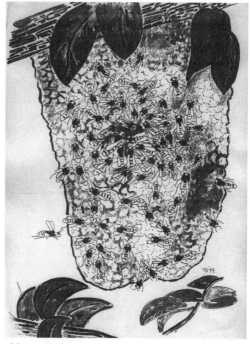

Hive mind.

In considering the power of the Santerian priest in connection with group mind theory, it may be suggested that classical European Wicca recognized the importance of the coven — often, but not invariably, thirteen in number. (European Wicca is the name given to the old nature religions and pagan religions that flourished in Europe prior to the arrival of Christianity and Islam. It still has followers today.) Working within such a group, as components of the group, individual members were apparently able to perform their magic more effectively than if they had been working alone. Yet it may be asked if there was rather more to it than that. Did the coven itself have some sort of pluralistic entity, some kind of communal self-awareness, greater than, and different from, the self-awareness, aims, and ambitions of any one individual member?

Various interesting theories concerning telepathy may, perhaps, shed light on the group mind phenomenon. Scientific neurologist Andrija Puharich conducted fascinating experiments in extrasensory perception in his laboratory in Maine in the U.S.A. He investigated telepathic reception and transmission and researched the effects of hallucinogenic mushrooms on both processes. He also looked into telepathic networks and the ability of some individuals to serve as unconscious relays during this process. His epoch-making conclusions are recorded in depth in *Beyond Telepathy* (1974). Puharich's findings may suggest an additional explanation for part of the power exercised by Santerian priests. If some part of Santerian achievement is due to the function of group mind phenomenon, then the power of the priest in certain cases may be due to his ability to function as what Puharich refers to as a *telepathic relay*. If the worshippers' thoughts are channelled through the presiding Santerian priest in something akin to Puharich's telepathic relay theory, then this could well be one of the sources of the priest's power.

It is not possible entirely to ignore the remoter possibility that Santerian magical instrumentation has some role in providing the priest with power. Taking the parallel with ancient European witchcraft once again, instrumentation was a prominently visible part of the earliest Wicca ceremonial. The cauldrons with their strange (and often unsavoury) ingredients, broomsticks, charms, and talismans might have been power sources — however unlikely that seems to modern, empirical, scientific thought in the twenty-first century.

This idea can be linked with the theory that emotional energy is capable of etching images into the fabric of buildings that are later reported to be haunted. The basic hypothesis is that powerful emotional energy will leave records of itself following bereavement, a murder, a battle, or some other major stimulus. The ghostly Roman legionaries processing through the cellar of the Treasurer's House in York provide a well-known example. The images of English Civil War soldiers re-enacting the grim seventeenth-century battle at Edgehill provide another. If the instruments used by medieval witches in Europe were impregnated with psychic, emotional energy in this way, perhaps that energy could radiate out of the instrument — cauldron or broomstick — to reinforce the spells and incantations the Wiccans were employing.

Is it not equally possible that the Santerian priest, using his wand, his precious stones, and his multicoloured robes, could draw forth from them some of the psychic energy recorded and stored inside them? The analogy of a rechargeable battery in a laptop computer or mobile phone helps to illustrate this instrumentation theory.

When Mesmer and the other pioneers of what is now generally called hypnosis or suggestion referred to *animal magnetism,* they might well have been talking about something qualitatively different. Mesmer used the word *animal* because of its Latin root that meant "breath." He believed that it was some sort of force or power that resided in all living bodies, human and animal alike. He also wanted to distinguish the strange force that he believed he had discovered from what were in his day being talked about as mineral magnetism, cosmic magnetism, and planetary magnetism.

Helena Blavatsky, writing in *Studies in Occultism* (Sphere Books, 1974, but originally published in her own magazine, *Lucifer,* in 1887), was convinced that Phrygian Dactyls had used this mysterious power of animal magnetism millennia ago. These Dactyls were an archaic race associated with Cybele, the Great Mother. They had great skill as metalworkers and may even have been in Tolkien's mind as the originals of those who forged the Rings of Power in *Lord of the Rings.* The three metalworking Dactyls of Mount Ida in Phrygia were Celmis the casting expert, Acmon the anvil, and Damnameneus the hammer. Another tradition had the Dactyls in the form of a human hand (in any case, *dactyl* means *finger*). Herakles (perhaps the first mention of the heroic Greek demigod?) was regarded as the thumb. The index finger was Aeonius, and his brothers, in order, were Epimedes, Jasius, and Idas.

From this, it may be inferred that what Mesmer thought of millennia later as animal magnetism was transferable by using the healer's hand to convey therapeutic power to the patients. What if Mesmer and his immediate disciples were right? What if — however remote the possibility — hypnotism and suggestion does not work *only* by empowering the patient's subconscious and superconscious minds, but by invoking this mysterious power of animal magnetism and enabling it to flow from the mesmerist to the patient? Here then is yet another possible source of priestly power in the mysterious syncretistic religions like Santeria and Voodoo.

Can the priest use what is conventionally understood in our twenty-first century as hypnotism and suggestion — undeniably powerful and effective things — and link them with what Mesmer believed he had discovered? The enigmatic Helena Blavatsky was a brilliantly intelligent mystic as well as an eccentric and controversial character. Her thoughts about the Phrygian Dactyls and their strange healing powers may have contained more than a grain or two of enigmatic truth. There is certainly a sense in which the Dactyls, shrouded as they are in myth and legend, have affinities with Loas and Orishas. Do the Santerian priests draw part of their power on some occasions from what Mesmer would have acknowledged to be animal magnetism? Was that same strange power known and used in Phrygia in ancient times?

The more deeply research penetrates into the powers of the priests of Santeria and the other syncretistic mystery religions, the more links appear to connect them with ancient Egyptian magic and with European Wicca. The mystery of the Voodoo Damballah provides an example of such a link. Where Santeria refers to the intermediate deities — those between human beings and the One Supreme God — as Orishas, followers of Voodoo call them *Loas*. (The name can also be spelled Lwa and L'wha.)

The Loas are very individualistic, perhaps even more so than the Santerian Orishas, and Damballah is regarded as the most important of the Voodoo Loas. He is at the core of much Voodoo magic, where he is seen as the serpent-god who devours his own tail. This symbolizes the concept of the "self turned inwards upon itself."

A wheel — like the traditional Wheel of Hecate — is used to represent Damballah, and Hecate herself provides another source of mystery and uncertainty. Best known today as a goddess of sorcery, Hecate was originally a deity of the wilderness and childbirth. In the famous old *Chaldean Oracles* that were edited in Alexandria, she was associated with a very strange, convoluted, spiral maze thought of as the labyrinth of knowledge. Hecate was credited with the power to lead humanity through this bewildering web of knowledge to the fire of life itself.

Rider Haggard's *She* (1886) is the story of an exceptionally beautiful and powerful woman who is apparently immortal, having bathed in the magical fire of life. Haggard had an extensive and detailed knowledge of Africa, including many of its mysterious ancient traditions, and it seems highly likely that his amazing protagonist, Ayesha (*She-who-must-be-obeyed*) was based on Hecate and the fire of life.

Hecate's circular knowledge-labyrinth is similar in many ways to the mysterious ring of Damballah. His symbol is complicated by its twelve spokes and three concentric circles. Each of the two inner rings takes the form of an *ouroboros*-type snake with its tail in its mouth. All of the spokes except one end with a serpent's head looking outwards, like sentinels guarding some important fortress, where the secret knowledge is preserved. Right at the top of this complex circle design is a magic square containing representations of the moon in its various phases.

This circular Damballah symbol with its protruding spokes is also connected with the spiked wheel associated with St. Catherine's martyrdom, a factor that provides another possible nexus between the Loa-Orisha sub-deities and several of the traditional Christian saints.

In some of the ancient African traditions, Damballah, as the primeval snake or serpent, is also reckoned to have a creative function, and the parallel with the serpent in Eden, the traditional site of creation, is difficult to avoid. In some other ancient traditions concerning Adam, his first wife was Lilith. She became a night-haunting screech owl demoness — the bitter enemy of young children sleeping on the flat roofs of houses in the Middle East. This transformation happened because the physical aspects of marriage so shocked and repelled her that she flew away from Adam in horror when

Serpent.

he attempted to consummate their union. Happily, he and his second wife, Eve, were far more compatible! Like Adam in this variant tradition of the Eden story, Damballah also married twice — although, unlike Adam, both his partners (the rainbow serpent Ayida Weddo and Erzulie Freda) continue to stay happily with him.

In the Voodoo tradition, it is usually the power of Damballah, chief of the Loas, that enters the priest in charge of the ceremony and empowers him. A further important aspect of this Voodoo perspective on the syncretistic mystery religions is that very specific gifts are offered to the individual Loas who are thought to be in possession of the priest conducting the ceremony and of other worshippers. The term used for this possession is "riding."

The offering of the correct and specific gifts, while the riding is taking place, is thought to increase the unification of the Loa and the worshipper, and, in the process, to augment and amplify the power available during the ceremony. Erzulie Freda, for example, is given beautiful fabrics, a comb, a hairbrush, jewels, and a mirror. Legba is presented with his traditional pipe, walking cane, and straw hat. Another very famous Loa, Baron Samedi, who was portrayed by Geoffrey Holder in the James Bond film *Live and Let Die*, is invariably given a cigar, sunglasses, and a top hat.

Objective, unbiased observation of genuine Santerian ceremonies — or the valid ceremonies of any other syncretistic mystery religion of the Santerian type — leads to the conclusion that something unusual, powerful, and very interesting is taking place, and that the priest is central to whatever it is that is going on. He clearly appears to possess demonstrable power, and he seems to be using that power effectively. What is it, and where does it come from? The analysis is far from simple.

It may be necessary to view the problem from the angle of those who feel the need for a powerful leader's help. In times of crisis, those who feel in need of help and healing may exert a psycho-social vacuum that has to be filled by someone, somehow. When things are bad enough the longed-for hero appears: Moses leads his people out of slavery; Joshua leads them effectually in battle after battle; David kills Goliath; Horatius holds the bridge over the Tiber and saves Rome; Arthur and his chivalrous knights defend their people; Robin Hood and his merry men help the poor and oppressed. Just as air pressure, or hydraulic pressure, can produce physical results, so socio-psychological pressure can produce results. Is it the case that when enough people are crying out for a leader, their cries can somehow bring one forth? Is there a case to be made for the theory that a Santerian priest's power is the result of his people's awareness of a power vacuum? Economists would argue that demand can create supply, and, conversely, supply can create demand.

Is it remotely possible that part of the priest's power is derived from hypnotism, suggestion, or animal magnetism? He may have a highly charismatic personality: the combined product of nature and nurture. He could have unusually effective telepathic talents. It is possible that he is the focal point of a power that is projected by the group mind of the worshippers who are sharing the ceremony with him. There may be abnormal psychic powers stored in the instrumentation that he uses.

There could well be a subtle combination of two or more — or even *all* — of these factors. It is not impossible for the Orishas, or Loas, whom the Santerian or Voodoo priest believes in, to enjoy some sort of *real* existence. If they, or other strange psychic forces and energies do exist, then some of the priests' powers may emanate from them.

Chapter 11

THE POWERS OF THE PRIESTESS

ALTHOUGH the general theories of priestly power in Santeria and the other syncretistic mystery religions apply to priestesses as well as to priests, there are certain specific aspects of power that apply exclusively to one gender or the other.

Since time immemorial, a mother goddess associated with fertility has personified the earth itself and its harvests of land and sea.

Variations of the nature and role of fertility goddesses occur in many of the oldest myths and legends of creation. There is an ancient Sumerian version, for example, in which Eve, best known from the Genesis account, turns up under the name of Ti, which means both "rib" and "mother of life" in ancient Sumerian. The Genesis version tells of Eve's encounter with the serpent, her eating of the forbidden fruit, the punishment of all concerned, and their expulsion from the Garden of Eden. In this old Sumerian account, which predates the Genesis version, Enki is the partner of Ninhursaga, the mother goddess, and they live on an island called Dilmun in her vast paradise garden. Like Eden, the garden is free of death, violence, illness, and the aging process. It contains seven vitally important sacred fertility plants that Ninhursaga tends with loving care. Unfortunately, during her absence one day, Enki eats them: something of a parallel with Adam eating the forbidden fruit, but not an exact one. As Enki is male, and unable to give birth to the offspring of the sacred, fertile plants, the angry goddess leaves him to die. News of the problem reaches the senior gods in conclave, and they order Ninhursaga to save Enki's life by producing the seven goddesses from various parts of his body. During this process Ti (alias Eve), "the mother of all," comes from one of Enki's ribs.

Adam and Eve.

Another mysterious, serpentine example can be found in the accounts of Shakti, the Indian goddess. She may be regarded as the life force behind all of creation. Even the other gods depend upon her. In some versions of the Shakti myth, she resides in every human body, but especially in women. She is envisaged as being serpent-like and occupying a position at the base of the spine. When religious contemplation and meditation waken this sleeping serpent, Shakti moves up the spine, reaches the top of the head, and enlightens the meditator, who is then freed from the endless circles of life and death.

There seem to be strange connections linking the serpent form of Shakti, Eve's conversation with the serpent in Eden, and Damballah's serpent form and connections with creation. A combination of these factors may suggest that Eve's willingness to talk to the serpent — and her possession of the necessary abnormal linguistic ability to do so — makes her something rather more than Adam's companion and assistant. Analyzing the Eden narrative from an alternative perspective could identify Eve as a person with the courage and intellect to prefer reason and knowledge to unthinking obedience and unchallenged acceptance.

Looking at her as possessing these strengths and virtues may also suggest that a Santerian priestess possesses similar distinctive qualities.

James Frazer, Robert Graves, and Marija Gimbutas have all supported the theory that a goddess, whom Graves describes in depth in *The White Goddess* (1948), was one of the earliest and most influential deities in Europe from earliest times. She was regarded as being in charge of birth, death, and love, and was closely associated with the phases of the moon.

It may be argued and conjectured, however, that ideas about this maternal female deity did not necessarily arise in Europe, nor were they

by any means confined there. Frazer, Graves, and Gimbutas all suggested that the concept originated in the matriarchal societies of neolithic times, millennia ago, and had pre-Indo-European roots.

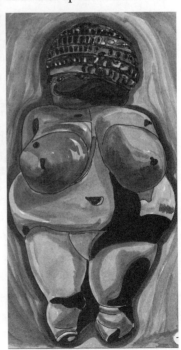

Above: Birth.

Right: Ancient Venus figure.

The famous Venus of Willendorf and many similar figurines may be intended to represent this most ancient of mother goddesses. What is less easy to establish is a chain linking them through generations of similar mother goddesses — and ultimately to the roles of the Santerian and Voodoo priestesses today.

Important early links in the chain are clearly visible in Sumerian mythology in the person of Ishtar, alias Inanna in Sumeria and Ninsun in Mesopotamia. The goddess appears again in Greece as Aphrodite and as the Canaanite Ashera. To the earliest Syrians, she was their beloved and revered Ashtart or Ashtarte.

In prehistoric Ireland, she was worshipped by her Celtic followers as the mother goddess Danu. To the Norse peoples, it seems that she became Freya. Another interesting northern speculation is that the character in the Beowulf saga referred to as Grendel's mother could have been a badly distorted, negative picture of an ancient mother goddess or prehistoric fertility goddess. The question immediately arises as to why the Beowulf legend makes her an evil, negative being. The traditional mother goddesses are benign, especially in their encouragement of physical love and fertility. Is Grendel's mother a distorted projection of fierce, instinctive, maternal protection? This is the she-bear protecting — or avenging — her cub, and is there not just a trace of something laudable in it, although in the case of Grendel and his mother both she-bear and cub are anathema to human beings?

Aegean and Anatolian peoples worshipped Cybele and Gaia, best known today through Lovelock's controversial Gaia Hypothesis, suggesting the unification of everything in the biosphere. If such an entity really exists, and possesses self-awareness, it might well have taken on the role of a mother goddess in ancient times.

The classical Greek pantheon included its fair share of earth mother goddesses, notably Demeter. Venus-Aphrodite, the radiantly beautiful love goddess of Greco-Roman theology, eventually became a mother goddess as well. She was credited with being the mother of Aeneas, who is regarded as the founding father of Rome (despite the wilder tradition of Romulus, Remus, and the she-wolf). By the start of the Christian era, and the savage Roman persecutions, Venus was referred to as *genetrix*, meaning "mother."

Ancient Siberians had a mother goddess, venerated by them as Umai, and there is an interesting linguistic connection here with an ancient Indian tradition that refers to Shiva's consort, Parvati, as Uma. Can they be one and the same maternal deity, and, if they are, in which direction did that nomenclature travel? Relevant again here is the Hindu belief in their mother goddess Durga. Her cult is an exceptionally old one, going back at least to the Vedic period — and possibly long before that. She is also credited under other names with being the earth mother who gave birth to the gods themselves. There is another sense in which Hindu theologians understand all their female deities to be different faces, or different aspects, of this one great primeval mother goddess.

There are groups of Christians who regard the Virgin Mary as a type of *spiritual* mother. In this sense, she is seen as a protector of human beings and a particularly caring and sympathetic member of the heavenly court who intercedes for them.

Mother and child.

Another female deity in some Christian thinking is Hagia Sophia — the personification of holy wisdom.

The mysterious and controversial Black Madonna statues have been interpreted by some researchers as evidence that syncretism is not a recent phenomenon. Are the origins of the Black Madonna to be found in a strange mixture of Christianity and ancient Egyptian religion, so that while the traditional Madonna statue represents the infant Jesus in the arms of the Virgin

Mary, the Black Madonna is the Egyptian goddess Isis cradling the infant Horus?

Whatever strange powers may, or may not, have been present in the ancient earth mother goddesses and their priestesses, there was certainly a great deal of inexplicable power in the priestess known as Marie Laveau, who worked in New Orleans in the turbulent nineteenth century. There are no definitive historical records of her parents or earlier antecedents, but she is thought to have been born in 1794 in a place called Vieux Carré, the daughter of Charles Laveau, a prosperous white planter, and one of his consorts, a beautiful mulatto girl named Darcantel Marguerite. Darcantel was also believed to have had some indigenous American ancestry. When Marie grew up, she was described by those who knew her as outstandingly beautiful like her mother, with masses of naturally curling black hair and very powerful, dark, flashing eyes.

She arrived in New Orleans as a youngster and was raised in the city. She was brought up in the Catholic faith at the Cathedral of St. Louis, where Father Antoine, the chaplain, was kind and supportive to her.

It was Father Antoine who conducted the wedding service for Marie when, at the age of twenty-five, she married Jacques Paris. Both were enthusiastic Catholics and worshipped regularly in the cathedral.

By all accounts, it was a happy marriage until tragedy struck a few years later: Jacques vanished mysteriously and was presumed dead. This allowed Marie, then known as Widow Paris, to marry her second husband, Christophe Glapion.

One of Marie's fifteen children, a daughter who was also named Marie, bore such a remarkable resemblance to her mother that once Marie junior was an adult, it was almost impossible to tell them apart. Both women were Voodoo priestesses. This uncanny resemblance between mother and daughter may have been responsible for several of the stories circulating in New Orleans during her heyday that she had miraculously recovered her youthful looks and had the power to appear in two places at once.

Marie Laveau came to fame when she was approached by the wealthy father of the accused immediately prior to the trial of a young suspect. Things were looking ominous for the boy before Marie's intervention. His father offered Marie anything if she could save his son, and she asked for his luxurious house in the best neighbourhood of New Orleans as her fee if she succeeded. She then concealed a number of mysterious Voodoo talismans and other magical objects in the building where the trial was being held. The verdict came in as not guilty, and true to his word, the boy's father gave Marie the house as promised. (After such a demonstration of her powers, he was unlikely to have tried to cheat her.)

Marie helped to nurse the wounded after the famous battle of New Orleans, and her high status and benevolent work were later acknowledged when she was a distinguished guest at the state funeral of General Jean Humbert.

Marie was an extraordinarily complex character, combining genuine care and compassion with her mixed Voodoo and Catholic beliefs. In addition to her work with the wounded after the Battle of New Orleans, she became a regular prison visitor and did her best for the prisoners awaiting execution on death row. She made gumbo (a traditional African stew with seafood ingredients that was a very popular dish in New Orleans) and brought it with her when she visited the convicts. It was alleged that she included Voodoo herbs and other secret ingredients that acted like modern antidepressants and reduced the mental anguish of those who were waiting to be executed. There were even stories that on some occasions she would deliberately overdose the gumbo so that the condemned man died "naturally" in his sleep before the executioner came for him. This attitude of hers sheds interesting light on the ideas inherent in Santeria and Voodoo concerning the ethics of euthanasia. If the accounts of the lethal drugs in the gumbo that Marie gave to the condemned on some occasions are correct, it suggests that the Voodoo ethic in her day was that death is preferable to suffering. This would be particularly the case in view of the Voodoo belief in an afterlife that was vastly preferable to life on earth. Supposing that this was known and understood by those who worshipped regularly with Marie, then part of her priestess powers may have been the solemn recognition that as far as the death row convicts were concerned, she was their priestess of life and death.

Although Marie used various Voodoo drugs, herbal preparations, talismans, dolls, and charms, much of her power seems to have come from her secret spy network. She herself was also a skilled hairdresser, and many of the rich and famous employed her in their own homes in that capacity. It seems that visiting hairdressers in nineteenth-century New Orleans were practically invisible, and their rich and powerful clients would discuss important, confidential matters in front of them as if they simply weren't there. Marie made mental notes of all that she heard and used the information later to great advantage. She persuaded many other slaves and servants to contribute to her ever-growing network of confidential information.

Her success in obtaining a verdict of not guilty for the son of her wealthy client may have resulted more from her secret knowledge than from whatever Voodoo talismans she secreted in the courthouse. With the intimate, confidential information that her network had gleaned for her, Marie might well have been in a position to hint to various jurors that if they decided to acquit the accused, certain things in their private lives would not be made public.

In addition to the information that her domestic spy network brought in from the homes of the rich and powerful, Marie owned the Maison Blanche brothel on the shore of Lake Pontchartrain. Just as the Nazis used the Salon Kitty Brothel in Berlin to obtain information from high-ranking clients, so confidential information obtained by the girls working in Maison Blanche reached Marie Laveau.

It was a remarkable combination of this secret information reservoir, her fervent and genuine belief in Voodoo magic, and her remarkable knowledge of potent herbs and drugs that made Marie such a powerful and influential person.

One of the most important Voodoo ceremonies in New Orleans during Marie's ascendancy was the Sunday dancing in Congo Square. She would arrive early before the main ceremony was

Marie Laveau's pet snake, Zombi.

scheduled to begin and would entertain the onlookers by dancing with her huge pet snake, Zombi, coiled around her. Here again the link with serpents and serpent symbolism is a prominent one.

Once a year on St. John's Eve, June 23, she would preside over the all-night Voodoo ceremony on the banks of the St. John Bayou. Like the Sunday services, the proceedings began with Marie dancing with Zombi coiled around her, and the evening became wilder and wilder as alcohol and Voodoo fervour took hold of the worshippers. Drumming and singing accompanied the nude dancing, while sacrifices were offered to the various Loas. The more enthusiastic participants were soon overcome and became ecstatic and entranced, believing that they were possessed by their Loas. They would then utter prophecies, give psychic advice, answer questions about the best courses of future action, and perform healings. Unsurprisingly, it was part of Marie Laveau's financial acumen to charge admission to the spectacular St. John's Eve festival.

Perhaps the most surprising thing about her, and one that emphasizes the power of syncretism in Santeria and Voodoo, was her continued devotion to Catholicism. She included numerous aspects of Catholicism in her own Voodoo services. There were many statues of the saints on display, and bells and candles were much in evidence at her ceremonies. Crosses, holy water, and incense were also used. The priests at the St. Louis Cathedral were favourably disposed towards Marie because she encouraged her followers to attend Mass there.

There was almost a Robin Hood element in her character, however, because although she charged the wealthy high prices for her services, she was very generous to the poor, the hungry, the sick, and the homeless.

Her grave in New Orleans is still visited regularly — the faithful believe that her powers as a Voodoo priestess have continued after death — and offerings are left there along with requests for her help. The routine is to make three chalk crosses on the side of her tomb and to knock three times on the stone when asking for her magical assistance. It is also believed that her spirit rises on June 23 each year and once more takes charge of a vast Voodoo ceremony.

In order to understand the relative powers and the paradoxical similarities and differences of the priests and priestesses of Santeria,

Voodoo, and other syncretistic mystery religions, it is helpful to analyze the ancient Chinese concept of yin and yang.

Most dictionaries define them as a generalization of the antithesis or mutual correlation between certain objects, and that is fine as far as it goes. The French anthropologist Claude Lévi-Strauss described a similar principle. He maintained that we understand life in terms of binary opposites and binary similarities. We understand size by looking at the opposites *large* and *small*. We understand temperature by considering *hot* and *cold*. In the realm of similarities, we understand *wealthy* in terms of *rich* and we understand *affection* in terms of *friendship*. Another way of looking at yin and yang is to suggest that they combine to form a unity of opposites. The similar Chinese idea of Liang Yi encapsulates the concept of heaven and earth — not so very distant from Socrates' ideas about the realm of eternal ideals and true realities contrasted with the world of imperfect forms that we perceive here on earth.

Yin and *yang* describe two primal forces that oppose each other and yet are complementary, and this paradoxical idea of being united in opposition has influenced Chinese religion, medicine, and philosophy for millennia. How much of it percolated through into other ancient civilizations is a matter of conjecture, but it can certainly be applied relevantly and effectively to the respective roles of the priest and priestess in Santeria, Voodoo, and the other mysterious syncretistic religions.

The yin element, as expressed in its original Far Eastern form, can be translated as somewhere that is shaded, overcast, and cloudy. It is pictured as a sheltered nook, or the south bank of a great Chinese river. It originally symbolized all that is feminine:

River goddess from Africa.

darkness, the night, passivity, and something that is striving like grav- ity to move downwards. In a system that recognizes the four-element theory, yin is air and water.

Yang, by contrast, is a bright, sunlit place. It is the north bank of the river. It is dynamically active and energetic, tending to rise like a Chinese kite. It seeks to move upwards and represents the light of day, as opposed to the darkness of night. It is masculine, and in the four-element theory it is earth and fire.

Another important aspect of the yin and yang concepts is that the op- posites are by no means absolutes: they move relative to each other. Chinese philosophers would say that everything in nature has interchangeable yin and yang states. There is an element of femininity in the most masculine males; and there is an element of masculinity in the most feminine females. Yin and yang do not epitomize stasis: there is constant movement between them. There is a very real sense in which yin and yang contain the seeds of each other — so neither can exist without the other.

Simon Baron-Cohen, director of the autism research unit at the University of Cambridge in England, has undertaken very interesting and important research into the differences between male and female brains. In essence, he has concluded that female brains are designed to be empathetic, while male brains are designed to understand the environment and to design and build systems relevant to it. His fascinating hypothesis is referred to as the E-S, or empathizing-systematizing, theory. It is interesting to observe that a psycho-neuronal theory at the cutting edge of twenty-first-century science is uncannily similar to Chinese thought from millennia ago. Both empathizing and systematizing are essential for human survival in the ultra-complex societies of today's sophisticated world.

Empathy can be defined as the ability to understand another indi- vidual's feelings and emotions, and then to respond to that person in an appropriate manner. Empathizers instinctively get inside another per- son's mindset and then do all they can to treat that person carefully and sensitively. Systematizers are driven to analyze what's going on around them in the environment, to observe any existing systems and functional institutions within it, to find out how they work, and then to construct new and improved systems.

The main similarity of yin and yang to Baron-Cohen's E-S theory is that both the male and female types of mind are essential to each other and interdependent. They need to work *together* in order to optimize their function.

A significant part of the power of the Santerian or Voodoo priest is his ability to analyze the Christian aspects of his syncretized religion, as well as the ancient African aspects of it. Having seen and understood both systems, he is in a position to devise a syncretized system that will work effectively for him and his people.

A significant part of the power of the Voodoo or Santerian priestess consists of her ability to enter empathetically into the hopes, fears, doubts, and aspirations of her people, to find out what they need and want and then to do her best to supply them.

A vital and particularly *feminine* power of the Voodoo or Santerian priestess is this ability to empathize with her worshippers — perhaps to an abnormally sensitive degree. In a way, this empathy can be seen as giving her something akin to Marie Laveau's spy network. The priestess's ability to feel what worshippers are feeling, to think what they're thinking, to

A pregnant female image connected to the fertility rites of the Olokun people.

get alongside them emotionally, to tiptoe through their minds and sense everything that's there: all this is an immense source of power — simply because knowledge *is* power.

Where the male Santerian priest can, perhaps, be seen to derive some of his power from his charisma — his aggressive, assertive, dynamic, commanding masculinity — the priestess may well derive some of her power from her physical attractiveness and feminine allure. It is one of the oldest and most basic of all male instincts to be drawn to, and to seek the company of, an attractive woman. Just as the priest will attract the attention of most of the female worshippers, so the priestess will attract the males.

This male-female attraction-chemistry is undoubtedly a factor in the success of Santeria, Voodoo, and other syncretistic mystery religions where both priests and priestesses lead the ceremonies and serve the needs of both genders in their local communities. It is particularly important in a religion and in a cultural system where sexuality is a straightforward and readily accepted part of life. Cromwellian Puritanism and Victorian prudery would be hopelessly at odds with the idea that attending worship was enriched and enhanced by having that worship led by an attractive member of the opposite sex. The semi-orgiastic rituals of some of the syncretistic mystery religions make it abundantly clear that — as far as they are concerned — sexual activity is something to be accepted, encouraged, and cultivated as part of natural human life.

The male systematizing tendency and the female empathizing tendency are as different and diverse as the principles of yin and yang: both, complementing each other, are vital to the success of the Santerian enterprise.

There is an important sense in which the powers of the priest and priestess in Santeria, Voodoo, Lucumi, and the other syncretistic mystery religions are gender free. The man or woman in charge of the ceremony, and of the worshipping community outside of their attendance at the ceremony, is granted his or her power by the consent and acceptance of the community.

There is an equally important sense in which there are clearly different and distinctive powers allocated to a priest or priestess, which are very much associated with that leader's gender. Using the analogy of parenthood, there are aspects of loving and caring parents that are gender specific. This gender specificity will vary from one historical period to another and from one culture to another, but it is recognizable. In every society and in all the ages of history, mothers have performed one set of functions while fathers have performed another. So it is with the priests and priestesses of Voodoo, Santeria, and similar faiths. One may be more likely to believe himself or herself to be possessed by a particular gender-associated Orisha or Loa than another.

The powers of the priest and priestess in these syncretistic mystery religions have clear similarities and equally clear differences. There are shared functions that are independent of gender, and there are shared power sources, but there are also gender-specific functions that are exclusive to a priest or a priestess.

Chapter 12

VOODOO DOLLS
AND TALISMANS

DOLLS, amulets, and talismans are an integral part of Voodoo, Santeria, and similar religions. They can be traced back to very ancient times and can take many forms.

The word *talisman* probably comes from the Greek words τελεσμά (*telesma*) or τάλήν (*talein*), which carry the idea of being initiated into mysteries. In its original form it signifies anything that protects the wearer and brings good luck. A

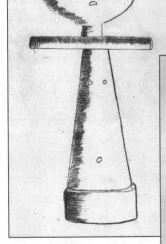

Above: Akua'ba doll carried to ensure beautiful children.

Right: European witch.

talisman does not have to be a solid, physical object, although this is how they are usually envisaged. It can be a word or phrase such as *vade retro satana*, meaning *Satan, go back*.

The witches' familiars — which could at a stretch be interpreted as talismans in the widest sense — were often living animals such as goats, snakes, toads, or cats. A talisman might be a protective plant, especially a magical herb such as wolfsbane (*aconitum vulparia*), also known as monkshood or aconite, which belongs to the buttercup family, *ranunculaceae*.

Aconite was frequently used in the magical potions of medieval European witches, and has been employed throughout the world as an arrowhead poison by both soldiers and huntsmen. Its association with lycanthropes of all types — from werewolves to were-bears and leopard-men — may have arisen because of its practical, toxicological use in killing ferocious animals. Conversely, it was also thought to have the power to turn a person into a werewolf.

Of all the talismans in history — including legend, folklore, and mythology — the magic ring is the one that is most frequently encountered. Sometimes these rings grant the wearer special powers, such as invisibility. At other times, they grant wishes. They are almost invariably benign and beneficial, but they can be merely neutral power sources and their use for good or evil is the choice of the individual who wears them and directs their powers. The symbolism inherent in the circularity of the magic ring makes it a talisman associated with eternity and immortality — the circle has neither beginning nor end. The magic ring of power worn on the finger is in an ideal position to be aimed, or directed, towards a point from which danger is threatening the wearer, or towards a point where the wearer wishes to send help or protection.

A magic ring.

In considering the importance of the magic ring as an especially potent and effective talisman, the source of its magical power needs careful investigation and analysis. Some rings began life as perfectly ordinary pieces of jewellery and then became magical in folklore or legend because they were touched by a divine being, a magician, or an enchanter. In Santeria, Voodoo, and similar syncretistic mystery religions, a ring may be regarded as magical and a powerful talisman because an Orisha or a Loa has possessed it or influenced it in some way — or because it is made of a metal that is associated with a particular Orisha or Loa. In this context, the ring may have a gem set in it, and it is this particular gemstone that is associated with the Loa or Orisha from whom the talisman ring derives its potency. There are even rings of power that are believed to acquire their strength because a powerful Loa or Orisha deigns to dwell *within* them at certain times. This may be thought of as a parallel situation to that in which an Orisha or Loa rides, or possesses, one of his or her worshippers.

The more powerful the deity or demigod associated with the ring — or other talisman — the more powerful that talisman was believed to be. The greatly revered and venerated ibis-headed Thoth, alias Hermes Trismegistus, who might possibly have been one and the same powerful and mysterious being as Melchizedek, the Priest-King of Salem, features in a remarkable talisman, an amulet from the New Kingdom's eighteenth dynasty that flourished three and a half thousand years ago.

In Santeria in particular — and in many of the other mysterious syncretistic religions as well — religious signs and symbols serve as amulets and talismans. The cross and crucifix are both prominent in Christian and syncretistic Christian-Yoruban cultures. Statues of saints and angels, of holy men and women, proliferate both in the worshippers' homes and in their sanctified meeting places.

A very popular amulet in Bolivia and Argentina represents the god Ekeko, traditional bringer of wealth and good luck. In some ways he resembles a cornucopia personified. He is regarded as a generous god of plenty, but, traditionally, he needs an offering before he will activate his benign, wealth-bringing powers on his worshipper's behalf. Many of the Ekeko talismans available in Peru, Bolivia, and Argentina have places where a banknote can be clipped. Ekeko also enjoys a cigarette. Many of his statuettes have his small, circular mouth open, ready and just the right size to take a lighted cigarette. In addition to bringing wealth to his followers, Ekeko accepts small offerings of grain in return for which he sends a good harvest. Traditionally, the statuette should be taken home and set in a comfortable place of honour in order to bring Ekeko's favour on the family. Smaller versions of him can be worn as pendants around the neck or carried on key rings.

Other talismans are associated with the zodiac and with birth months. Each has its particular jewel, although traditional stone and month associations vary over time and from one location to another. These zodiacal birthstones can be seen as parallels with the gems that are associated with particular Loas and Orishas: January is garnet, February is amethyst, March is aquamarine or bloodstone, April is diamond or sapphire, May is emerald, June is pearl or moonstone, July is ruby, August is carnelian, September is sapphire, October is opal or tourmaline, November is topaz, and December is turquoise.

Other amulets and talismans can take the form of drawings or special designs. Writing in 1671 in his *Traité des Talismans,* Pierre de Bresche said:

> A talisman is nothing more than a seal, figure, character, or image of a heavenly omen, a planet, or a constellation. It is impressed, engraved, or carved upon an appropriate stone or upon a metal that corresponds to the planet. The man who carries out this work must have a mind that is settled and fixed upon his task and the culmination of his efforts without being distracted by other unrelated thoughts. His work must be done on the appropriate day and at the precise hour of the planet. It must be carried out in a suitable place, during good, fair, calm weather, and when the planet is in the best astrological aspect that may be in the heavens. This will more strongly attract the proper influences to produce a result when using the talisman depending upon the power of the talisman and on its virtues.

When considering talismans and amulets as designs, in the sense that Pierre de Bresche explained them centuries ago, it is relevant to examine the idea of today's sigils and sigil magic. Some of the shapes and patterns found throughout Santeria, Voodoo, Lucumi, and the other syncretistic mystery religions may well be sigilistic in nature. The word *sigil* comes from an old Latin root *sigilum*, which has the sense of *seal.* There is an even more ancient Hebrew word, הלוגס, or *segulah*, that means something that has a powerful spiritual effect. This "something" can be a written or spoken word, a physical object such as the Ark of the Covenant or the mysterious holy stones Urim and Thummim that the ancient Jewish priests knew how to use; it might also be an action that was spiritually effective, such as a priest raising his hands to bless the congregation, or a worshipper making the sign of the cross at an appropriate point in the service.

When the technicalities of handwriting and typography are analyzed, what is termed a ligature occurs where two, sometimes more, letter forms are joined together to form a single glyph. A relatively modern example can be found in the Initial Teaching Alphabet (ITA), a forty-four symbol phonetic system designed to help young children to learn to read. Instead of the normal *i-n-g* to represent the sound of *ing* as encountered in words such as *ring, bring,* or *thing,* the ITA system used **ŋ**. This ITA symbol is a ligature formed from joining *n* and *g*.

Similar things happened in runic scripts many centuries ago and they were then known as bind runes. Rarely found in inscriptions from the period of Viking ascendancy itself, they proliferated in pre-Viking runic inscriptions and during the medieval post-Viking period. Seafaring warriors — no matter how great their skill and courage — would certainly have felt a compelling need for the protection that magical talismans and amulets were believed to provide. If bind runes were rare during the Viking Age, it may have been because the Vikings felt that something stronger than a sign or symbol was needed. Nevertheless, the Vikings and other peoples of their time used the yew-tree rune *(Eoh)* as a defence against black magic, witchcraft, and evil in general. They also depended upon a non-alphabetical rune resembling the mighty Thor's battle hammer, which was a talisman that was believed to be particularly effective against thieves.

There are traditions that some groups of Viking navigators had a form of magnetite, a type of iron oxide (Fe_3O_4) known as lodestone, which they used both as a navigational aid and as a talisman. There is clear evidence that the Chinese knew about it in the fourth century BC: it is referenced in a book of that period entitled *The Book of the Master of Devil Valley*. Joseph Needham's detailed academic treatise *Science and Civilisation in China* sheds valuable light on the history of the lodestone. By the middle of the eleventh century, a Chinese mathematician and astronomer named Shen Kua was reporting the use of magnetic compasses, as was his contemporary, Alexander Neckham, an English monk, the author of *De Utensilibus*, which dealt with various instruments and pieces of equipment that he had heard about.

Modern Santerian amulets and talismans include magnetic hematite bracelets on which are engraved images of Jesus, the Virgin Mary, Saint Martha, Saint Jude, a guardian angel, and the Virgin of Guadalupe.

Ancient Egyptians considered amulets and talismans most effective when they were directed towards very specific aims. Many of these Egyptian charms included a representation of an Egyptian god such as Isis, Osiris, or Horus, together with the ankh, the T-shaped stem with an oval top — the key to immortality. Khepri the scarab-god was also a popular amulet in ancient Egyptian times, and his popularity has spread globally in the twenty-first century. Khepri, or a design that looks very much like him, is seen among Santerian talismans and amulets — as well as those associated with the other syncretistic mystery religions.

Some contemporary Voodoo practitioners and other magicians construct sigils today by choosing words that are associated with power. A combination such as *stone, steel,* and *strength* might be selected. The words of these sigils are always represented by capital letters. First, they are written side by side with no spaces, and then letters from the first word that also occur in the second and subsequent words are omitted from those subsequent words: STONESTEELSTRENGTH becomes STONELRGH.

STONELRGH is the sigil that can be carved on stone or written on parchment or paper and carried as a talisman. The magician's intention is that it will confer the strength of steel and stone on the person who carries it — usually the magician who constructed it. A similar sigilistic talisman might be intended to endow the user with health, wealth, and knowledge. If the health component is placed first in the sigil, it produces HEALTHWKNODG. The wearer then believes that this talisman will bring protection from illness and injury and will increase his or her riches and wisdom.

An African amulet from Tanganyika was made from a dog's gallbladder. This making of amulets and talismans from animal sources was an integral part of the ancient African traditional beliefs that eventually syncretized with Christianity to form Santeria and similar religions. It was thought the power of the animal from whom the talisman was made would be encapsulated inside the talisman and would be available for the protection and success of the talisman wearer. Other biologically based talismans included a baby's caul and a rabbit's foot. The rabbit's foot may have been intended to endow the wearer with the speed of escape and fertility of a rabbit, while the baby's caul may have been intended to represent a new life, a new start, a renewal of youthful vigour. Yet another biological talisman was a bag manufactured from the skin of a dead crane. This was believed to attract treasure, the symbolism being the powerful flight of the crane and its ability to capture "treasure" — its food — from the water.

A Chinese variant of this belief involved using a live cricket as a talisman to attract good fortune. The boundary between a pet and a live talisman is not a sharp or distinct one. The medieval European wizard or witch might well grow very fond of a pet goat, toad, or cat, while also valuing it as a familiar and a talisman.

Talismans also related to varieties of age-old sympathetic magic. Strewing coins on the floor or on a tabletop was though to attract wealth. Scattering rice in a similar way was thought to "attract" more rice in the form of a good harvest. Co-author Lionel's grandmother, a village blacksmith's daughter born in the late nineteenth century, would always try to leave one last coin in her purse "to attract some more."

There is a sense in which the Jewish prayer shawl known as a *tallis* (plural *talleisim*) can be regarded as a talisman in the broadest sense of the word. There is certainly strong similarity in the name. The tallis reminds the wearer of the eternal presence of God, and that as a faithful worshipper he or she is under God's protection.

An interesting and sophisticated Jewish talisman is referred to as the *kimiyah*, or "angelic text." The names of angels, or extracts from the Torah, are written by rabbinic scribes on parchment *squares* — the shape is important. These texts are then encased in silver and worn as jewellery.

Geometrical shapes and designs of all kinds have been incorporated into amulets and talismans for many centuries. The regular polygons — beginning with the equilateral triangle — have been particularly favoured, and have found places in Santeria and the other syncretistic mystery religions. The triangle reminds the wearer that he or she is protected by God the Three-in-One: Father, Son, and Holy Spirit. It also represents the threefold creation — Heaven, Earth, and Hell. The triangle talisman is also seen as representing the three dimensions of normal, physical space in which we live and move and have our being. There are also three concepts of time encompassed by the triangle talisman: past, present, and future. The wearer believes that the triangle protects him or her throughout all three spatial dimensions and within every aspect of time.

As noted above, squares are also very important shapes when used as the basic design of talismans and amulets. They represent the four cardinal points of the compass, and so are thought to protect the wearer all over the world. The square also represents honesty and integrity — hence the phrase *square dealing*. It has powerful ancient masonic and proto-masonic connections as well: "being on the square" indicates the highest ethical and moral principles. The four Christian gospels are thought to form the four corners of the talismanic square, and so in some of the syncretistic religions it is believed that the four gospel writers can be identified with four of the wisest, most powerful and benign Orishas or Loas.

The five-sided regular polygon, the pentagon, and the five-pointed star, the pentagram, are of great importance and significance as talismans and amulets. They are regarded first as protective, and secondly as a means of attracting power, wealth, love, and loyal obedience.

In addition to the talismans and amulets fastened to the wrist, hung around the neck, or worn as rings or in the ears, there were special types of healing amulets and talismans that could be placed near the sufferer's bed or dipped in the water in which the infirm person was bathed. Other types were actually eaten as a form of magical medicine. The Voodoo or

Santerian healer would inscribe the design of a healing talisman on some suitable foodstuff and feed it to the patient.

The Bible, or the holy book of some other religion, was often used as a talisman, especially in cases of sickness. A copy would be placed under the patient's mattress or pillow.

Another form of applying the talisman or amulet as closely as possible was to have it tattooed into the skin of the believer who sought its protection. Coptic Christians in Egypt used this technique, which is also practised by the Haida peoples of Canada. Where totemism is an important aspect of a religion, and tattooing is practised by that culture, it is not uncommon to find that some tattoos represent the totem of the clan.

Umbanda, Quimbanda, Santeria, and Voodoo all use drawings as talismans and amulets. These may be pictures of the Orishas and Loas themselves or of specific things that appertain to them or are closely associated with them: rivers, waterfalls, lightning, trees, foodstuffs, gems, or representations of fertility. Colours are very important in these talismanic drawings because of the colours that are associated with particular Orishas and Loas.

Arguably, certain essences and fragrances have also been regarded as being very similar to talismans or amulets by their users. Garlic, for example, has long been used as a protection against vampires. The fragrance of incense has been thought to attract the favourable attention of saints, angels, Orishas, and Loas.

Soldiers have been known to wear amulets and talismans with an image of the Sacred Heart of Jesus and the slogan *détente bala*, which is a literal order to the bullet to stop. The St. Christopher medallion is carried by many traditional Christians as an invocation to St. Christopher to protect them while travelling. The contradictory background legends of St. Christopher are particularly relevant to a study of the processes by which religions sometimes unite and syncretize, and of the opposite processes by which they separate and differ.

The Roman Catholic background to St. Christopher makes him out to be a Roman of huge build — a giant as big as the biblical Goliath. In this version he was originally named Reprobus and converted to Christianity. A second Catholic source calls him Offero and locates him in what was originally Canaan — indirectly implying that he might have been one of the later descendants of Goliath. In either version, the giant consults a wise old Christian hermit and asks how he can serve Jesus. The hermit recommends going to a river crossing where the stream is fast-flowing and dangerous, and offering to help travellers to ford it safely. He took the hermit's counsel and began to help people across by carrying them on his mighty shoulders. One of those who asked for the giant's help was a small boy, but when Reprobus started to carry him over, he found the weight was greater than that of any other traveller whom he had carried. The child explained to the kind-hearted giant that he was in fact Jesus Christ, and that he himself carried the sins of the whole world — hence the enormous weight that Reprobus was now bearing as well. Jesus then baptized the giant and bestowed on him the new name of Christopher, Greek for Christ-carrier (*Christospherein*). Just as with the Joseph of Arimathea legend giving the origin of the Glastonbury thorn, Jesus told Christopher to plant his staff in the ground. It grew into a beautiful flowering tree. This miracle led to mass conversions, which infuriated the Roman emperor Traianus Decius (201–251), whose widespread persecutions of the Christians included the martyrdom of Christopher.

In the Eastern Orthodox account of St. Christopher, he was a gigantic Marmarite from Cyrenaica with the head of a dog instead of the head of a human being. Despite this, he became a Christian, and the accounts converge when he was martyred on the orders of Traianus Decius. However, the miracles that accounted for the vast numbers of conversions attributable to Christopher consisted of his continual defiance of Decius's attempts to kill him. When the cynocephalic giant finally allowed Decius's men to martyr him, his corpse was taken to Alexandria by Peter of Attalia.

These legends provide fascinating parallels with some of the early African ideas found in Voodoo, Santeria, and the other syncretistic mystery religions. The concept of a huge and powerful Loa or Orisha with the head of a dog and the ability to defy death is a significant one. The concept of the animal-headed god also links in with various members of the ancient Egyptian pantheon. The successful defiance of Emperor

A dog-headed entity.

Decius is another significant idea, and it should be remembered that Decius and his son and co-emperor, Herennius (227–251), were both killed by King Cniva's Goths at the battle of Abrittus — it was as though some sort of paranormal vengeance, or nemesis, had overtaken the Roman emperors at that battle.

Christopher's Greek Orthodox adherents sang a special hymn to him, which broadly translates as follows:

> Your body was great and most powerful but your face was terrible to behold;
>
> You willingly suffered terrible injuries from your own race;
>
> Both women and men tried to arouse passion within you — then followed you to the death of a martyr.
>
> You are our good and powerful protector, O Christopher, for you are a true martyr.

The Voodoo, Lucumi, and Santerian travellers' equivalent of St. Christopher medallions is the talisman or amulet depicting the symbols of the Loa known as Agwe, or Agoue, regarded as the personification of the ocean.

His rituals are held in the proximity of the sea, and his offerings are floated out to him on small rafts. Although his protection of travellers makes him an equivalent of the Christian St. Christopher, Agwe is often associated with St. Ulrich (890–973), who was the fearless warrior-bishop of Augsburg. When fierce Magyars attacked Germany, they swept all before them until 954 when Ulrich's charismatic courage and military skill halted them at Augsburg. Emperor Otto arrived on August 10, 955, and defeated the Magyars at Lechfeld. There are traditions that Ulrich and his men broke through the Magyar lines from the north and greatly helped Otto's victory.

Agwe's talisman.

This provides another parallel with the characteristic courage and ability of a benign Loa or Orisha such as Agwe, who first halts the attack of any danger to the travellers he is protecting — as Ulrich halted the Magyars at Augsburg — and then overthrows and destroys those hazards completely — as Ulrich and Otto did together at Lechfeld.

Another very important talisman for followers of the syncretistic mystery religions is one dedicated to Guede. He is regarded as the Ruler of Death, Lord of the Underworld, King of Darkness and Night. He is about as far removed from the European representations of death as it is possible to be. There is nothing slow, solemn, or morbid about Guede. Full of life and joy, he requests fast, rhythmic music whenever he arrives at a Voodoo ceremony. He jumps about ecstatically and laughs and jokes with all the worshippers present at the service. He is closely associated with sex as well as with death.

His talisman, or amulet, is a potent one and is believed to have the power to open psychic portals and to make it possible for the user to

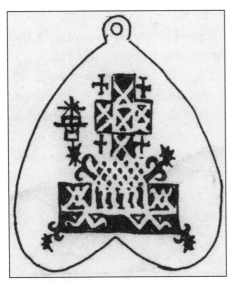

Guede's talisman.

Talisman of Ogun the Warrior.

contact helpful spirit guides. It is even thought that wearers of Guede's talisman are able to contact their guardian angels when they are in special need of angelic power and support. Those who own this amulet tend to think of it as the equivalent of a psychic lens, or spiritual amplifier, enabling them to see, hear, and feel benign psychic entities in the spiritual realm.

The amulet of Ogun the Warrior, another very powerful Loa, is also highly prized. The spellings of his name vary and include Ogoun, Ogum, and Ogou. He is recognized as the Orisha or Loa who has control over politics, warfare, hunting, iron, and fire. In representations of him, Ogun swings a lethal sabre or large machete, and he enjoys alcohol (mainly rum) and tobacco. His wives include Erzulie, Osun, and Oya. His attributes can be linked with those of Ares and Hephaestus from the classical Greek pantheon. Those who carry the Ogun talisman believe that it gives them magical powers that protect them from attack — Ogun the fierce and habitually victorious warrior will attack those who attack his followers. His warrior qualities inevitably link him with blood — his own shed in battle or that of the enemies he has slain. This leads to his being regarded as a healer in some areas — especially where the illness involves a blood condition.

Historically, followers of the syncretistic mystery religions believe that it was Ogun who inspired and empowered the slaves during the Haitian Revolution in 1804. In his twenty-first-century role as an inspirer of politicians, Ogun is on the side of the underprivileged and under-represented and has many aspects. In the Christian side of the syncretized religions, Ogun can appear as a wounded warrior in an almost Christlike pose, suffering for his people — yet triumphant in the end on their behalf. As Ogun Feraille he is a strength-giver; and as Ogun Badagris he carries his people almost as St. Christopher did, protecting travellers like Agwe. In all his aspects, even the most benign of them, Ogun is a very fierce, aggressive, dominant Orisha of power and victory.

Not surprisingly, in view of Peter's use of his sword leading to the wounding of the High Priest's servant's ear, Ogun is linked with St. Peter when Orishas and saints are thought to share an identity in Santeria and Palo Mayombe.

In Yoruban teaching, Ogun is believed to have a sanctuary in the ground. He is thought to sink into this refuge, to rest there but not to die. This sacred place is known as Ire-Ikiti, and he is venerated by the people of Ire because he fought fearlessly for them at all times.

In Dahomey teachings, Ogun is referred to as Gu, their god of war and of blacksmiths and other craftsmen. It is part of the Dahomey religious teaching that Gu was sent to earth in order to make it a good, safe, and happy place to live. It is also part of their teaching to explain that he has not yet accomplished all that he was sent to do, but is never discouraged, and keeps on working at it. To followers of Candomblé in the state of Rio Grande do Sol, Ogun becomes St. George the dragon-slayer. In other regions he may be identified with St. Sebastian.

Another powerful and much sought after talisman or amulet is the one associated with Brigitte. She is the Loa of wealth and money, as well as burial grounds and tombs, and there is a theory that it was her powers that were invoked by servants of the Chase Elliott family when the heavy lead coffins were inexplicably disturbed in the sealed vault at Christchurch, St. Oistins, in Barbados in the early years of the nineteenth century. Graves in Haiti are still dedicated to her, especially if it is the first woman's grave in a new cemetery. Brigitte's husband is Baron Samedi;

Brigitte's talisman design.

her traditional colour is purple, and black chickens are sacrificed when her aid is invoked.

The Irish Saint Bridget could well be a Christianized version of the ancient Irish worship of the pagan goddess Brigit — as a form of syncretism practised long before Santerian syncretism blended the Orishas like Brigitte with the traditional Christian saints from the eighteenth century onwards. Brigitte the Orisha is believed to be capable of holding on tenaciously to the good fortune and prosperity that her talisman is alleged to attract for her adherents.

The talisman or amulet of Erzulie is believed to attract love. Honoured and revered as the Haitian love goddess, Erzulie is regarded by her worshippers as the personification of attractiveness, sensuality, sweetness, and love. Like the Christian St. Nicholas, Erzulie is renowned for generosity, but she also resembles the Greek Muses in being an inspirational goddess of the arts — especially dancing. She controls waterfalls, rivers, and streams, and uses their pure, clean, limpid waters for healing her devotees. Erzulie is also understood to be one of the most sympathetic and approachable of all the semi-divine beings, and welcomes mediums and other perceptive, psychically gifted humans who want to contact the spirit world.

Erzulie's talisman.

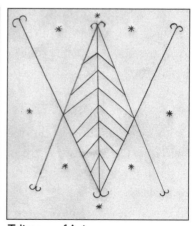

Some of her devotees credit Erzulie with three very different and distinct aspects. As Erzulie Freda, she is a virgin goddess like the Roman Vesta, goddess of hearth, home, and family. As Erzulie Dantor, she is the goddess of sexual passion. As Erzulie la Siren, she is the goddess of the sea and maternity.

The talisman or amulet of Loko (also spelled Loco) is a believed to be a great healing charm. In the syncretized mystery religions, Loko is a herbalist with great knowledge and wisdom of plants — especially trees. He is venerated as a particularly effective doctor, and his herbal remedies are highly regarded and sought after. His wife, Ayizan, is a goddess of trade and commerce, and is a very important Loa, sometimes referred to as a "root Loa." She is especially involved with initiation rites, known as *kanzo*, for those joining the syncretistic mystery religions like Voodoo and Santeria.

Talisman of Loko.

Talisman of Ayizan.

Her counterpart in Christian hagiography is St. Clare, who lived from 1194 until 1253 and was a devoted supporter of St. Francis of Assisi. Born Chiara Offreduccio, Clare devoted her life to helping and organizing women who wanted to follow the example set by St. Francis himself.

The talisman or amulet of Legba is believed to bring great power and success to the believer who wears it or carries it. Legba is one of the most revered and admired of the entire Voodoo pantheon. He is spoken of respectfully as Vye Legba, meaning old Legba, or more familiarly as Papa Legba. Theologically, he is rather a complex character — the one who opens the way between the world of the Loas and the human world, as well as *being* the way, or road, itself. Because of this dual property that he possesses, he is sometimes called Gran Chemin, which translates literally as "The Big Road." His followers also revere him as the backbone or spinal column, the central pivot, of the entire Voodoo world.

Talisman of Legba.

His followers regard him as the demigod in whom humility and communication blend into a special kind of perfection. They love Papa Legba because — in spite of his very senior and important place among the Loas — he never asks for elaborate or expensive sacrifices and ceremonies. According to his worshippers, Papa is more than content when he is given a mug of coffee and a few roasted grains or nuts. Like several other Loas and Orishas, he is an inveterate smoker, but Papa's pipe is a very modest one made from bamboo and a corncob. Mirrors are an important part of Papa Legba's symbolism, and he is frequently referred to as Legba do Miwa, meaning Legba on the rear of the mirror. This again is a tribute to his humility. Wise old Legba holds up the mirror of truth so that

Ancient mirrors.

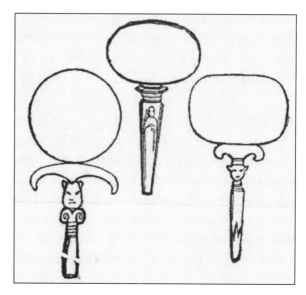

his followers can see themselves as they really are — and then try to make any improvements that are needed. He himself has no illusions and no vanity. The back of the mirror is good enough for the Loa of humility: he does not need to admire himself. He is truth, and he is the road to truth.

Legba is one of the most amiable and friendly of all the Loas and Orishas. Traditionally his colours are red and white, and, being renowned for his great age, Papa Legba is identified with the Christian St. Anthony. This remarkably saintly centenarian lived from 251 to 356, and was a prominent leader of the holy men known as the desert fathers. Traditionally, St. Anthony miraculously cures infectious skin complaints.

The amulet or talisman of Eshu is believed by its wearers to protect them from all harm and all evil. Eshu the Orisha, who is otherwise known and revered as Exú, Eleggua, and Elegba, has a wider range of attributes than many of his peers. He protects travellers as Agwe does; he is a god of roads and pathways, which brings him close to Papa Legba's work; and he presides over good fortune and bad. Within the syncretistic mystery religions, Eshu is thought of as being so important that magical ceremonies, or any rituals involving enchantment, should begin with prayers and offerings to him. He is identified with the enormously powerful Christian St. Michael, the Archangel. Michael is seen as the Commander-in-Chief of the Army of God, and in Daniel's vision it is the immensely powerful Michael who comes to assist the angel Gabriel in his contest with the angel of Persia. Much of the detail about Michael was taken from the Midrash, and reached Christianity via the Book of Enoch. In medieval times, Michael and George were thought of as the patron saints of knighthood and chivalry. The British honours system includes the Order of St. Michael and St. George, which was founded in 1818, and many paratroopers, soldiers, and police officers still think of him as their patron saint. Most Catholic Christians refer to him as Archangel Michael, while members of the Orthodox Churches call him the Taxiarch Archangel Michael.

The amulet or talisman of Simbi is thought to have the power to protect its wearers against unemployment and to keep them in steady work with good prospects of advancement and promotion. Although recognized by followers of the syncretistic mystery religions in general, Simbi is particularly significant in Haiti, and Governor General Michaëlle Jean of Canada, who was born in Haiti, features two simbis as part of her coat of arms.

Simbis are water serpent Loas or Orishas who were part of the ancient religious traditions of west central Africa and the Congo. Simbi d'l'Eau, also spelled Simbi Dlo, simply means Simbi of the *water*, and Simbi Andezo is a title meaning Simbi of the *two waters*. In Haiti, Simbi

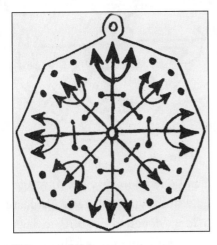

Talisman of Eshu.

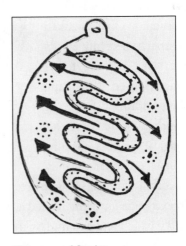

Talisman of Simbi.

Makaya is regarded as a great and powerful magician, sorcerer, and worker of enchantments. He is also associated with secret societies. In a different zone of paranormal power and influence, Simbi Anpaka is believed to be a Loa of herbs, plants, and leaves — especially toxic ones. Other Voodoo authorities regard Simbi as the equivalent of Mercury, or Hermes, the messenger god, who serves Papa Legba. As well as carrying communications, this version of Simbi is a carrier of souls.

The extremely popular and widely venerated Orisha known variously as Shango, Xango, or Chango is seen as a father-god of the sky, and, like Zeus-Jupiter of the Greco-Roman pantheon, as a commander of lightning and terrifying thunderbolts. Historically, Shango was the third king of the Oyo people and an ancestor of the Yoruba people. From the enormous energy symbolized by his dynamic sky powers and shown in the lightning and thunder, Shango is also regarded as the Orisha or Loa of sexual potency.

One of the myths re-lating to Shango's birth concerned his parents, Obatala the Wise (known as the King of the White Cloth) and Aganju, the god of fire, who was also a ferryman. Obatala asked Aganju to take him across the river, but the ferry-man refused. The king then withdrew from the riverbank and used his magical powers to turn himself into an irresistibly

Talisman of Shango.

beautiful woman. He then returned and offered to have sex with Aganju in exchange for being ferried across the river. Aganju agreed with alacrity, and Obatala retained his female form long enough to give birth to Shango, whose personality was thus explained as a mixture of his father's fire and the rational wisdom of his "mother."

Traditionally, Shango duly became the husband of three wives: Oshun, Oba, and Oya. Their stormy relationships, as explained in some of the myths, were attributable in part to his fire-god ancestry.

Oshun, also known as Oschun and Oxum, is one of the three wives of Shango but has a talisman in her own right. Those who wear or carry it believe that it will bring them substantial business success and significant financial prosperity. Oshun is the Orisha who reigns over love, physical attractiveness, money, and diplomatic negotiations between individuals and nations. She is normally kind, generous and loving — although she has a furious temper when angered.

Talisman of Oshun.

She is identified with Cuba's patron saint — Our Lady of Charity — La Virgen de la Caridad del Cobre. Her sacred metals are copper and gold, and her sacred colour is yellow. Peacock feathers are suitable gifts for her, and so are mirrors.

In addition to talismans and amulets of the kind examined above, there are traditional dolls, or poppets, that feature prominently in Voodoo, Santeria, and the other syncretized mystery religions.

The doll, or poppet, is an integral part of sympathetic magic. When the poppet is created to represent a particular person, the theory of sympathetic magic suggests that whatever is done to the poppet will have an effect on the person whom the little figurine represents. Various materials can be used to make the poppet. Wood, clay, and wax are frequently used, as is cloth. Poppets can also be filled with magical herbs and spices, which vary according to the type of spell that is being cast on the person represented by the doll. Most Voodoo magicians try to incorporate what are known as *taglocks* into the doll. These might be personal items worn by the person being represented, or a few of that person's hairs or nail clippings.

Once the poppet and the person have been linked by the enchanter working the sympathetic magic spell, the sorcerer endeavours to make things happen. Suppose, for example, that the intention was to exile the victim from the magician's life zone. In this situation, the Voodoo sorcerer has no malign intention such as injuring or killing the victim — he or she simply wants to be entirely separate from the person.

The poppet could be made from grey or black cloth, black wax, or very dark wood. Herbs placed inside it could include rue and garlic. Binding the legs of the doll would be to prevent the exiled person from

A poppet.

tracing the magician who had worked the spell. Binding the wrists of the doll would indicate that the person would no longer be able to meddle in the magician's affairs or intervene to cause problems. The doll would then be taken to a swift-flowing river and dropped into the water so that the current carried it far away from the magician. This would indicate that the unwanted person was being swept out of the magician's life sphere.

The ancient African religions that provided the foundation stones of much that is now associated with the syncretistic mystery religions such as Voodoo and Santeria were undoubtedly in contact with Egyptian beliefs and practices millennia ago.

Sympathetic magic of the kind that employs dolls and poppets was in use more than three thousand years ago, and was actually employed during the plot against Pharaoh Rameses III, who reigned from 1186 BC to 1155 BC.

One of his wives, Tey, was responsible for triggering a harem revolt against him, because she wanted her son, Prince Pentawere, to succeed him. The conspirators included a number of "magicians" who probably relied on poison as well as their sympathetic magic involving the waxen images of Rameses. The conspirators were arrested and most of them were executed — but Rameses died before the trial ended. Had he been poisoned? Or was it the image magic that killed him?

The ancient Greeks also used poppets to practise their version of sympathetic magic. These Greek images were known as *kolossoi,* and could be made from wood, clay wax, or metal — silver, bronze, and lead were popular choices. Parts of the figurine were often twisted and distorted to incapacitate the person against whom the kolossoi magic was being directed. Kolossoi were often pierced with nails or needles, and it was customary to use thirteen of these. In some cases, animals' teeth were used to pierce the kolossoi.

The basic idea behind these Greek kolossoi was to *bind* the opponent rather than to kill him or her. Each of the thirteen nails, needles, or animal fangs was strategically placed to paralyze a limb or to cause blindness or deafness. Sometimes the kolossoi were decapitated and the head was buried away from the rest of the figurine. It was believed that this would completely confuse the opponent and prevent him or her from taking any effective or appropriate action against the "magician."

On happier occasions, kolossoi were used as love-binding magic. In "The Witch" by Theocritus, written during the third century BC, there is a reference to an enchantress named Simaetha who tries to bring back her errant lover, Delphis, by using the Greek version of sympathetic poppet magic.

Contemporary practitioners of poppet magic who are adherents of the syncretistic mystery religions frequently use fabric as a basic material.

These fabrics are selected carefully so that their base colours, patterns, and designs are appropriate for the poppet-maker's purposes.

Green, gold, or silver base colours with a design suggesting pounds, dollars, or Euros would be ideal for a prosperity spell poppet. Scarlet or crimson would be best for a love spell with a design of stylized lovers' hearts and roses on the fabric. A hostile poppet spell would be likely to employ black or dark grey cloth and to have crossed swords or axes as a design. The warm red and creative colours of gold, orange, and yellow would be right for a creativity enchantment to help writers, artists, sculptors, and composers of music. Solar designs or patterns involving salamanders would be appropriate too. Red and white fabrics are recommended for poppets involved in protection spells, and their patterns could include castle gateways, turrets, ramparts, and steel fences. Keys and locks are appropriate too, as are sturdy portcullises and raised drawbridges. For a poppet magician who is trying to heal a sick pet, the poppet needs to be made in the shape of the animal, not in human form. The ideal fabric colour would be fawn or brown, and the design would incorporate animals, birds, or scenes from nature. For poppet-makers seeking to enrich their spirituality, blue fabric is recommended, with a design of stars, planets, the moon, and representations of the zodiac.

The poppet is then filled with appropriate herbs and spices and the all-important taglocks linking it to the person it represents. In addition to the lock of hair or nail trimmings, a photograph or the person's signature is believed to be effective.

Poppet-makers regard it as a very important part of the process to *tell* the figurine whom it represents, and actually to name that person. It is thought by devotees of the syncretistic mystery religions that this naming and identifying process is central to the poppet's effectiveness.

The challenging question that arises over the poppets, talismans, and amulets cherished by followers of Santeria and the other syncretistic mystery religions is that those who believe in their efficacy swear by them. Is it remotely possible that they really *do* provide the protection, healing, or success in love or business that is claimed for them?

Is there a parallel factor here with belief in the ability of seers and prophets to forecast the future accurately? Psychology suggests that human perceptions are not always reliable. The memory can be an arbitrary and selective piece of mental equipment. If nine out of ten prophecies and forecasts come to nothing, those nine are quickly forgotten — if they register at all. If one in ten actually comes to pass, however, that's the one the prophet's adherents remember, talk about, exaggerate, and multiply.

If the talisman wearer recovers quickly from a serious accident, wins the love of a hitherto unattainable dream partner, or makes a fortune from a new business venture — these are the things that will be remembered and widely publicized, with all the credit for them being accorded to the talisman or amulet of the particular Loa or Orisha associated with that talisman.

The universe is a strange and mysterious place, and the most advanced twenty-first-century technology is not yet able to assign the precise links binding every cause to every effect. As the famous quotation from J.B.S. Haldane (1892–1964) points out, "The universe is not only stranger than we suppose — it is stranger than we are *able* to suppose." What if, amidst all that Haldanean strangeness, there really are connections between wearing amulets and talismans and bringing about certain desired ends and goals? It seems that almost nothing is totally impossible — but some things are far less likely than others. As the millennia roll by, science becomes aware of more and more proven causes and effects. Yet, year by year, month by month, and even day by day, new discoveries are being made, fresh technologies are being developed, new connections between causes and effects are being traced. There may actually be some genuine and effective connection — which scientists prefer to dismiss because it sounds like magic — between wearing a talisman or amulet and bringing about the benign results with which that talisman or amulet is traditionally associated by members of the syncretistic mystery religions.

The power of the mind is grossly underestimated. Thought is a form of energy. Energy and matter are interchangeable under certain circumstances. Theoretically, if its full powers are released and directed, mind ought to be able to accomplish what most people would describe as miracles. Mind may need focal points in order to channel its vast powers. The greatest mental powers appear to be generated at a level either above or below normal, everyday consciousness. Is the real power of a talisman or amulet its ability to act as a focal point for the mind of the wearer who believes in its power? If mind energy is capable of influencing its environment, does it do so by thinking that an Orisha or Loa is working via a talisman or amulet on the believer's behalf to make the desired things happen? Is it the power of the subject's own mind that stimulates the immune system to destroy the pathogens causing the believer's illness?

Does this mind power work within groups of believers? Are many unidirectional thoughts like the numerous tiny strands of hemp in a thick rope? If enough Santerians or Quimbanda devotees think the same healing thoughts, or will the same love and prosperity together, does that group mind power bring things to pass?

Talismans and amulets dedicated to particular Orishas and Loas *seem* able, on occasion, to create real, external, objective, and desired benign effects. Quite *how* this happens still remains conjectural.

Chapter 13

SPELLS, INCANTATIONS, AND MAGICAL INGREDIENTS

ENCHANTMENTS, incantations, spells, and their magical ingredients such as blood, bone, herbs, and spices are an integral part of Voodoo, Obeah, Santeria, and the other syncretistic mystery religions.

Spells have seemingly been part of ancient magic from the beginning of time. There are numerous classical and biblical references to them, such as the dramatic "magical" conflict between Moses and Pharaoh's court magicians in Exodus, Chapter 7. In order to persuade Pharaoh that Yahweh wanted the Israelites set free, Aaron casts down his staff, which becomes a serpent. At Pharaoh's command, the Egyptian magicians do the same with their rods, which also become serpents. Aaron's serpent then swallows theirs.

In the adventures of Odysseus (Ulysses) he encounters Circe, the

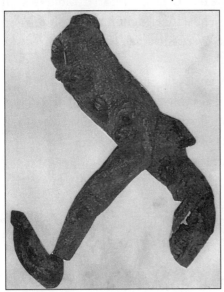

enchantress, whose Greek name Κίρκη (Kirkē) means "falcon." She lives on the Isle of Aeaea. Circe is no ordinary mortal: she is the daughter of Helios, god of the sun, and Perse, who was one of the oceanids. Circe's magic relied very much on her vast knowledge of herbs and drugs. She also used a wand to complete the spell that turned Ulysses' men into pigs.

Mandrake root — often used in spells.

On his way to rescue his men, Ulysses is met by the god Hermes, who tells him to use *moly* (μῶλυ), a herb with a black root and white blossoms, as a protection against Circe's magic. Hermes also warns Odysseus that although Circe is irresistibly sexually alluring, she is also treacherous. By following Hermes' advice, Odysseus survives a year with Circe and then sets off again for Ithaca.

How does a wizard, a witch, a sorcerer, or a hungan set about performing what he or she believes to be magic? And what does such a magician regard as the *purpose* of such magic? The goals of Pharaoh's magicians and Circe were clear: they were attempting to use their magical powers to achieve particular objectives. The targets and purposes of contemporary spells may be as varied as the magicians and their clientele, but the fundamental goals have not changed: people use magic as an attempt to achieve some desired end.

There is also a sense in which, while respecting the ancient, traditional ingredients and methodology, every worker of spells is an individual with his or her own refined, creative ideas. The expert who has reached the traditional cordon bleu standards in cookery via one of the international centres of excellence, such as the world-renowned Canadian Cordon Bleu School in Ottawa, will nevertheless have his or her own special, personal perspective on the cuisine that is being prepared. Modern spell casters work along similar lines. While adhering to the time-honoured basic methods of traditional magic, every enchanter will put a distinctive, personal signature on a spell.

Almost every known spell — from hunting spells created millennia before the Christian era to spells aimed at solving the problems of advanced computer technology in the twenty-first century — contains elements of what magicians would regard as *sympathy* and the *law of similars*.

There is also a sense in which words are an essential part of many Santerian spells. The etymology of the word *spell* provides interesting corroboration for this emphasis placed upon the importance of words during magical practices. The Anglo-Saxon term *spel* means a story or an aphorism. The Icelandic term *spjall* means a saying or an utterance. The Gothic word *spill* means a story with a meaning or a fable. The law of similars can be seen here yet again: by using the *name* of a deity, an

Orisha, a Loa, or a jinn, it was believed that the magician could produce the same effects as if the paranormal entity was actually there with the client and the miracle worker.

By adhering to this principle of similarities, a spell caster believes that a symbolic object, when used correctly in terms of its magical potential, can act on the environment. This influence on the environment — including the human inhabitants of the environment — is believed to function effectively simply because it has a sympathetic relationship with the target.

For example, if a blacksmith or farrier has accidentally injured his hand while putting a nail in a horse's shoe, the spell caster who has been called in to cure his friend the smith will put healing ointment on the farrier's injured fingers, *as well as on the hammer and the nail.* The tools that caused the problem of the hand injury are seen as being in a sympathetic relationship with the victim and with the specific injury that they inflicted upon his hand. By putting healing salve on the hammer and nails — as well as on the injured human being — the magician is implying that the tools have somehow been reconciled to their owner and he is, therefore, protected from future injury from them.

According to the magical law of similars, which is understood and practised by Santerian magicians, Voodoo hungans, Obeah workers, and others, there is what might be described as a type of *godly essence* or *divine blueprint* that pervades and underpins the whole of the natural universe. According to the law of similars, this celestial pattern hidden throughout the universe is full of clues to the true spiritual nature of animate and inanimate objects. The skilled, experienced, and perceptive Santerian magician believes that he or she can read and interpret these baffling patterns and matrices.

Leaves in the stylized shapes of human hearts often form part of love spells. The colour red can signify blood and can therefore figure in a healing spell to cure a disease of the blood. The colour blue can be used in a spell to heal and reduce varicose veins. Mosses and delicate ferns are employed in spells that reverse hair loss, because they resemble prolific human hair. Bright, transparent jewels and clear, shining glass can be regarded as similar to bright eyes and clear vision, and so may be used as components of spells aimed at helping to restore sight. Seashells, treated with holy oil or holy water, rubbed with appropriate herbs, and then blessed, can be placed against the supplicant's ear as part of a spell to bring news from distant places — including the spirit world.

This law of similars is sometimes applied in areas outside magic in its generally understood sense. Salvador Dali (1904–1989) had all the outstanding intellectual power, talent, and charismatic self-confidence to have been a noteworthy priest-magician had he been a believer in Santeria, Voodoo, Obeah, or one of the other syncretistic mystery religions. He knew the law of similars very well, and he understood its powers over an audience. While delivering one of his lectures aimed at exploring the deep theological and philosophical issues that intrigued his amazing mind, Dali dressed up in an old-fashioned deep-sea diving suit. Those of his entranced audience who understood the law of similars saw the point immediately: depth of water *similarized* depth of thought.

One of Dali's many superb but challenging canvases is entitled *Dream Caused by the Flight of a Bee around a Pomegranate a Second Before Awakening*. It was painted in 1944, when the artist was forty, and shows a beautiful sleeping girl, whom Dali identifies as Gaia. There are two pomegranates in the painting — a very large one and a normal-sized one. From the large one emerges a fish and from this fish emerge two tigers that seem to be springing towards the exquisite sleeping Gaia. There is also a rifle with a fixed bayonet in the picture. It is descending from the sky. The bayonet is pressing into Gaia's arm — like the sting of an insect — and waking her. (The Second World War was coming towards its end when Dali created this work.) The picture also contains a strange elephant-like creature on enormously long, telescopic legs.

Over the years, various art experts have attempted to explain the symbolism in this canvas as Dali's surrealist attempt to interpret the theory of evolution. He has almost certainly been influenced here by Freud's ideas about the subconscious mind. Dali seems to be working through a series of semi-Freudian ideas about dreams in a dreamscape. The power in the picture is largely derived from its near-magical qualities, which proceed along the lines of the *law of similars*. The mystical Gaia-goddess's beautiful form, for example, is shown as *similar* to an exquisitely attractive human girl. The audience is instantly drawn to her. This very positive symbol stimulates the viewer to feel a similar attraction to the Earth itself and to Nature personified in the biosphere. The huge fish shows life emerging from the sea. The tigers are dangerous predators. The bayonet touching Gaia's arm suggests that war and violence are a threat to all life on the planet. It wakes her from the peace of sleep and pleasant dream images into a hazardous reality. The bayonet symbol — like the sting of the bee circling the pomegranate — is similar to the suddenness with which life can change from peace to war: from pleasantness and stability to horrendous suffering and chaos.

Dali's other famous symbols — perhaps the ones for which he is best known — are the soft, drooping, and melting watches. They say so much about the mystery of time as Dali conceived it. The plasticity and flexibility of Dali's watch images follow the magicians' law of similars. The surrealistic image of the unreal watch is Dali's method of conveying his message about the weird and incomprehensible nature of time.

Another general category of magic, well known among Santerians and followers of the other syncretistic mystery religions, includes the ancient fire spells. These go back to extremely early times. More than one Orisha and Loa is associated with fire, but Shango is one of the best known in this field. In Haiti, Ogun is revered as a fire Loa.

The ancient Greeks told in their myths and legends how Prometheus brought fire to earth and was punished for it by the other gods.

Indigenous American myths and legends include an intriguing story of how the coyote stole fire from the powerful and mysterious Fire Beings and brought it back to be shared by men and all who needed it for warmth in winter.

Learning how to create and use fire was one of the most important turning points in ancient history, ranking alongside the domestication of animals and the discovery of the wheel.

Fire spells like these are very much part of the priest-magician's stock-in-trade today. They can be extremely simple: all that the fire enchanter needs to begin work is a fireproof container such as a ceramic bowl or a metal bucket filled with sand as an extra precaution. Fire spells are normally performed outside, so that the smoke can rise to the realm of the Orishas, Loas, and spirits of the departed. However, fire spells on a sensibly small scale can also be performed indoors, near an open window, so that the smoke is free to rise through it. The smoke is also understood to be carrying the magician's *intent* as well his or her prayers and supplications. The choice of twigs from different trees, bushes, and shrubs is important. Practising fire-magicians know which twigs and dried leaves are appropriate for each particular spell. Favourite fuels for different spells on different occasions and with different objectives can include applewood, rosewood, pine needles, pine cones, lavender, bay leaves, and eucalyptus.

The spell worker lights the selected material and then concentrates on the flames, thinking deeply about what the power of the fire is to achieve, what he wants the fire gods, the Loas and Orishas of flame, to do for him or her. Some fire magicians endeavour to go into a flame-induced trance at this stage to release their mind powers. Once the flames have died down to embers, the enchanter adds more aromatic herbs and expresses the purpose of the spell in words of intent and prayers. One format uses the phrases, "Hear my wishes and my prayers, O great and wise ones. / Of your goodness and kindness grant me the blessings / Of love, joy, health, safety and success in all that I do."

The third and concluding part of a fire spell such as this one is to make a thank-offering to the Loas and Orishas on whom the priest-magician has called. Some enchanters add paper currency to the fire; others give incense, tobacco, a cigar, or a few drops of rum or liqueur. They also regard it as very important to *thank* the Orishas and Loas on whom they have called.

The Republic of Suriname (formerly called Surinam) in the northern region of South America has a significant number of the descendants of former African slaves among its population. Many early members of this group had intermarried with the indigenous peoples of the region and syncretized ancient African beliefs with the old, established local faiths.

An eyewitness account of a fire-dance ceremony in Suriname records how a virgin priestess went into a trance while participants danced among the flames and stepped barefoot over very hot embers without injury. It was believed by the dancers, however, that if the priestess was woken from her trance suddenly, or unexpectedly, they would no longer be immune from the effects of the fire.

Joseph Chilton Pearce's theories in *The Crack in the Cosmic Egg* deal with alternative realities that can, perhaps, be invoked by mind power. His ideas about such reality shifts are as interesting and significant as J.W. Dunne's famous theories on the nature of time. In one of these hypothetical alternative realities, suggests Pearce, fire would not burn in the way that it does in our experiential, terrestrial reality. Was the entranced virgin priestess creating a temporary, localized, alternative reality in which the fire dancers were safe — *as long as she was maintaining the parameters of their alternative reality?*

Fire-walking plays a significant role among the Voodoo rituals in the Caribbean, and Trinidad has fire-eaters as well as fire-walkers. Haiti is also noted for the large numbers of fire-magicians of various kinds who follow the traditions of the syncretistic mystery religions.

Dr. William Sargant (1907–1988), the brilliant author and psychiatrist, studied Haitian Voodoo for many years. He saw connections linking Haitian Voodoo not only to ancient Congolese belief systems, but via Arabian traders, through Asia Minor and Persia, all the way back to ancient shamanism as practised by Tartars and Mongols. In the course of his extensive researches on Haiti, Dr. Sargant studied ceremonies where the participants felt that they had to fulfill the wishes of Ogun Badagris by drinking a fiery mixture of rum and pepper, and by dancing on live coals.

Fire magic of these various kinds has always been understood — again in accordance with the law of similars — to be symbolically associated with the metaphorical fires of human love and sexual passion. In Santeria, Obeah, Voodoo, Lucumi, and most of the other syncretized mystery religions, love and marriage spells abound. One particularly popular and allegedly successful spell of this type begins with selecting a red rose. The client requesting help from the spell worker is then instructed to write the name of the loved one on the petals of the flower. A very thin brush and silver or golden paint is thought to be especially effective for this. Once the petals have been duly inscribed with the desired person's name, they are dipped in rose water either by the magician or the client. During this baptism of the petals, which is believed to give them additional magical powers, they are strewn near the house of the loved person — ideally by moonlight.

Money, and the power it can bring with it, is the central objective of many spells incorporated into Santeria, Voodoo, and similar religions. Two of the principle ingredients are what are usually described by the ritualists as "mysterious African soap" and "mysterious African candles." These are obtainable from a range of specialist

An Orisha or Loa surrounded by candles.

"magical" shops found all over the world, but especially in Haiti, the Caribbean, Africa, and South America.

The client seeking money has to rise early in the morning on the day of the full moon. The law of similars can be seen operating here because the full moon resembles a very large silver coin. Before speaking about anything else, the magician's client has to say how much money he or she wants. The client then bathes from head to foot using the mysterious, magical soap. Nothing else has to be done until midnight. The client then takes an egg that has been boiled hard and lights the mysterious, magical candle.

An important incantation then has to be repeat-

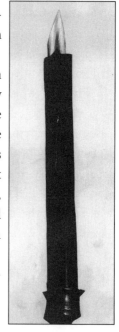

A black candle of the sort often used in spells.

ed: "May money always surround me as the silver-white of this egg surrounds the golden-yellow of its yolk. May the money that surrounds me make me safe and secure — as the shell of this egg protects the white and the yolk."

The shell is then removed from the egg and the client places the whole egg in his or her mouth. The tradition emphasizes the importance of not cutting up the egg before placing it in the mouth. (Obviously, great care must be taken not to choke on the egg at this point.) The candle is then extinguished. The ceremony is repeated twice more on successive nights.

In addition to acquiring the specific magical ingredients such as candles, flower petals, eggs, bones, herbs, and spices, spells are believed to work at their fastest and strongest when the appropriate magical *instruments* are used in the right way, at the right time, and in the right place.

Priest-magicians who practise Santeria, Voodoo, Obeah, and the other syncretized mystery religions will use magical implements and instruments very similar to those used by spell workers all over the world

A Seer using a crystal ball.

 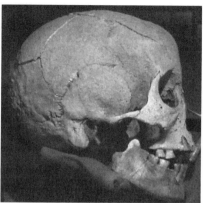

A cauldron used in magic.   Human skulls featured in spells.

— and throughout many millennia. These magical tools and accessories include an altar, a censer, a chalice or sacred drinking vessel of some kind, a tripod, a sacred sword, a wand or magical staff, a trident, and a cauldron or mixing bowl. All of these need to be made from special materials as prescribed by the oldest and most expert enchanters, and sanctified by special rituals and liturgies before being used.

Another important aspect of spell casting in Voodoo, Santeria, Lucumi, Obeah, and the other syncretized mystery religions is the importance of *numbers*. As well as being a brilliant pioneering mathematician, Pythagoras (580–490 BC) was also a numerologist. He argued that numbers enveloped, impregnated, and percolated through everything in the universe — the spiritual worlds as well as the physical ones. For Pythagoreans, the number one stood for unity and God. Two was the number of duality and represented an evil force — the devil, Satan, Lucifer, or his equivalent — *something* that was opposed to God and to the divine, loving plan for the well-being of humanity.

Pythagoreans regarded four as a very sacred and holy number, and it was the number on which they swore their most solemn oaths. Five was the number that signified marriage. Pythagorean numerologists also allocated numbers to the celestial bodies and to the elements of their creation theory. The sun, like God, was allocated the number one. The moon, with its sinister influence, shared the number two with the forces of darkness. As well as symbolizing marriage, five was the number of fire, harmonizing here with earlier ideas about the ecstatic fires of love, as well as the flames of fire the element. Earth was given six for its number, and the Pythagoreans associated air with the number eight. For them twelve stood for water.

Later numerologists, such as Cornelius Agrippa writing in the sixteenth century, had very different ideas from the Pythagoreans. For the numerologists among the Santerians and similar syncretistic religious groups, three and seven are particularly good and important numbers. They frequently figure in spells. Nine is the source of inspiration from Loas and Orishas. Ten represents completion and fulfillment, and twelve (which adds its one and two to make the very powerful and benign three) is the number of signs in the zodiac, tribes of Israel, the apostles of Jesus, and the gates of the ancient holy city of Jerusalem.

The spells used by the priest-magicians of Santeria, Voodoo, Obeah, and similar syncretistic mystery religions are based on sympathetic magic and the laws of similars. They also involve word magic and secret incantations. They are mixed from strange ingredients and they employ special magical instruments and implements. Times and locations are thought to make them more powerful in their effects. Trance, or at least semi-trance, states are often resorted to by the spell workers, and elements of subconscious and supra-conscious mind power are often in evidence. Numerology also has a significant role in these spells. The spell workers believe that their Loas and Orishas are the real power behind their spells, the paranormal entities who control the forces that make the spells work. The Orishas and Loas concerned with literal fire and flame — as well as with the metaphorical flames of burning love and passion — are believed to have major roles in making Santerian spells effective.

Chapter 14

SEXUAL MAGIC

AN IN-DEPTH understanding of the powerful sexual element in magic benefits greatly from a survey of the personality theories of Abraham Maslow (1908–1970). His 1943 publication *A Theory of Human Motivation* sets out the idea that there is a hierarchy of needs that every human being experiences simply as a consequence of being human. There were a few important thinkers like Manfred Max Neef, the distinguished Chilean philosopher and economist, who disagreed with Maslow, but no criticism of Maslow's basic hypothesis succeeds in totally dismantling the truth of his largely sound and well-reasoned argument.

At the foundation of Maslow's pyramid of needs is the physiological one. First and foremost, human beings need oxygen to breathe, water to drink, sleep to restore and refresh them, procreative sexual activity, biological homeostasis, and excretion of their waste products.

After those vital, basic physiological needs have been met, Maslow argues that the next stratum up consists of human safety needs. He lists these as bodily security, security of employment — including self-employment or being independently financially wealthy — moral security, and the security of an individual's health, family, and property.

Maslow's third layer up is categorized as a need to belong, a need to give and receive love, a need for close, warm friendships, and for a higher level of sexual intimacy that expresses love as well as raw desire and is more refined and sophisticated than the simple, basic mating urges included among the fundamental physiological needs on level one.

The fourth level of Maslow's pyramid is concerned with the need for esteem. In Maslow's mind, people need to give and receive respect. They need to develop a high level of self-esteem — to see themselves as having real value — and to learn self-confidence. They need to achieve

Sex god and goddess.

things and to have those achievements recognized. The great C.S. Lewis phrased it this way: "When we have learnt to love our neighbours as much as we love ourselves, we are then permitted to love ourselves as much as we love our neighbours."

The final layer that reaches all the way up to the summit of the pyramid of needs is normally defined as self-actualization. When human beings have satisfied every other need, says Maslow, this is what makes them truly and fully human. It is here that they gain satisfaction from solving problems, from understanding morality and ethics and living by whatever their own idiosyncratic standards demand of them. They accept facts boldly and bravely; they are creative, autonomous, and spontaneous.

How do Santeria and the other syncretized mystery religions set out to fulfill human needs as described by Maslow? Part of Santerian charity, ethics, and morality is to see that as far as possible, homeless people are sheltered, hungry people are fed, and sick and injured people are nursed and healed. It would be an integral part of the ethics of a loyal and devout Santerian to protect anyone who was vulnerable — especially children, the frail, and the elderly.

With the exception of the special and unusual religious duties of a virgin priestess at a fire-walking ceremony (and that is a role she is free to leave and to pass on to another celebrant, if she later wishes to marry and lead a normal life), Santeria and similar syncretistic religions discourage celibacy for both clergy and laity.

The ancient African roots of the faith can be traced back to a dynamic, prehistoric hunter-gatherer culture in which frequent and vigorous sexual activity contributed to racial survival and was also practised as part of their fertility religion.

As their level one and two needs were satisfied, those Paleolithic peoples, among whom Santeria's deepest and most ancient African roots grew and developed, discovered a need *beyond* simple survival and safety. They wanted companionship, friendship, and intimate sexual activity that reflected their love as well as their urge to procreate.

If the concept of the purpose of magic as a way to fulfill human needs is linked with Maslow's pyramid of needs, it may be suggested that magic attempts to fulfill the sexual needs of level three as well as the more basic ones at the foundation level. How do Santeria, Voodoo, Lucumi, Obeah, and the rest of the syncretistic mystery religions approach these human demands?

A general theory of sexual magic that is widely — but not universally — held is that human sexual energy, or libido, is the most powerful drive a human entity has at his or her command. If this energy can be controlled, harnessed, focused, and directed — then the magician in charge of it can reach goals and objectives that are not normally attainable.

Sexual magic approaches the use of the orgasm in two different ways. The first theory suggests that it is the power of the orgasm itself, as a massive release of energy, which somehow empowers the magic. This hypothesis considers the magical objective, say a wealth or power spell, to be the missile. Orgasmic energy is then regarded as the essential, explosive force, the equivalent of cordite or TNT in a cartridge, which launches the projectile. The orgasm is seen as the powerful wind that fills the sails of the magician's boat and carries the spell to its destination. Another particularly relevant and appropriate analogy is the archer's bow: tension builds up as the bow is drawn back. That tension is suddenly

The archery analogy of orgasm.

released at the moment of orgasm and the energy so created speeds the arrow-spell towards its target.

Parallel thinking can often be detected between the oldest forms of European Wicca and the syncretized mystery religions including Santeria, Voodoo, Lucumi, and Obeah. There is a strong probability that they shared a number of primeval sources going back as far as the oldest of the African, Egyptian, and Chaldean roots of magic and the wisdom known to have existed in the Indus Valley since time immemorial.

Sexuality in creation stories.

Wiccan sexual magic centres on what is referred to by practitioners as the Great Rite. In its oldest, purest, and most genuine form, this consists of actual sexual intercourse. The priest represents the male lover god, while his priestess represents the maiden goddess. Variations involve a male god of the sun or sky with a female partner representing the earth, nature, or the terrestrial biosphere.

In its ritual form, semiological representations of intercourse are often employed. The priest inserts the athame, a ritual knife, wand, or magical rod — prepared from one of the Wiccan sacred trees — into a magical vessel filled with wine and held by the priestess. Members of the congregation can be called upon to perform either the direct rite or the symbolic rite under the direction and guidance of the officiating priest and priestess.

Samael Aun Weor (1917–1977) was what would have been called a true Renaissance man had he lived a few centuries earlier. This brilliantly intelligent Colombian philosopher was also an anthropologist, psychologist, occultist, and academic esotericist. His expertise extended to an analysis of sexual magic and the place of the orgasm in such magic. In Samael's view, the explosive release of sexual energy via orgasm did not achieve the best and most effective magical results. He believed that sexual energy should be sublimated into what he thought of as higher, purer, creative spiritual energy. Samael did not regard the ecstatic physical pleasure of an explosive orgasm as merely the power that *carried* magic to its destination — for him, sexual power had to be translated and transformed into creative spiritual magic.

Another man with great understanding of the sexual elements in magic was the American Dr. Paschal Beverley Randolph (1825–1875). He was a competent and caring medical man as well as an expert on occult matters and a prolific writer. His medical qualifications and experience gave him an objective and open-minded approach to sex, and he is also reputed to have been one of the first Rosicrucians in the U.S.A.

As a young man, Randolph worked on a sailing ship and his travels took him as far as Persia, where he learned a great deal about mysticism, the occult, magic in general, and the sexual elements of magic in particular. In the course of these travels, Randolph recorded that he had met a group of fakirs near Jerusalem, possibly even a branch of Nusa'iri, an ancient tribe from Syria with a long history of secret wisdom.

Based on what he had learned during his travels in the Middle East and beyond, Randolph taught a type of sexual magic that was the epitome of the first orgasmic theory. In his own words, "true sex-power is god-power."

He believed that when orgasm took place the lovers were in contact with cosmic powers and therefore anything that they wished could be accomplished. Randolph believed that orgasmic sex enabled the participating lovers not only to reach new heights of spirituality and cosmic awareness but also to accomplish anything from wealth and temporal power to the highest peaks of physical health and fitness.

Randolph was also a trance medium and an influential supporter of the American nineteenth-century spiritualist movement. He was thought to have been associated with an organization known as the Hermetic Brotherhood of Luxor, with which Madam Blavatsky was also linked. Other prominent nineteenth-century occultists interested in sexual magic included Carl Kellner (1851–1905) and Theodor Reuss (1855–1923). Both were strongly influenced by Randolph's ideas, as was Aleister Crowley.

Kellner, who was financed by his successful chemical paper business, founded and led the Ordo Templi Orientis. He was eventually succeeded by Reuss, and Crowley took over as leader when Reuss died in 1905.

During the years that Randolph, Kellner, Reuss, and Crowley were developing and deploying their theories of sexual magic, the syncretistic mystery religions were also increasing in strength and influence.

There would almost certainly have been significant and continuing contact between these two major strands of nineteenth and early twentieth century religious thought and practice.

Traditionally, the Languedoc region of France also had a long history of magical involvement, which was still flourishing at this time.

The authors were giving a series of lectures on the Rennes-le-Château mystery a few years ago at Penarth in South Wales. A member of the audience, Bremna Howells, who was very knowledgeable about magic in general, came up with a fascinating theory about how the mysterious

Father Bérenger Saunière, priest at the church of St. Mary Magdalene in Rennes, had become so unaccountably wealthy. His sudden and inexplicable access to wealth lay at the heart of the mystery.

This lady had a friend who was an *Ipsissimus*, a rank in certain magical circles that is by definition "beyond the comprehension of the lower degrees." An Ipsissimus is said to be totally autonomous — free from the needs and wants of all the subordinate ranks of less skilful and less experienced magicians. An Ipsissimus is thought of as one who has attained perfect harmony and balance, not only with this universe but with *all* universes — physical and spiritual. An Ipsissimus has, by definition, attained all that there is to attain.

Following the first Rennes lecture, Bremna had discussed the Saunière mystery with the Ipsissimus. In his opinion, the secret of the priest's acquisition of great wealth after 1885 was centred on the sex-magic spell known as "The Convocation of Venus." One of the curious things about the planet Venus — always associated with Venus-Aphrodite the sex goddess — is the way that the planet appears to make a pentagonal pattern every eight years.

There are also tenuous connections linking Mary Magdalene with Yemaja, also spelled Yemoja and Ymoja, the Orisha and Loa connected with seas, oceans, sexuality, and fertility. Yemaja is sometimes regarded as another persona of the goddess Venus.

Strange, mythological, hagiographical connections have also been made between Mary Magdalene and the ancient mermaid legends, forming yet another nexus between Mary and Yemaja. An association of this kind, however, may simply be a coded reference to the stories of Mary crossing the sea from Israel to France during the first century. Couiza Montazels near Rennes (Saunière's birthplace) has a very old fountain decorated with mer-people known locally as *griffouls*.

More significantly, the area near Rennes-le-Château has a pentagram of landmarks: two of these have Templar connections; one is the ancient church in the village of Rennes itself (the church dedicated to St. Mary Magdalene, who is associated with Venus-Aphrodite); another is marked by a mysterious menhir; and the fifth is a large, white stone near Granès. In the centre of this curious pentagram is an area called La Pique, also known

Co-author Lionel with one of the mysterious griffouls.

as the hill of Coume-Sourde. The mystical Rosicrucian saying "as above so below" might well apply to the Rennes-Venus pentagram phenomena.

According to the information supplied by the Ipsissimus, the Convocation of Venus spell is a remarkably accurate predictor of future events. In his opinion, Saunière's wealth came from selling the prophecies that resulted from the successful performance of the Convocation of Venus — the magic being made triply effective by being performed within his Church of St. Mary Magdalene, in contact with the ground pentagram reflecting the celestial pentagram of Venus the sex goddess.

Sexual activity was the essential core of the spell, and the Ipsissimus concluded that this was performed by Saunière and Marie Denarnaud. She was his attractive young housekeeper — many years his junior — and utterly devoted to him. Marie would almost certainly have done whatever he requested of her.

Whether or not the Ipsissimus was right, the *possibility* that Bérenger and Marie were carrying out sex-magic together in the church as a form of worship to the goddess Venus is supported by the story of Bérenger's deathbed confession on January 17, 1917. Allegedly, he told his confessor,

Father Rivière, something so traumatic that Rivière left the dying man without absolving him. It was also widely alleged that Rivière — hitherto a calm and cheerful man — sank into such morbid depression that he was unable to carry out his priestly duties for months. Did Saunière confess to performing sexual magic with Marie in the name of a pagan goddess? A pious, sincerely devout and celibate priest like Rivière would have found Saunière's behaviour shocking, repellent, and incomprehensible.

Supposing that the prophecies obtained via the Convocation of Venus *were* surprisingly accurate, where did that knowledge really come from?

In the authors' opinion, human beings have valid choice, genuine decision-making powers, real autonomy, and free will. How can seers view what has not yet come to pass? They can't and they don't. At every moment of their lives, human beings can choose to take one path or another. That moment-by-moment choice steers and shapes their futures — and the futures of those associated with them.

There are avant-garde physicists who think that these unfulfilled futures — these choices that people did *not* make — these *wheels of if* — still have some kind of quasi-existence. What seems probable, then, is that gifted seers like Mother Shipton and Nostradamus have the ability to perceive some of these probability tracks. From time to time, the seer will glimpse one of the probability tracks that actually develops into shared, objective, experiential reality. Perhaps the seer's powers actually include an *evaluating* gift as well as a perceptive one — so that he or she can discern which of the kaleidoscopic probability tracks is most likely to become experiential reality.

Enthusiasts for sexual magic like Randolph, Kellner, Reuss, and Crowley would possibly have argued that whether or not the goddess Venus existed — or was involved in any way with the Rennes ceremonies enacted in her name — the sexual magic working between Bérenger and Marie would have been powerful enough on its own to increase their perceptiveness of probability tracks and their ability to evaluate them.

Evaluations of the sexual elements in Santeria, Voodoo, and similar syncretistic mystery religions need to include the part played by tantra — and its profound influence on so many other religio-magical practices.

The word *tantra* is an old term from Sanskrit that can convey the idea of "braided or woven together, knitted together." Like many other ancient root words, however, *tantra* has associated meanings. One of these refers to "growth" and "expansion" combined with "emerging" or "being revealed." Some etymologists reach this meaning by splitting the word into *tan*, signifying "growth and expansion," combined with the suffix *tra*, which carries the sense of "appearing" or "coming into view."

A few ancient versions of Hindu worship and religious exercises seem to have included the veneration of human sexuality, either in actual practice or in symbolic form.

The earliest forms of tantric yoga go a long way further back into prehistoric human twilight than the famous erotic carvings on the Khajuraho Temples in India, built by Chandela rulers during the tenth and eleventh centuries, which are often thought of in connection with sexual magic and tantra practices. Experts on tantra history have suggested that it was being practised in the Harappa culture that flourished in the mysterious Indus Valley around five thousand years ago.

There were almost certainly trading connections between the Harappan peoples, Egyptian and sub-Saharan Africans, and the ancient Chaldean civilizations. An exchange of items for trade almost invariably led to exchanges of social, cultural, and religious ideas among the traders.

The sexually oriented worship known generally among scholars and historians of pre-Hindu religion and magic as Shaktiism and Shaivism was

Sexual representation from Benin Palace.

concerned with the goddess in her various personas as well as the god —
and this worship emphasized their distinctive female and male attributes
and characteristics.

Their religious practices varied between the use of sexual statues
and carvings and actual participating human partners. The ceremony
honouring female aspects of the goddess was described as *yoni puja*. The
ceremony venerating male aspects of the god was described as *linga puja*.

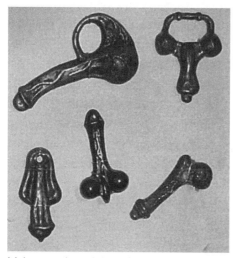

Male sexual models and replicas.

Sheela na Gig, symbol of female
sexuality.

Authoritative archaeological theories concerning the history of
religion have taken into account the ubiquitous discoveries of these
carved yoni and linga at Stone Age sites all around the world. This
raises the question as to whether attempts to control the environment
by performing sexual magic (together with some very early forms of
simplistic belief that might justifiably be described as "sex worship")
were among the earliest religions.

Over the millennia, many forms of sexual religion and sexual magic
have evolved and developed from these primeval sources. These have
included Kundalini yoga, the famous left- and right-hand paths of tantric
yoga, tantric Taoism, and karezza.

There are unmistakable sexual connotations in the drumming,
music, and dancing that form a prominent part of many Voodoo and

Obeah gatherings. The colours and designs of the female costumes are sexually eye-catching and are intended to attract and — consciously or subconsciously — to appeal to male partners in the congregation as well as to honour the male Orishas and Loas believed to be present at the ceremony.

As the drum rhythm pervades the congregation, it too has powerful sexual connotations; so does the irresistible music to which the rhythmic percussion gives structure. There are also climactic factors in both the melodies and the drumming that again have unmistakable sexual connotations.

Some extreme, puritanical forms of Christianity seem to have found the whole idea of sexuality strangely disturbing and frightening and to have retreated from it, condemned it as sinful, or suppressed it. The syncretized mystery religions — with their powerfully liberating ancient African input — are free of this weakness and fear and are able to welcome and enjoy sexuality as one of the greatest gifts bestowed on humanity by a loving God. Followers of Santeria, Obeah, Lucumi, and the other syncretized faiths are able to understand and appreciate that sexual feelings and religious feelings match each other in intensity. Far from regarding these two powerful, primary emotions as being at war with each other, adherents of the syncretized mystery religions often see them as complementary. For them, sexuality and spirituality can be powerful allies, completing and enriching the two most dominant dimensions of human personality.

Followers of the syncretized mystery religions employ large numbers of spells that are directed towards love and sexuality.

The invisible forces of their Orishas and Loas are frequently associated with the invisible powers of the breeze, especially when the wind is blowing on a night when there is a full moon. One of the oldest and simplest of the syncretistic religions' love spells is in harmony with these ideas about the additional powers of the Loas and Orishas on a worshipper's behalf when the moon is full and a night breeze is blowing.

According to this very simple spell, all that has to be done is for the spell worker to stand silently beneath the window of the loved one's room and whisper his or her name three times. The spell is alleged to be even more effective if the name is whispered seven times. A slightly more complicated variation involves dropping seven blood-red rose petals — one at a time — below the loved one's window each time the name is whispered.

One of the most frequently used sex-magic love spells is aimed at recovering a lost lover. Its users claim that it is so powerful that even if the lost lover has established a relationship with a new partner, the former partner can use this spell to re-establish the original relationship. The central aspect of this spell — like a significant number of others — is a bath. The names of Venus-Aphrodite, Lakshmi, or Oshun are invoked to bless the water. Patchouli, cinnamon, verbena, rose, and other herbal essences are put into to the bath. A few drops of almond oil, musk, and vanilla are then added. A lock of the lost loved one's hair and a few of his or her nail clippings are mixed with a lock of the enchanter's hair and some of his or her nail clippings. The hair and nail clippings are then placed in red paper — strong, vivid reds like scarlet and vermilion are preferred. The magical characters for love, prosperity, and joy are then written in gold ink on this bright red wrapping paper. This can be done using Japanese, Chinese, or Greek characters as shown below:

繁體中文版

or

愛喜悅繁榮

or

ευημερία χαράς αγάπης

The spell worker's name and the name of the lost love that is to be recovered are then written close together on the other side of the wrapping paper, again using gold ink. As with every spell that is genuinely believed in by the spell-maker, there is a note of warning. The originator of the spell cautions anyone who feels like using it that it has to be taken seriously. Failure to comply with the instructions can, according to the spell writer, result in disharmony and unhappiness instead of the desired effect of recovering the lost lover.

By adding the *identifiers* — the hair and nail clippings — the spell user is putting part of himself or herself into the spell and, although this adds power, it is also thought to be the psychic equivalent of a motorist's SatNav equipment: it focuses on the spell worker and the lost lover, so that any errant or misdirected magical force will cause problems for both of them.

Tolkien used this basic magical theory when he described how part of Sauron's personality had been integrated into the One Ring. When the One Ring was destroyed in the volcanic depths of Mount Doom, Sauron was destroyed with it because part of him was *in* it.

Many of the sex-magic love spells involve candles, which Freud would immediately have identified as linga, or male sex symbols. The mysterious Henri Gamache was apparently the collector, editor, and creator of a great many of these candle spells. Historians of magic are not certain of Gamache's true identity, but interesting magical writings under his name came out during the Second World War in the U.S.A. His Afrocentrism makes him particularly relevant to a study of Santeria, Voodoo, and the other syncretistic mystery religions.

There is a modified version of this spell in his collection. It is intended to attract a loving and sexually enthusiastic partner of either gender. The spell begins with elaborate directions for laying out the spell worker's altar. Preparations should ideally start on a Friday when the moon is waxing. The altar is said to need a photo or drawing of the desired partner, along with a lock of hair and nail trimmings if they can be obtained; a Bible; white candles in cross formation, which need to be anointed with what the spell workers call magical altar oil; a red candle anointed with lavender drops, or love oil; a candle of the appropriate colour for the love object's zodiacal sign; and finally, another candle of the spell worker's zodiacal colour.

The magician then reads from the Song of Solomon — the chapter chosen depends upon the magician's gender. Incense can be burnt during the Bible readings, and the candles representing the magician and the love object are moved slowly closer to each other until they are touching — so that their melted wax *combines* as it flows down.

Other varieties of love and sex spells are focused on physical performance and potency once the desired partner has been attracted to the magician. One of these involves honey and cinnamon, different magical perfumes, and flowers with bright golden or orange petals. There are numerous magical powders available from specialist shops that cater to followers of Voodoo, Santeria, and the other syncretistic mystery religions, and two of these allegedly magical ingredients are referred to colloquially as "Love Me" and "Love Me More" or as "Want Me" and "Want Me More." Priest-magicians recommend these powders for inclusion in this spell. Different perfumes such as lavender and rose are also recommended. If there is plenty of water available in the spell worker's house, or in the temple where the spell is being performed, several baths full can be used. According to some versions of the spell, however, the ideal location is out of doors, near a stream of pure, clear running water. An essential component is a drawing or photograph of both partners close together with their arms affectionately around each other and looking lovingly and longingly towards each other.

As the lovers stand close together, they pull the golden petals from the flowers and drop them into the water. The petals are followed by the sticks of cinnamon, the honey, and the two magical powders. The intimate picture of the lovers is placed in their bedroom, while the lovers bathe together in the stream into which the ingredients were thrown. During the bathing, they repeat each other's names lovingly and excitedly.

Like most spells, the instructions emphasize that its power is greatly increased if it is repeated three times, or even seven times.

Analysis of numerous love and sex spells of this type seems to suggest that they are intended as forms of sympathetic magic at its most direct and obvious level. The portraits or photographs represent the people, the loving sex partners, whom they depict. The sweetness of the honey carries the connotation of the sweetness of intimate affection. The removal of the petals represents the removal of clothing — and inhibitions. The throwing of the petals and other ingredients into the water symbolizes the lovers' total immersion in physical passion. For this reason the flowing stream is preferred to the static indoor bath. The sympathetic magic of the flowing water carries the lovers along on a tide of passion into which everything has been thrown. Nothing matters to them now except their physical love. The jettisoned perfumes represent the warm, natural scents of amorous human lovers embracing passionately and energetically. Placing their picture in the bedroom puts them into the location where their love finds its fulfillment. The repeating of each other's names focuses on their personal identities. This is not just any man having sex with any woman: these are not merely anonymous representatives of human maleness and femaleness personified. These Santerian lovers are real people, genuine and unique individuals. They have names. They truly matter to each other. Each cares deeply about the other. Each is concerned with the partner's pleasure as well as his or her own. The repetition of the spell three times, or seven times, symbolizes the permanence of their love and the desire to repeat the ecstatic experience of physical love as often as they can.

The syncretistic mystery religions with their honest and direct ancient African roots understand and accept the force of sexuality as a natural and very significant part of human life.

Chapter 15

CASE HISTORIES

WILLIAM Buehler Seabrook (1884–1945) was a fearless and effective member of the French army who was gassed during the action at Verdun and awarded the Croix de Guerre. He was a journalist on the *New York Times* and a world traveller specializing in strange, weird, bizarre, and paranormal phenomena. In the 1920s, he entertained Aleister Crowley for a week and wrote a book about the experience. In 1927 he went to Haiti and wrote about it in *Magic Island*, which was published in 1929. He married Marjorie Muir Worthington in 1935, but they were divorced in 1941. Seabrook died from a drug overdose in 1945.

During his experiences in Haiti, Seabrook encountered several examples of zombiism. He described one of them as having a face that was incapable of registering expression. Its eyes, he said, were the worst part of that frighteningly emotionless face. They were like the eyes of a corpse. They stared at him without being focused. They were not blind, but they did not see. Seabrook went on to describe how the *bokor* (the Voodoo sorcerer) put his victims through the zombification process using a combination of drugs and spells. Once it was complete, the victim was to all effects dead to his or her past life, and could do nothing except obey the bokor.

A great many case histories come out of the New Orleans area, and a significant percentage of these concern Voodoo practitioners who claim to be able to transform themselves into creatures. European shape-shifters are often credited with the ability to become wolves or bears. The Voodoo magicians are usually credited with the power to become big cats. This may well go back to their ancient African origins. Leopards were often associated with the Egyptian Osiris, and leopards were also thought to have the mystical power to guide the souls of the dead.

An African leopard statue.

An African leopard water pot.

The Nigerian leopard cult has existed for many centuries, perhaps for millennia, and is also well known in Sierra Leone. Its members mutilate and murder their victims with steel claws that make it look as if a wild carnivore was responsible. It is a belief among the leopard men that a magical drink known as *borfima* enables them to transform themselves into leopards and bestows superhuman power on them.

Other case histories from the New Orleans area tell how Voodoo magicians have terrified their victims into believing that they had been cursed by having magical animals inserted into their bodies. These Voodoo animal invaders included frogs, toads, snakes, lizards, slugs, and snails. In a number of cases, witnesses testified to seeing these strange creatures leaving the dying victim in much the same way that rats are known to leave a sinking ship.

The magician setting out to curse someone in this way would use a spell that included powder made from the body of the creature that was to be inserted — or blood from that creature. This blood or powder would then be secreted into the intended victim's food or drink, and an incantation would be recited.

Other Voodoo magicians would be employed to neutralize the animal-internalizing spell and administer special purgative herbs and spices that would expel the dangerous animals from the intended victim.

As a defence against these internalized animals and other forms of curse, many people in Voodoo areas such as New Orleans — including the intelligent and well-educated — carry what are known as *gris-gris* bags. These little leather or cloth pouches are filled with herbs and spices that are believed to have magical powers to ward off harm in all its forms.

Knowing what went into the magical gris-gris bags was the domain of wise old masters of the Voodoo arts such as Jean Montanet, sometimes referred to as "the last real Voodoo priest." Real he undoubtedly was — and a Voodoo expert he certainly was — but he was by no means the last of his kind.

Jean Montanet died at the age of one hundred in 1885. He was also known as Jean la Ficelle (John the String), Jean Latinié, Jean Racine (John the Root), and Jean Macaque. His most lasting and memorable titles, however, were simply Dr. John and Voodoo John.

He was descended from the noble Bambaras people of Senegal, and was believed to be the son of one of their princes. Strong, muscular, and broad-shouldered, John had a commanding voice and a dominant, charismatic personality. His adventures began at the end of the eighteenth century when Spanish slavers abducted him and sold him in Spain. He was then transported to Cuba, where he became an outstandingly good cook, and a grateful owner appreciated John's talents so much that he rewarded him by giving him his freedom. John left the sea to work as a cotton-roller, where his immense physical strength was a great asset and singled him out from the other workers. His employers soon noticed that he had other more subtle powers that made him a natural choice as foreman and overseer.

It was also recognized that John had strange psychic abilities and claimed to be able to read the future from the random markings that occurred on bales of cotton. No two bales would be exactly identical, and

John would gain meanings from them in the way that others would read Tarot cards, the I-Ching, or tea leaves! This fortune-telling ability made John rich, and he bought land on Bayou Road extending as far as Prieur Street. As well as telling fortunes and making psychic predictions, John became famous as a magical healer and caster of spells.

He sold potions that made hair grow; that protected his clients from spells and curses cast against them; that helped people to recover stolen property; and that helped them to win love and, having won it, to demonstrate a high degree of virility and potency.

John's "consulting rooms" contained his table and chair, pictures of the saints, Santerian cowry shells for reading the future, an elephant's tusk, and packs of magical cards with holes burnt in them. During his ceremonies and consultations, Dr. John burnt large quantities of candles of various colours. His own special gris-gris pouch contained bones wrapped in black string — which is, perhaps, where his title of *Ficelle* came from.

His ancestry as a Bambaras prince led to his acquiring a harem of nearly twenty black wives whom he bought as slaves and by whom he had numerous sons and daughters. The queen of his harem, however, was a lively and attractive white girl, who was in charge of his other wives and also gave birth to several of John's children.

To give John his due, he was a caring and generous man. Having been a slave himself, he was a kind and considerate master — and a generous benefactor to those in need. He gave food to the poor continually — even cooking it himself on occasion.

As a case history of an outstandingly successful Voodoo magician, Dr. John clearly combined the two paradoxical strands of the syncretistic mystery religions: he was dominant, powerful, charismatic, and full of genuine, ancient African secrets. His ethical beliefs made him loving and companionable to his many wives and kind to his servants and slaves. Yet he laughingly boasted that some of the so-called spells and remedies that he sold to the rich at exorbitant prices were nothing more than water in which he had stewed a few harmless herbs. On the other hand, he took parts of his spell-casting and fortune-telling very seriously indeed — and *seemed* to believe in it himself.

Dr. John was also a paradoxical character insofar as he had his weaknesses as well as his strengths. He was often out of his depths where money was concerned: he had no confidence in banks or other investment institutions. He would go to great lengths to hide his money by burying cash — and then forgetting where he had concealed it. Towards the end of his colourful career, he was dependent on the loyal support and charity of his many children — and it says much both for them and for him that he was properly looked after.

It was, of course, assumed by followers of Santeria and the other syncretistic mystery religions that powerful enemies — presumably bokors whom Dr. John had defeated in his heyday — had levelled curses at him and cast spells against him to destroy his previous prosperity.

As a twenty-first-century comparison, one of the many practising Voodoo priestesses is Miriam Chamani, who is described as a servant of the Orisha or Loa named Ayizan, the ruler of the marketplace and the bringer of mysteries to the ordinary human world. Her name in the original Fon language is derived from "earth" and "sacredness," so she is also regarded as a benign earth goddess. Among her many other duties, Ayizan is the Loa who guides and guards priests and priestesses of the syncretistic mystery religions and supervises their initiation ceremonies. She also protects her followers against curses, negative spells, and evil magic. A great healer-goddess, she works alongside her husband, Loco, who is the foremost Loa expert in the use of healing herbs. Ayizan is thought of overall as the bringer of health, power, and energy.

As a servant of Ayizan, the priestess Miriam Chamani is totally dedicated to healing and helping those who consult her. Miriam looks after those who consult her by giving African bone readings, arranging Voodoo weddings, and consulting Damballah and Erzulie for her clients.

A stark contrast with the good side of Voodoo as represented by the positive priestess Miriam Chamani and her faith in the benign Loa Ayizan is the case of what happened to David St. Clair, the Voodoo author and researcher. Many of his strange experiences are included in *Drum and Candle* (1971). David had moved to Brazil, where he apparently came under attack from a Quimbanda technique referred to as "closing the paths."

Quimbanda itself is based on very ancient African religio-magical traditions, and is currently popular in Brazilian cities including Rio de Janeiro, Pernambuco, and Maranhão. Although related in some ways to the more conventional Umbanda, Quimbanda is becoming increasingly distinct from it. The name is derived from the old Kimbundu language of Angola and carries the basic idea of the work of a healer and seer.

Quimbandan practitioners are often interested in making amulets, talismans, and magical concoctions, and in receiving advice from various Orishas, Loas, and spirit guides.

David's problems in Brazil began when his girlfriend left him and a substantial amount of money that was due to him did not materialize. He became ill with malaria and was then involved in litigation concerning an inheritance. As a sensible, pragmatic realist, David thought of these difficulties and problems as nothing more than chance, or a run of bad luck.

He had a Brazilian friend, a practising Macumban with psychic powers, who told David that Quimbandans were working against him and had "closed his paths." St. Clair's first reaction was to dismiss this warning as Brazilian religious superstition. He changed his mind when he was informed via other psychic messages that his maid was a practising Quimbandan and was performing negative magic against him. According to the information that David was given, it was alleged that this girl was systematically purloining items of his clothing and taking them to a Quimbandan ceremony.

He was informed that the stolen clothing — identified with him via sympathetic magic — was buried. Spells were chanted over the place and candles were lit in ceremonial patterns around it. David's psychic informants also warned him that the girl was adding curious magical powders to his food to strengthen and reinforce what was being done to his clothing.

Although he was not yet convinced of the effectiveness of the magical closing spells that were supposedly being used against him, David decided to attend a Macumba service and enlist the help of a priest or priestess there.

The opening parts of the service followed the normal lines of music, drumming, and exotic dancing, and several of the worshippers became possessed by Loas or Orishas. At this stage, the priestess in charge was wearing the conventional Macumba costume, including a white blouse and a golden cross around her neck. To David's surprise, the priestess left the temple for a few minutes, and when she came back, David could scarcely believe the transformation in her. She was now wearing badly torn and stained red satin clothing; the golden cross was gone and she had a small human skull suspended around her neck instead. There was a dead snake hanging from the eye sockets of this skull, and the jaws were fastened together with macabre black tape.

As David watched in amazement, the dramatically transformed priestess gulped down half a bottle of powerful local rum and shouted ecstatically that she was now possessed by Exu, that for the time being she *was* Exu. He is a particularly difficult Loa or Orisha to understand, even by long-standing practitioners of the faith. He is associated with St. Peter when saints are syncretized with Orishas and Loas.

It may be argued that without an untamed streak, a wild, irrational, unpredictable component to the human personality, life would be monotonous, dull, boring, repetitive, and scarcely worth living. Exu is the Orisha that supports this element of humanity. He is said to have a tendency to do things that are requested of him in reverse order — or in ways that are totally different from what his worshippers had expected. Exu is opposed to unthinking, unswerving obedience to authority or to any accepted and established traditions. For his

Symbols of Exu.

followers, ritual and liturgy obscure meaning. Exu teaches his worshippers to be constantly on the lookout for fresh ways of doing things, to experiment and to try out new ideas.

His traditional location is the crossroads, and his worshippers gather there to meet him and learn from him. Crossroads are symbolic meeting places of new and old ideas. Crossroads are scenes of interaction: places where things happen. In a sense they represent the reactions of different chemicals. Sodium comes down one road. Chlorine travels along another. The metaphorical crossroads where they meet is the birthplace of sodium chloride. Fresh directions can be taken when life-roads cross other life-roads.

Exu is seen as the ruler of intelligence, knowledge, and the means of manipulating it advantageously. He is also said to be the guardian of the bottomless well of wisdom. He is the ultimate cosmic chess master — and it is interesting to note that Aleister Crowley was a world-class chess player. Among his many other psychic interests, Crowley may well have been an Exu worshipper.

The demon of Rennes who once held a trident.

Like the strange figure of the demon — often thought to be Asmodeus — immediately inside the church at Rennes-le-Château, Exu carries a symbolic trident. The three prongs are supposed to represent the future, the present, and the past — as well as negative, neutral, and positive states of morality and ethics.

Exu is regarded as the interpreter, the message-carrier and spokesperson of the gods — in this aspect he is rather like Hermes Trismegistus, or Thoth, scribe of the ancient Egyptian pantheon. Unlike the other Orishas and Loas, each of whom works in one or two specific areas, Exu is free to travel anywhere and to exert his influence in every sphere of activity. He can concern himself with thunder, lightning, the sun, the desert, the mountains, the sea, and the rivers. He can help his worshippers with sex, love, human relationships, financial success, and worldly power. There is another aspect of Exu worship in which he is seen by Umbandists as the great *enabler* — a sort of power cable enabling Orishas and Loas to communicate with their people on earth.

Despite Exu's vast powers, unfathomable knowledge, and lightning fast intelligence, there is a strange sense in which his human devotees can mould him into their ideas of him. Those who regard him as evil will find that he manifests himself to them in a negative way. Those who regard him as benign and supportive will encounter him as an ally and sponsor. Those who conceive of him as something non-aligned — like the laws of natural science — will find him to be neutral.

He also has a female consort known as Pomba-Gira, who is the essence of female beauty, irresistible allure, and insatiable desire. Like Exu, she has access to unlimited wisdom and unfathomable knowledge.

In David St. Clair's case, the priestess was possessed by Exu in a benign phase. Speaking through her, he told David that he was lifting the closed path curse that had been put on him by the maid and her Quimbandan associates. He also announced that those who had directed it against St. Clair would find that it was rebounding on them with quadrupled fury.

According to David's own account of events, from that moment onwards, things seemed to go back to normal. His depression lifted. His confidence returned. He began a happy new love relationship, and his financial affairs improved spectacularly.

In a life-threatening situation in Kenya, Dr. John C. Barker, a psychiatrist, became involved in a case in which a senior officer at a medical station was apparently cursed by a witch doctor. A magical package was found concealed over the cursed medical officer's door. The spell worker had placed it there so that every time the victim entered or left his house, he would supposedly come under the influence of the negative spell. Dr. Barker, with his sound professional knowledge of how the human mind works, mixed a revolting-looking and foul-tasting spell of his own, which was actually perfectly harmless in spite of its obnoxious smell. He told all the suspects that it would kill the man who had caused the spell to be put on the medical officer — but would harm no one else.

Under this threat, the client of the witch doctor confessed. Barker ordered him to fetch the witch doctor and have the spell removed from the medical officer. The guilty man sped away to do what he was told, and came back with the witch doctor, who bent over the hex victim, whispered something to him, and left. Within hours, the sick man made a full recovery.

It was a case that even a professional psychiatrist like Barker did not find easy to explain.

Dr. Barker's colleague was more fortunate than fifty-three-year-old Finis P. Ernest, an Oklahoma nightclub proprietor. He and his mother had been prosperous business partners but he decided to sell the business against her wishes, and she allegedly threatened terrible things would happen to him if he did. Finis went ahead with the sale in spite of her threats.

Despite years of previous good health, he was taken ill repeatedly *whenever he went to visit his mother*. On August 23, 1960, Finis died after making a telephone call to her.

An even stranger case concerned a young woman who died on the day before her twenty-third birthday in 1966. Doctors in the world-renowned Johns Hopkins University in Baltimore attended her: no other place could have offered her better or more up-to-date treatment or more caring attention.

The girl came from a remote part of the famous Okefenokee Swamp area that straddles the Florida-Georgia state boundaries. She was born on Friday, August 13, 1943, as were two other baby girls. The midwife in attendance told their parents that because of the date, all three of them were doomed. She warned their mothers that the first would not see her sixteenth birthday and the second would die before she was twenty-one. Sadly, both of these prophecies came to pass. The third baby was the girl being attended in August 1966 by the team of outstanding Johns Hopkins doctors led by Dr. Gottlieb Friesinger at the Baltimore City Hospital. The midwife had told her mother that she would die before her twenty-third birthday.

Every test had shown that she was in good health, apart from being understandably anxious and overweight, but she began to develop serious heart irregularities and an erratic pulse. Her breathing became uncontrollable and she broke out in an abnormally heavy sweat. On Friday, August 12, 1966, despite everything that Friesinger and his assistants could do for her, she died. The autopsy could not reveal any natural causes.

This selection of case histories and the preceding studies of Santeria and the other syncretized mystery religions raise the central question about Voodoo, Obeah, Quimbanda, and the rest: when Voodoo works, *how* does it work?

Chapter 16

WHEN VOODOO WORKS, *HOW* DOES IT WORK?

FROM THEIR earliest infancy, human beings begin to learn about the nexus between cause and effect. It is the basis of survival and progress. As children mature and gain more and more experience of life and the sophisticated relationships that exist among a complex array of people, objects, and events, they gradually discover that there are inexplicable *irregularities* in the cause and effect scenario. A personal example illustrates the point.

When co-author Lionel was a small boy, his father took him fishing from the quayside in Gorleston in East Anglia. Periodically, his father would ask his mother to take Lionel to the local sweet shop and buy him a bar of chocolate or some sweets.

Having been to the shop, Lionel would return to the quayside to find a fish on his hook. As a result, he came to believe that the shop was lucky — that somehow a visit to the shop induced a fish to take the bait. A child's diagnosis of cause and effect is frequently erroneous. As we grow and gain experience of this mysterious universe, we become more critical. Visiting the shop had no magical effect on the fish. His father simply took advantage of Lionel's absence to buy a fish from another fisherman and put it on the boy's hook.

One of the most dangerous fallacies known to logicians is the one labelled *post hoc ergo propter hoc*: after this, therefore because of this. A Voodoo priest or priestess casts a spell, lifts a curse, restores health, or creates prosperity or a happy, loving relationship for a previously lonely client. The client is naturally delighted. But *how* and *why* did the magic work? Was the spell really effective in some way, or was it simply another fish-and-sweet shop phenomenon?

The twenty-first century's most advanced science is still a long way from understanding the universe's deepest secrets and solving its most profound riddles. When new solutions do come to light from time to time, they usually raise more questions than they answer.

One partial explanation of the apparent effectiveness of some types of magic may be that certain things are able to work in lower concentrations and at greater distances than was hitherto understood.

Dr. Christopher Clark working at Cornell University analyzed data that showed that whale noises can travel from one ocean to another, and can be detected up to two thousand miles away.

At the other end of the size scale, certain species of insects are attracted to their plant or animal targets by the odours that their hosts give off. These pheromone chemicals seem to be detectable in minute quantities by the insects that are highly tuned to various chemical stimuli at great distances from the target. Pheromones also attract the insects to one another intraspecifically for mating purposes.

Sharks can detect blood when it is diluted to as little as one part per million. They can also detect their prey by sensing its electrical field. The shark's head contains hundreds — in some species thousands — of electroreceptors, which are known to marine biologists as the Ampullae of Lorenzini. These guide the shark to the electromagnetic field radiating from its prey. Their ampullae can also enable sharks to orient themselves and navigate using the earth's magnetic field — something almost analogous to the SatNavs fitted in cars.

There are further biological navigational mysteries surrounding the ways that bees search for nectar-bearing flowers and then return to the hive to inform other bees of the flowers' location by performing a communication dance. Research has suggested that bees are able to navigate using the position of the sun, but the bees' precise steering mechanisms are not yet fully understood.

These long-distance communication mysteries in the natural world may have some relevance to the world of magic. The whale song that can travel thousands of miles through the oceans, insects' sensitivity to pheromones, sharks' ability to detect electromagnetic fields produced by other living creatures, and bees' solar navigation and honey-dance communications all suggest that distance and the smallness and faintness of a signal are no object to its having a profound effect.

The Santerian incense, coloured candles, talismans and amulets, strange chemical ingredients of a spell, vibrant music, and chanting, drumming, and incantations could, perhaps, operate in ways that are not yet understood — but resemble the natural mysteries demonstrated by whales, sharks, and some insects.

Another group of magical theories that set out to explain the methodology of Santeria, Quimbanda, Obeah, and the other syncretistic mystery religions starts from the premise that the priest-magicians are genuinely in contact with paranormal psychic beings whom they refer to as Loas and Orishas. These entities, which are paralleled to some extent by the Christian concepts of saints and angels, can be called upon by Voodoo experts and other priest-magicians. They will then be begged for help with problems such as poor health, poverty, loneliness, or unhappy relationships.

If these supernormal beings exist, if they are benign, and if they really do have power to influence people, objects, and events, then Santerian miracles of healing, happiness, and financial prosperity are explained in terms of their benevolent intervention.

A skeptical and cynical approach to an explanation of what *appears* to be magic would be the diametric opposite of a belief in Orishas and Loas and their interventions in human affairs. This set of theories says that every case that has ever been recorded — from zombiism to miraculous healings; from abject poverty to a millionaire lifestyle — has been misunderstood, misreported, wildly exaggerated, or simply caused by chance. What has been fondly thought of as magic has been something perfectly natural, normal, and ordinary *viewed from an unusual angle.*

In the authors' opinion — based on more than forty years of serious research into every aspect of the paranormal — the real answer lies deep within the mystery of the human mind. The brain contains 10^{14} neurons. That's a figure one followed by fourteen zeros. A single thought is an electrochemical connection between any two (or *more*) of these neurons. The possible permutations reach a number so close to infinity that the difference is inconsequential. The human brain can think as many thoughts as there are atoms in the known universe. In our normal lives, even the most academic scholar, the most daring researcher, and the most imaginative creative writer uses only the tiniest fraction of the brain's capacity. Are what people call "magicians" simply those gifted men and women who have learned how to use a few more of their neurons?

The bulging archives of magic hold countless records of happenings that the cynics and skeptics cannot realistically or convincingly explain away. In the great majority of these cases, the common denominator has been human will, mind-power, and a determination to succeed against all the odds. The best-known magicians and miracle workers have almost invariably been men and women who would never take no for an answer. If magic exists at all — it exists within indomitable human minds.

Where Santerian magic — and the magical elements in the other syncretized mystery religions — becomes most effective is within an environment that is conducive to releasing the hidden powers in the human mind. The drumming, the music, the rhythmic dancing, the incense, the chanting, the belief in possession by Orishas and Loas — these are all conducive to the release of mind-power.

The electrochemical pathways in the brain can be classified as forms of *energy* — and it is energy in one form or another that keeps the wheels of life turning. The more priest-magicians think, the harder they concentrate, and the more focused they are on the magical objective, the more likely it is that they will be able to work mind-magic on behalf of those who have come to them for help. The awareness that those around them believe in their powers reinforces those powers. It also seems probable that trancelike states, periods of altered consciousness, also increase magicians' mind-powers.

The Christian gospel accounts of healings and other miracles, and the history of miracles in the early church, all indicate that *faith* is of vital importance: the greater the faith, the greater the achievement.

What, then, is the *real* secret of magic? Is it the result of processes that are not yet fully understood but that will succumb eventually to the rigorous probing of hard science? Will strange, but perfectly natural and explicable, connections be found between magical spells and enchanters' rituals and substantial changes in objective reality? Does the secret of magic belong in the same category as the shark's ability to employ the Ampullae of Lorenzini, or the bee's ability to dance her directions to the nectar sources? Do Orishas and Loas really exist? Do they have strange superhuman powers? And are they willing to *use* those powers when the magician-priest begs for help?

Or are all human beings rather like Dorothy in *The Wizard of Oz?* Does everyone already *have* the power — as symbolized by Dorothy's ruby slippers — to perform miracles and achieve their goals *if only they would use it?*

The first two sets of theories regarding magic remain unproven and unresolved. There *may* be connecting power of an unknown type that operates over space and time when spells are cast. It's an area worth investigating objectively and scientifically — but the jury is still out. The further science progresses, the more we learn about the amazing complexity of causes and effects. Magic may be shown to work in ways as mysterious as cetaceans, bees, and sharks. Orishas and Loas *may* exist and *may* be willing and able to assist Santerian priest-magicians to help and heal people in need. If skilled veterinary surgeons can help animals in ways that the animals do not understand, why shouldn't Loas and Orishas help human beings who don't understand how Loa power operates? Again, the jury is out.

Magic and mind-power, however, seem to be almost synonymous. Thought may be a form of magic, and magic may be the expression of projected and directed thought. The wise St. Paul advised his readers to concentrate their thoughts on things that were pure and good and lovely. He was a very knowledgeable man, and he may have had something truly profound in mind when he wrote those words.

BIBLIOGRAPHY

Anonymous. *Hamel, the Obeah Man.* Jamaica: Mcmillan Caribbean Publishing, 2008.

Baron-Cohen, Simon. *The Essential Difference.* London: Penguin Press, 2004.

Blavatsky, H.P. *Articles from her 'Lucifer' Magazine (1887–1891)* reprinted in *The Dennis Wheatley Library of the Occult.* Great Britain: Sphere Books Ltd., 1974.

Bradbury, Will (Ed.). *Into the Unknown.* Pleasantville, NY: Readers Digest Ass., 1981.

Brittman, Barry & DeFail, Anthony *Maze of Life.* Meadville, PA: TouchStar Productions, 2007.

Brookesmith, Peter (Ed.). *Cult and Occult.* London: Guild Publishing, 1985.

Brooks, Noah. *Washington in Lincoln's Time 1895.* New York: The Century Company Publishers, 1895.

Butler, William Vivian. *The Greatest Magicians on Earth.* London: Pan Books Ltd., 1977.

Carey, Margret. *Myths and Legends of Africa.* London: Hamlyn, 1970.

Carroll, Latrobe. *Death and its Mysteries.* London: T.Fisher Unwin Ltd., 1923.

Clayton, Peter A. *Chronicle of the Pharaohs.* London: Thames and Hudson Ltd., 1994.

David-Neel, Alexandra. *Initiations and Initiates in Tibet.* New York: University Books, 1959.

David-Neel, Alexandra. *The Secret Oral Traditions in Tibetan Sects.* San Francisco: City Lights Publishing, 1964.

David-Neel, Alexandra. *With Mystics and Magicians in Tibet.* New York: Dover Publications, 1971.

Dodson, Aidan. *Monarchs of the Nile.* London: Rubicon Press, 1995.

Earle, William. *Obi; or, The History of Three-Fingered Jack*. Peterborough, Ontario: Broadview Press, 2005.

Fairley, John, and Simon Welfare. *Arthur C Clarke's World of Strange Powers*. London: W. Collins Sons & Co. Ltd., 1985.

Fanthorpe, Lionel and Patricia. *The Holy Grail Revealed*. California: Newcastle Publishing Co. Inc., 1982.

———. *Secrets of Rennes le Château*. Maine: Samuel Weiser Inc., 1992.

———. *The Oak Island Mystery*. Toronto: Hounslow Press, 1995.

———. *The World's Greatest Unsolved Mysteries*. Toronto: Hounslow Press, 1997.

———. *The World's Most Mysterious People*. Toronto: Hounslow Press, 1998.

———. *The World's Most Mysterious Places*. Toronto: Hounslow Press, 1999.

———. *Mysteries of the Bible*. Toronto: Hounslow Press, 1999.

———. *Death the Final Mystery*. Toronto: Hounslow Press, 2000.

———. *The World's Most Mysterious Objects*. Toronto: Hounslow Press, 2002.

———. *The World's Most Mysterious Murders*. Toronto: Hounslow Press, 2003.

———. *Unsolved Mysteries of the Sea*. Toronto: Hounslow Press, 2004.

———. *Mysteries of Templar Treasure and the Holy Grail*. Maine: Samuel Weiser Inc., 2004.

———. *The World's Most Mysterious Castles*. Toronto: Hounslow Press, 2005.

———. *Mysteries and Secrets of the Templars: the Story behind the da Vinci Code*. Toronto: Hounslow Press, 2005.

———. *Mysteries and Secrets of the Masons*. Toronto: Hounslow Press, 2006.

———. *Mysteries and Secrets of Time*. Toronto: Hounslow Press, 2007.

Faraone, Christopher A. "Binding and Burying the Forces of Evil: The Defensive Use of 'Voodoo Dolls' in Ancient Greece." *Classical Antiquity Magazine* 10, no. 2 (1991): 165.

Frazer, Sir James George. *The Golden Bough*. New York: The Macmillan Co., 1922.

Gettings, Fred. *Encyclopedia of the Occult*. London: Guild Publishing, 1986.

Gettings, Fred. *Secret Symbolism in Occult Art*. New York: Harmony Books, 1987.

Gimbutas, Marija. *The Civilization of the Goddess*. London: HarperCollins, 1992.

Graves, Robert. *The White Goddess*. New York: Farrar, Straus and Cudahy, 1948.

Graves, Robert (Intro.). *Larousse Encyclopaedia of Mythology*. London: Paul

Hamlyn, 1959.

Grimal, Nicolas. *A History of Ancient Egypt.* Oxford: Blackwell, 1988.

Guerber, H.A. *Myths and Legends of the Middle Ages.* London: Studio Editions Ltd., 1994.

Guiley, Rosemary Ellen. *The Encyclopedia of Ghosts and Spirits,* New York: Checkmark Books, 2000.

Harrison, Michael. *The Roots of Witchcraft.* London: Tandem, 1975.

Hay, George (Ed.). *The Necronomicon: The Book of Dead Names.* London: Skoob Books Publishing, 1992.

Hitching, Francis. *The World Atlas of Mysteries.* London: Pan Books, 1979.

Hougham, Paul. *The Atlas of Mind, Body and Spirit.* London: Octopus Publishing Group, 2006.

Lawrence, Richard. *The Magic of Healing.* London: Thorsons, 2001.

Lévi-Strauss, Claude. Jacobson, Claire. (Trans) *Structural Anthropology.* New York: Basic Books, 1963.

Lloyd, Gwynedd (Ed.). *Lotions and Potions.* London: National Federation of Women's Institutes, 1968.

Martin, Lois. *The History of Witchcraft.* Hertfordshire: Pocket Essentials Publications, 2007.

Maslow, Abraham. *Motivation and Personality.* New York: Harper, 1954.

Michell, John, and Robert J.M. Rickard. *Phenomena: A Book of Wonders.* London: Thames & Hudson, 1977.

Needham, Joseph. *Science and Civilisation in China.* Cambridge, UK: Cambridge University Press, 2000.

Newton, Toyne. *The Dark Worship.* London: Vega, 2002.

Ogden, Daniel. *Magic, Witchcraft and Ghosts in the Greek and Roman World: A Sourcebook.* Oxford: Oxford University Press, 2002.

Owen, Iris, and Margaret Sparrows. *Conjuring up Philip.* New York: Harper & Row, 1976.

Pearce, J. *The Crack in the Cosmic Egg. (Revised Edition of the Classic Back in Print Edition.)* South Paris, Maine: Park Street Press, 2002.

Playfair, Guy Lyon. *The Unknown Power.* St. Albans, Hertfordshire: Granada Publishing Ltd., 1977.

Puharich, Andrija. *Beyond Telepathy.* London: Souvenir Press Ltd., 1974.

Reeves, Nicholas, and Richard H. Wilkinson. *The Complete Valley of the Kings: Tombs and Treasures of Egypt's Greatest Pharaohs.* London: Thames & Hudson Ltd., 1966.

Sargant, William. *Battle for the Mind*. London: Penguin Books, 1961.

Schwartz, Gary E.R., and Linda G.S. Russek. *The Living Energy Universe*. Charlottesville, Virginia: Hampton Roads Publishing, 1999.

Seabrook, B. *The Magic Island*. New York: Harcourt Brace, 1929.

Sharper Knowlson, T. *The Origins of Popular Superstitions and Customs*. London: Studio Editions Ltd., 1995.

Shaw, Ian. *The Oxford History of Ancient Egypt*. Oxford: Oxford University Press, 2000.

Singer, Marian. *Everything you need to know about Witchcraft*. Newton Abbot, UK: David and Charles, 2005.

Spence, Lewis. *The Encyclopedia of the Occult*. London: Bracken Books, 1988.

St. Clair, David. *Drum and Candle*. New York: Bell Publishing, 1971.